Between the Frames

Between the Frames:

Thinking about Movies

Heidi G. Dawidoff

Archon Books

1989

First published 1989 as an Archon Book, an imprint of
The Shoe String Press, Inc., Hamden, Connecticut 06514

Printed in the United States of America

The paper used in this publication meets the
minimum requirements of American National Standard
for Information Sciences—Permanence of Paper for
Printed Library Materials, ANSI Z39.48–1984 ⊗

Library of Congress Cataloging-in-Publication Data

Dawidoff, Heidi G., 1937–
Between the frames : thinking about movies.
Bibliography: p.
Includes index.
1. Motion pictures—Aesthetics.   2. Men
in motion pictures.   3. Women in motion
pictures.   4. Love in motion pictures.
5. Motion pictures—United States—History.
I. Title.
PN1995.D35   1989   791.43′09′09353   88-35083
ISBN 0-208-02238-4 (alk. paper)

Set in Bembo by Coghill Composition Co., Richmond, VA
Designed by Kathryn Frederick

Contents

v

Part IV: Problems of Aesthetics

For Nicholas and Sarah

Acknowledgments

I am most grateful to Robert Dawidoff for his warm encouragement during the early stages of writing, when only a few chapters existed; to Gloria and Bill Broder and Rebecca Folkman and Jonathan Aaron for their equally warm encouragement during later stages, when the full manuscript was done. Davis Weinstock took an interest from the very beginning and kept it up, generously sustaining my faith in the book with his enthusiasm and helpful advice. I owe special thanks to Betsy Weinstock, and James Thorpe III, my publisher, for their imaginative, rigorous, unerring, and irresistible criticism; and to my nephew, Jonathan Wiener, for his inspiration for half of the book's title. Finally, I should like to thank the Board of Trustees at the Hopkins School for granting me a sabbatical leave in 1987, thus enabling me to complete the book.

Introduction: *Thinking about Movies*

Most children I grew up with followed the conventional cinematic course: they went weekly to the movies. In my rather strict and culturally lofty home, a trip to the movies resembled a carefully planned voyage: undertaken only rarely; the stopping points chosen with marked decision. Other children went to local theaters on Saturday afternoons in company with each other, ate popcorn during the show, and got to see funny movies, silly movies, happy movies, energetic movies. I went dressed up, accompanied by both parents, to early evening shows (evoking in my parents' minds, perhaps, the annual gift to young Viennese children of a night at the opera), and saw excellent movies, which were invariably too adult for a little girl: *Wuthering Heights* one year; *The Philadelphia Story* another; *The Green Years* yet another. Fed sparingly yet well on such choice fare, I missed Hollywood's joyfully profuse productivity and the careless, roistering crowds of happy Americans who knew how to relish mass entertainment with hearty appetites. Even so, I saw what I was missing on the occasion of my first movie, *Wuthering Heights,* when the *Movietone News,* featuring a smiling President Roosevelt swimming in the White House pool, was followed by the previews of *Meet Me in St. Louis.* Three minutes of that movie revealed a way of life, a pace, an attitude, a freedom of form, and a commitment to joy that the story of gloom and thwarted passion, of course, could not. What was striking about the experience, however, was precisely the contrast between the aching drama of impossible love and the cheerful musical in which so much was possible. It would probably have been the same if I

1

had seen *Meet Me in St. Louis* and had only glimpses of the darkly, broodingly romantic *Wuthering Heights*.

From his professorial height, my father determined the movies by which I should be transported and, by extension, what I should remember and savor, for he screened everything I saw for suitability. The heavy interim between movies bred in me a longing for them that he, in judiciously concerning himself with the cultivation of my taste and judgment, may not have expected. Adolescence brought me some freedoms. Trips to movies became jaunts, even weekly jaunts, with friends or by myself, to first-run theaters, revival houses, Harvard's film societies—any place where I could catch up. I saw *Johnny Belinda, Beat the Devil, A Place in the Sun, Angels in the Outfield, Singin' in the Rain,* and, finally, a Bette Davis vehicle: *Of Human Bondage;* and again it was the rich sense of movies' protean power brought out by the contrasts among such a sampling that struck and delighted me.

Movies are made for entertainment, but so is all art. Part of the entertainment is the transportation—what people, with reference to movies, generally call escape—it makes possible. For a brief time, one is taken beyond one's life. But the effect of the transportation lingers, and that experience of remembering and savoring, once we've returned to the business of our own lives, is also part of the entertainment. If art failed to transport us, it wouldn't be art at all. Art is supposed to give us life as we don't really live it; as we might live it; as we should like to live it; as we never imagined we could live it; even sometimes as we daren't or mustn't live it. That is the purpose of a movie's dissolve, which moves us silently and serenely from a completed scene to a new one, thus omitting the life between that we, in reality, hobble through minute by minute. That is the purpose of Busby Berkeley's dances—those unending metamorphoses formed by perfect patterns of beautiful girls, whose lovely figures and smiling faces outdo the kaleidoscopic fragments they imitate. That is the purpose of all the happy rescues, coincidences, endings; of all the ghouls, monsters, villains; of all the synchronization, stylization, composition. They water our imaginations, intensifying life's experience, spurring us to be less ordinary, not necessarily in what we do with life but certainly in how we think about it. For art is meant to give us ideas, to give us a heightened sense of possibility, to set us thinking.

Despite flaws in any or all of its component art forms—drama, acting, photography, music—the graceful union of these parts that comprises a whole movie pleased and prompted my young imagination in ways otherwise the prerogative of great art. Movies don't have to be, and mustn't try to be, great art in the usual sense of poised, still perfection captured by a great painting, for example, to achieve artistic grace and power. In fact, all too often, directors who have set out to create "an artistic masterpiece" along the lines of a great painting have succeeded only in foddering the art house crowd with fresh stupidities and boring the multitude with a massive piece of inert affectation weighed down by deathless (but nonetheless quite dead) symbols and poetic (but nonetheless quite prosaic) camera work. However beautiful particular shots may be, a movie requires cinematography; it won't do to give a slide show. A movie becomes art in its own way, a way that gains force and integrity by a lively amalgamation of several art forms, by its intrinsic promulgation of energy in motion. The movie, after all, sweeps us up in its moving pictures—those hours and hours of life imagined and arranged for us between countless frames whose organizing principle satisfies us while their borders remain as invisible as drawings beneath a painting or outlines behind a novel.

I make no secret of my preference for Hollywood movies of the '30s and '40s. Their wholehearted enthusiasm for and faith in a new art form prove ever irresistible to a person raised on New Deal optimism. In their profusion and variety, moreover, they deal with all of life's big subjects, sometimes tritely and formulaically, but, more often, imaginatively, honestly, and intelligently. They have something to say—the way any work of art has something to say about human life and the human spirit, something which transcends the particular occasion and becomes good for all time. It is life's big subjects—relationships between people being the biggest of all—as they are dramatized through decades of movies that unite the chapters and give the book its coherence. The chapters are roughly chronological, but with much backtracking and advancing as I compare movies of different periods.

Part I focuses directly on the subject of relationships. Parts II, III, and IV are indirect treatments of the same subject, even though they explicitly name other approaches to thinking about movies. The various failures in relationships, discussed in part II, constitute the movies' clearest manifestation of the sort of demoralization that landed them, the characters, and the stories they dramatize "in the doldrums." Movies about actors deal with the subject of acting, as both profession and recreation, largely in terms of the way it affects the actors' relationships. Even problems of aesthetics, so often theoretical, have a direct bearing on the subject of relationships. How to present sex on the screen, how to "talk about" art, how to turn a novel into a movie, and how to conclude a movie—since moviemaking began, moviemakers have had to, and will continue to, confront and resolve these problems if they hope to reveal something believable about human nature and human relationships.

My early ventures in thinking about movies taught me that thinking has a great deal to do with keeping experiences alive long enough to understand them. Thinking may reveal sad truths or lead to dead ends, but its true function is to invigorate an idea, to enhance our attachment to a subject by confirming its importance in our minds. In this way, thinking gives life some shape and continuity, a narrative quality, as if our ideas, impelled by enthusiasm, were running through our minds like movies.

Part I:

Relationships

1.

The Rock that Turned to Sand

"What do women want?" In an exasperated lapse from brilliance, Sigmund Freud asked this silly, provocative, and above all unanswerable question. Why people have troubled themselves with it or, indeed, why people have seriously undertaken the study of women as if they were a separate species unto themselves probably suggests more about the general isolation and alienation people feel these days than about an inherent separation of the sexes. The ladies of *Love's Labour's Lost* knew exactly what they wanted, while their scholarly lovers, to Shakespeare's amusement, were muddled men who needed good-humored assistance to rescue them from folly; the gentlemen of *Princess Ida* also knew exactly what they wanted, while the scholarly princess, to Gilbert's amusement, was a misguided maiden who needed the same good-humored assistance to rescue her from loneliness. The makers of *A Letter to Three Wives* (Joseph Mankiewicz) and *Adam's Rib* (George Cukor) show us that in 1949 people still believed that it was possible to know what women wanted and that what they wanted was neither different from nor incompatible with what men wanted. The rock men and women built upon was a relationship with each other, a relationship of equals, a relationship, moreover, that was seen as giving the partners freedom to be fully, independently themselves (when a career was often seen as variously degrading, compromising, or effacing to the individual). By the 1970s, however, such beliefs had crumbled; movies like *Klute* (1971), *Scenes From a Marriage* (1973), *Shampoo* (1975), *Looking for Mr. Goodbar* (1977), and *Shoot the Moon* (1982) show us men and women drifting

7

through the universe with much more free time than their '40s forebears, much more intense longing, and no idea of what they want. An examination of these movies—all about relationships between men and women—should yield some interesting, though disheartening, insights into the declining faith in such relationships and in people's potential to create and prosper through them.

A Letter to Three Wives is a study of three marriages, largely from the women's points of view. In each relationship, the man and woman struggle to maintain their independence. What threatens the individual's independence turns out to be not the marriage tie or the spouse's actions or demands, but instead an individual's childish need for dependence. It is that childish dependence, moreover, that threatens the marriage, for the marriage can thrive only on independence.

When Deborah (played by Jeanne Crain) broke away from her hayseed background and joined the Navy, she met the wealthy Brad (played by Jeffrey Lynn), who fell in love with what appeared to him a strong, independent woman. As soon as the war is over, they marry and settle down in Brad's posh house, where both betray the social insecurities and concern with appearances that lay dormant beneath their handsome, democratic Navy uniforms. Their scenes in the movie are fights about what Deborah will wear and how good they'll look as a couple, with Brad choosing her clothes while still keeping the photograph of her in uniform on the piano; with Deborah buying the clothes that he picks out and then fuming over her own weakness in capitulating in such a childlike way. In their opening conversation, Brad informs Deborah that he may not be back from a conference in time to take her to the annual spring dance at the country club; she puts up a mild protest against going alone, and he erupts, scolding her the way an impatient parent might: "What are you afraid of, Deborah? You don't have to fly into a panic." At bottom, it is very important to Brad that his wife be independent, even though, with all his worries about image, he confuses and restricts her with mixed messages.

Rita and George (played respectively by Ann Sothern and Kirk Douglas) are a more interesting married couple than Deborah and Brad. George is a high school teacher who loves the work that pays him poorly but gives him intellectual freedom; Rita writes a soap opera for a radio station that pays her lavishly but robs her of sleep as well as freedom as a writer. Their scenes are fights about the way a career can truncate one's independence and self-esteem. George makes little money, but he values the freedom he has to pursue his idealism about teaching Shakespeare to the young. He doesn't mind Rita's making good money; what infuriates him is her having become a slave to the advertisers who call up constantly to demand revisions in what he regards as a contemptible form of writing. He tells her forcefully that she used to be an attractive, independent woman, a lively companion, a perfect partner, before she took on the job and became a mouthpiece for uncultured sellers of deodorants. What doubles his fury is her having tried to sell him out, too, by wangling a job for him out of these boors, her bosses, thus conveying an utter disregard for his feelings and interests. (The idea that a career may be constraining and relationships liberating comes up again in Mankiewicz's *All About Eve,* an idea that centuries of men must know something about, but one that today's women don't want to hear, judging from the hisses that greet Margo Channing's "A woman and her career" speech in movie revival houses.)

Lora Mae and Porter (played respectively by Linda Darnell and Paul Douglas) have the most complicated relationship of the three. She wins him, her boss, as a husband by holding her own, by refusing to become his mistress. The more she asserts her independence, the more he is drawn to her. Later, once they are married, we see that these two socially ambitious people, who have raised themselves right off the tracks (when the train goes by, Lora Mae's whole house shakes and the refrigerator door opens), confuse their feelings for each other with their desire for what Porter calls "class." They fear that a show of tenderness will make them look silly, mistaking distance for independence. Their scenes are fights about the price tags they've put on each other, thus making the marriage an extension of the business world in which both have been so successful, fights which implicitly cry out for loving reassurances but which only inhibit shows of affection until the two are almost estranged. These two have raised themselves socially with great energy and speed, but they haven't learned how to deal with feelings. Both are sensitive and passionate, especially about each other, yet they are ashamed to say how they really feel.

Though each marriage is threatened and each woman believes

that her husband may leave her, the problems are ultimately re-solved and the marriages survive. Part of the resolution comes through reawakened love, or an awareness of feelings that have lasted. The women really want to come home from their Saturday at the settlement house trip, a charitable donation of their time which these surburban women give to unfortunate urban children, and find their husbands there waiting. The resolution also comes through the ubiquitous but unseen Addie Ross, author of the tantalizing letter. She is the woman each husband admires for her social fluidity, her freedom to have all kinds of relationships, her freedom to be generous; in short, her independence. All three wives want secretly to live up to her, but they don't know how until each is prompted once more to assert her own independence, which frees her to feel and show love. Once each woman recovers her independence, she need no longer worry about the attractive fantasy Addie Ross stirs in her husband's mind. Each of these husbands would much rather have the real woman he married than the imagined ideal he turns to when his marriage totters. We are thus left to assume that Deborah and Brad will stop fussing about clothes and concentrate on each other instead. Deborah does go to the dance without Brad and that, presumably, will give her some confidence to behave like the independent woman he fell in love with. Rita and George openly celebrate her polite defiance of her boss. She keeps her job but firmly resists being pushed around, and that's the independent woman George loves. Lora Mae and Porter happily hit the dance floor after she has brazenly and lovingly kissed him full on the lips in public. What has moved and delighted her so deeply is Porter's having confessed that he indeed ran away with Addie Ross and then changed his mind. In this way, he comes as close as his embarrassment about feelings will permit to telling Lora Mae that he loves her. She reads his imperfect but heartfelt words correctly. Her kiss is an act of initiative and reconciliation. Instead of teasing him with her independence, Lora Mae can now use it to guide Porter to emotional maturity.

In *A Letter to Three Wives,* the women learn about what they want by remembering their fights with their husbands. These fights are instructive, of course, because they reveal the way in which dependence, whether on a person, or social convention, or on image, makes people childish and unattractive to each other.

The fights are about what drives them apart, but they represent at the same time their frantic efforts to get back together.

Adam's Rib is also full of fights. In fact, it isn't until Adam and Amanda Bonner (played respectively by Spencer Tracy and Katharine Hepburn) start fighting in private that they achieve the marriage they really want. The fight begins in public, as they oppose each other in court, he prosecuting a woman who has shot (but not killed) her adulterous husband, Amanda defending her.

When we first see Amanda and Adam, they live out a modern fairy tale: they are rich, employed, and childless; they have an apartment and servants in town, a farm and dogs in Connecticut. Gradually, as the fight in court—a fight Amanda is winning as she proves that the law's unfairness to women protects an adulterous man and condemns a woman who fights to save her family—invades the serenity of their perfect home, they must confront each other and learn what it is that they want from the relationship. Adam is greatly threatened by his wife's performance in court, and well he might be: she humiliates him there. He then humiliates her at home by spanking her hard on the bottom; she retaliates by kicking him in the shins. The ideal, modern marriage has deteriorated into an uncivilized, loveless feud. They've brought their careers into the relationship (as did Lora Mae and Porter), which proves very costly in terms of the personal independence, self-control, and maturity each values so highly. (Since, in both marriages, the husbands and wives truly value each other's professional competence, they will have to find a way to integrate their personal and professional lives, as Rita and George are able to do.) As Amanda regrets the fact that her professional victory might have destroyed her marriage, leaving her prey to a foppish but very attentive neighbor, the once eminently respectable Adam wanders about the darkened city streets, a scowl on his face, violent thoughts in his head, a revolver (that turns out to be made of licorice) in his hand.

In this movie—as in *A Letter to Three Wives*—the problems are resolved in part because the two know and are struck anew by how much they love each other. That might not help them out of their now violent conflict, though. What they want from each other is respect. It is on the Connecticut farm (Connecticut is always a choice setting for recovery in movies; see Stanley Cavell, *Pursuits of*

Happiness, Harvard University Press, 1981), where they have gone to put their relationship in order, that Adam can praise Amanda for the good work she did in court. She responds to his praise and to his announcement of his nomination for a judgeship by saying, "I'm proud of you," only to hear him answer, "I'd rather have you say that than anything." It wasn't her independence he ever objected to; it was the way she cast him into a childish role—brought out his speech defect in public, had a hefty female circus performer lift him off his feet in court—that made him lose his sense of his own independence. He felt stupid and undignified, like a child, just as George felt when Rita bargained over him with the advertisers. In turning to each other again, Adam and Amanda have understood that without the relationship they would cast themselves adrift; they would not secure independence but only loneliness, and loneliness threatens the capacity to be independent. That is to some extent what Adam means when he shouts hooray for "that little difference" between men and women as he and Amanda are about to jump into bed. The little difference is the independence you can celebrate when the person you love respects you; when you can tell each other you've done a good job; when you know the relationship means most in your life.

In both of these movies from 1949, people discover what they want, strong marriages in which the individual remains independent. Both movies affirm a faith in the possibility of such a relationship. The fights are long and hard, but people prove willing to grow up, to win the benefits of civilization. By the '70s, there doesn't seem to be much civilization left to have faith in. The world is a wild forest region. Adam and Amanda had a glimpse of the world that way too, but they worked their way out of it to the restorative balm of the farm. Porter also saved himself from a perilous misstep by leaving Addie Ross in "the city" and returning to Lora Mae. When people can't work their way out of it—or when all that lies beyond the wild forest is a desert waste—they are doomed to a life at least partly savage, and that is what the movies of the '70s show. In *Klute, Shampoo,* and *Looking for Mr. Goodbar,* the main characters all have freely chosen careers which are not fulfilling, and they have countless sexual contacts which never turn into relationships. They are all roaming wild and lonely, scavengers in forlorn lands without even the capacity to know what they want, although they spend most of their lives hungry with desire that has none of the uplifting compensations of romantic longing. The hair stylist of *Shampoo* carries on like Fielding's Tom Jones, but he never has any fun. His story ends with the loss of the one woman for whom he could have matured into an independent person to a crude, paunchy man who has kept her as his mistress.

In these relatively recent movies, so much effort goes into, and so much time is wasted on, avoiding the strong relationship. Sometimes a career seems easier to handle; it's a part of life one can control more easily, perhaps because one can at least play the part of a grown-up convincingly without having to be one. Being on one's own can make us look independent as we march bravely down city streets. Just look at Jane Fonda of *Klute* and Diane Keaton of *Looking for Mr. Goodbar:* the confident stride; the assertive look; the fearlessly inviting smile. But they're both little girls, in their short skirts and blue jeans, only playing the role of independent women. Ultimately, the playacting only drives them into their lonely selves, another wild region where they are not safe, rather than into some kind of relationship. In *Looking for Mr. Goodbar,* Theresa's sister (played by Tuesday Weld) ironically calls her "my Rock of Gibraltar," an adept way of underlining for us her crumbling personality. Indeed, the professional life may seem simpler and more gratifying than the personal life, but it makes its own great demands by drawing so much from the person that nothing is left for a personal life. Theresa is a magnificent teacher, intelligent and dynamic in her classroom. It's when she comes home that the helpless, unresourceful baby in her comes out. She wants to watch television; she wants a drink; she wants sex; she wants and wants. (When Sam Craig says to Tess Harding in *Woman of the Year,* "The outstanding woman of the year isn't a woman at all," he means that her career has made her careless and unfeeling in her relationships, less than human with him and the little boy she has adopted to enhance her professional image.) A close relationship may not be believable, attainable, or even desirable in the context of these '70s movies, but, as dramatized on the screen, it remains a test of a character's independence nevertheless. The characters in these '70s movies are shown repeatedly in their quest for companionship that demands nothing of them, making them voraciously

hungry and self-indulgent. It is to be expected, but ironic nevertheless, that the self-indulgence always leaves them feeling empty.

In *Scenes From a Marriage* and *Shoot the Moon,* the marriages
disintegrate because they have come to exact too much—too much
closeness, too much commitment, too much maturity. The men
want out, and yet both are already in what will be their second
marriages. In both movies, the second marriages represent choices
that leave the individuals some freedom, different, however, from
the freedom of independence: it is freedom from the pressure to be
fully responsible, mature, self-controlled. The choices of new
mates are invariably less interesting and less challenging versions,
emotionally and intellectually, of the first choices. The first marriage, in both movies, was the setting for civilization. The couple
kept house, worked hard, had children, and believed in fidelity.
The second marriage is the setting for a retreat from (not an
abandonment of) civilization, as if to say the first marriage failed
because the capacity and desire for independence weren't strong
enough. Now that the couples are settled into new marriages that
don't demand so much maturity, they can play with their former
mates. They actually express more love for each other in their
childish adultery than they did when they were married. These
couples, then, do achieve some sense of what they want. They
want easy relationships: some love; some attachment; some conversation, but not too much. In the 1978 comedy *Same Time Next
Year,* Alan Alda sighingly sums up his satisfaction with his adulterous arrangement, "one beautiful weekend every year, with no
cares, no ties, no responsibilities." It is exactly this sort of relief
from depth and intensity that Bergman's couple also achieves.

The movies of the '70s emphatically show our world as an
unfriendly place that frightens us and never comforts us. The world
has always been an unfriendly place in one way or another, to
someone or other—Hamlet found it "weary, stale, flat and unprof-
itable" sometimes—but people were not so frightened by it. They
could, and did, in times of pain and sadness, turn to each other and
speak, "Ah, dear, let us be true to one another," as Matthew
Arnold advised, and even Hamlet, in the depths of disgust with
life, the world, and almost everybody in it, found comfort in
talking to Horatio. In movies about contacts rather than relationships, like *Shampoo, Klute,* and *Looking for Mr. Goodbar,* relation-

ships themselves are perceived as frightening: they demand too much; they threaten one's sense of self or one's preoccupation with self; they limit and degrade the individual. The skepticism about relationships manifests itself by meager dialogue. Diane Keaton's Theresa Dunn rejects the one man who has love and conversation to offer her in favor of the host of mumbling strangers she brings home to bed. All the verbal fights of *A Letter to Three Wives* and *Adam's Rib* bring the couples to resolution and reconciliation. All the sexual acts of the call girl in *Klute,* the hair stylist in *Shampoo,* or Theresa Dunn in *Looking for Mr. Goodbar* neither advance nor comment on relationships. Instead of dialogue, these movies give us screaming bouts—the words, if any, are indistinguishable and unmemorable—that end in physical violence: George of *Shoot the Moon* wrecking the tennis court; Theresa succumbing to her murderer in *Looking for Mr. Goodbar. Shampoo* ends peacefully, however, with a conversation between the hair stylist and the woman he has discovered he loves. The signal for his readiness to mature, to recognize a definite wish, to choose one woman, is a sudden wealth of dialogue. After a movie composed largely of human grunts, squeals, and groans, mechanical hair dryers, motorcycles, and televised convention noises, the last quarter is rich in conversation. The hair stylist, no longer mute or inarticulate, talks when he can love. In movies, if not also in real life, actions don't equal words in effecting and expressing a close tie between people.

In the two 1949 movies, as in almost every movie of the '30s and '40s, people find each other interesting to talk to and are able to sustain long conversations eagerly, relishing them, even, if not especially, when they fight with each other. Fights bring out their verbal agility, honesty, wit, and they indicate, above all, that people have something to say to each other, which indicates further that they have independent minds. Indeed, Lora Mae's kiss marks the happy ending to a crucial conversation between two people who were barely on speaking terms, who, in the course of the movie, had to learn how to speak their love to each other in order to recognize its full force. Adam and Amanda Bonner jump happily into bed at the "closing curtain" after a successful reconciling conversation. In the more recent movies, people don't seem interested in conversation; the use of language imposes the burden of having ideas, and people can't find subjects for conversation. The use of language evidently also imposes the burden of holding one's own in a relationship, and people can't find the will to be subjects (for all the kicking and screaming about being turned into objects). Hence, there are often in movies of the '70s so many barren stretches of silence while the lonely camera roves over blank terrain, seemingly in search of its own subject. Such a problem never plagues a movie like *Modern Times,* though, where the mimed intimations of closeness between the main couple evoke their conversations for us. Woody Allen's '70s movies abound in talk, of course, which is not the same as conversation at all. His one-liners, whether glib, funny, or frantic, are invariably directed toward himself in some way and constitute a flimsy disguise for foreplay. It is sexual action, after all, that delimits his personal ambitions; he knows it and feels bad about it. The very fact that he can't work or wait for a relationship becomes his subject in *Annie Hall* and *Manhattan.*

The dearth, or death, of language as a means for carrying on relationships is a sign, a warning, that something has gone terribly wrong with the way men and woman see themselves and each other in movies. They are no longer building on the rock of relationships. They no longer consider themselves or anyone else worth the effort or risk. The movies of the '70s indicate a period of discouragement about the human capacity for steady affection and reason. This is not a study in social history but rather a comparison of observed portrayals and attitudes in movies from two periods. The source of the discouragement might be found in any combination of causes: the demeaning frustrations of cold war; the preponderance of machinery in our lives; men's and women's emphasis on careers to the neglect of relationships; television's usurpation of conversation time at home; Hollywood's own self-indulgence in cashing in one sensation; the shift to screenplays about relationships between men; the demise of the great screenwriters. Whether such causes are pertinent to this particular look at these particular movies is possible but also doubtful. Movies, even bad movies, are art rather than social science. They express the general and varied conditions of a society in a number of ways, constituting reference points for their times. They specifically express the attitudes of the individuals who collaborate in making movies, notably writers and directors, just as a "wasteland" or "hollow men" may or may not be images for our society but are certainly images for T. S. Eliot's perceptions of it. During any period, moreover, many, even opposing, attitudes find expression and adherents. After all, Prufrock moped and sighed through deserted streets while Ogden Nash found sunny sociability everywhere and Robert Frost swung merrily in birches. Within the year that Hamlet called the world "an unweeded garden," Sir Toby capered blissfully in Olivia's backyard. And so it is with movies too.

The movies of the '70s discussed here suggest that one may find integrity in one's professional life, but the human being may not be capable of personal integrity. (Isn't that sad disparity exactly what we see in Liv Ullman, mature, accomplished actress, star of screen, and Liv Ullman, pitiful, confused little girl, author of *Changing?*) Like the universe, these movies lament, we are composed of random particles that prompt random desires that, in turn, prompt random encounters. The two movies of 1949 suggest that the individual can find integrity; we can integrate our professional and personal lives because, like the Rock of Gibraltar, we are strong and firm and can understand what we really want.

If Matthew Arnold bemoaned the lost "sea of [religious] faith" in 1867, how would he weep and wail now that the sea of humanistic faith has dried up? There is consolation to be found, though, in the almost old-fashioned *10* and *Arthur*. Like the movies of 1949, these Dudley Moore vehicles rest on the power of conversation, personal growth, and independence. Gorgeous as Bo Derek's Jenny is in *10,* she nevertheless makes herself repellent, on the very brink of sexual consummation no less, by expressing her complete indifference to her wedding vows with a coldly mocking "Wow!" Her perfect wantonness is too much for her new lover, to whom adultery without guilt or attachment is unthinkable and to whom being treated as a sex object heralds a revelation about the value of being treated as a person. Out of bed he jumps, barely, but technically, faithful, to return to the good, middle-aged woman who loves him and will ever hold up her end in a good argument. The valet-guardian, played by John Gielgud in *Arthur,* is important precisely because he has important things to say, while no one else takes time to talk sense, or even much nonsense, to the silly, drunken Arthur. In these two movies, learning that one wants to grow up into an independent person and be true to another independent person still runs strong.

2.

Woman's Work in Movies
of the '30s and '40s

Women are terribly important in movies of the '30s and '40s. Just as they occupy the center of most nineteenth-century novels, so they carry the central and pivotal roles in many movies. In neither form do they necessarily assume worldly roles; rather, they play out their importance through the conventional roles of secretary, governess, girlfriend, wife, and mother. Conventional as the roles are, the characters created to fill them are certainly not, if a conventional woman's role suggests, as it usually does, a subordinate position, a life lived in the service and shadow of a man, not to mention an image of "the little woman"—sweet, uninformed, vulnerable. For nineteenth-century writers and for Hollywood's Golden Age screenwriters, women were fascinating subjects, worthy "centers of interest," as Henry James called them, because, unlike men, their freedom from "the world"—from schedules, business, politics, commerce, and from the numerous impersonal contacts they involve—gave them the advantage of time to cultivate character, to concentrate on people, to acquire a kind of expertise where both the inner life and relationships are concerned. "Writing about men," said Joseph Mankiewicz, "is so . . . limited. They're made up, for the most part, of large, predictable, conforming elements. Men react as they're taught to react, in what they've been taught is a 'manly' way. Women are, by comparison, as if assembled by the wind. They're made up of—and react to—tiny impulses. Inflections. Colors. Sounds. They hear things men cannot. And, further, react to stimuli men either can't feel or must reject as 'unmanly.' "[1]

All women's conventional roles involve them in relationships, usually with men, but in these relationships the women are instrumental in shaping men's characters and determining the direction of their lives. They are hardly dolls, happy homemakers, or even "the angel in the house" that Virginia Woolf deplored. (Such women, in fact, are routinely ridiculed, when they do appear in movies, for their passivity, implied stupidity, and materialism, until the '50s, when attitudes toward both men and women suffer unhappy changes, resulting in characters who look weak and foolish. See chapter 5.) The limitations of their opportunities notwithstanding, many women in movies of the '30s and '40s, without benefit of a man's kind of job, are full of initiative, ready to act, rich in many-sided intelligence. An examination of a few movies in which women play conventional roles might tell us something first about how such roles were themselves regarded, especially by men, and, second, how women in those roles fared and functioned.

Hollywood saluted the New Deal with a peerlessly ebullient musical called *Footlight Parade*. James Cagney is the producer and Joan Blondell is his secretary. The job of secretary has understandably become unpopular since 1933, conjuring up visions of servile women, compromised and degraded by their bosses. No one is going to compromise or degrade Joan Blondell, however! She's smart, tough, worldly-wise—a boon to her boss precisely because she's alert and independent. He alone can never get his ideas to work; he alone is vulnerable to glamorous, rapacious women; he alone has flawed judgment. Before he is aware of his exact circumstances, while he is still spinning in confusion and wondering why his plans won't work out, he is not left to toil alone, for he has a perfect partner in his secretary. Her reason, shrewd judgment, and good sense save him from professional ruin, personal folly, and marital calamity. Her assets of character enable her to act, to take decisive measures in casting the shows, getting them booked into theaters, and dismissing the gold diggers. Furthermore, it's only a matter of time before her boss will see and value her rightly. She won't have to, and doesn't want to, gloat secretly over the "only joke" that "every woman knows" she has on those idiots called men. For her boss isn't an idiot any more than she is. Without his imagination, her practicality would be of little use. Without his honesty, her good judgment about people would serve no moral end. It's the partnership that counts, and the secretary is the only person in his life equal to such a relationship. Unlike the assorted chiselers and gold diggers who intrude, onstage and backstage, parasites and pirates all, the secretary, neither granting nor asking for favors, works for a living and for a relationship.

Six years after *Footlight Parade* toasted America's honest, dedicated workers and rejoiced at their chances for employment, Jean Arthur, as Saunders the secretary, sat in the nation's capital waiting for James Stewart, as junior senator Jefferson Smith, to arrive. What transpires between these two is very similar to the secretary-boss story of *Footlight Parade*. Jean Arthur's secretary is just as worldly-wise as Joan Blondell's, but Arthur's experience in Washington has jaded her. At first, Jefferson Smith, bathed in idealism, looks like an idiot to her. But, as he needs her to help him through his awakening to corruption in people and politics, so she needs him to reawaken in her the faith she once had in people's goodness. Both the producer and the junior senator are imaginative, honest, and naive. Both are prone to fall in love with their own wild ideas, their grand projects; they pay too little attention to people, don't understand them very well, run the risk of being exploited by some and of overlooking those whom they need. They both need someone who will respect them enough to tame but not to undermine their ideas and, in so doing, to teach them something about people. In both movies, it's the secretary who wins that part—a part that is complicated, delicate, and pivotal. Without her, there can be no success; without her, the producer would lose his show; without her, the junior senator would go home to Ohio in tears.

Governess and teacher are other conventional jobs women held. Bette Davis, who probably outran all actresses in the variety of women she portrayed on the screen and in the dynamic force she gave a scene just by making an entrance (in *Cabin in the Cotton*, everyone seems slumped over until she comes on screen and revives all in sight, including the audience), succeeds as governess and teacher, too, and succeeds, moreover, as the two secretaries did, in upsetting or redefining the conventional ideas associated with such roles. Admittedly, it would be hard for Bette Davis to be ordinary in any movie, but the very fact that such a strikingly individual actress was cast in some conventional women's roles suggests that such roles could be "centers of interest," catapulted beyond their imagined limits by the force of women's characters.

In *All This and Heaven Too,* the duchess (played by Barbara O'Neill) is the woman with tremendous power on her side—she is noble in her own right; married to a nobleman; in league with an abbot; friend to the king—but these obvious credentials for success avail her nothing. It is Bette Davis as the governess, in all her meek, polite servility, who assumes a kind of leadership in the duke's house because she is of superior mind and judgment. She has the credentials that make a person independent in a psychological sense, which bears more weight even than her financial independence. Everyone except her eventually succumbs to the madness generated by the duchess. While the duchess alternates between vain adornment of her person and sex-starved raving, the governess draws close to people, sheltering the duke and his children in the embrace of her peaceful reason, enriching her own life with the warmth of close ties. Mother as well as teacher to each of the four children, friend to the duke, loved "above all bargains" by all five, the governess nevertheless loses everything except her greatest asset: her strong character that enables her to suffer loss without being essentially diminished. It is her capacity for what Henry James called "affronting one's destiny," of meeting horrible circumstances that one cannot fully control with heroic patience and resilience, that writers of novel and screenplay have assigned to women leading quite conventional lives. Whether this is the way women are or the way writers wish them to be is of small account here. That they are perceived and presented in this way says enough.

Seeing clearly, exercising restraint, making practical choices, and accepting limits—these are among the gifts women bring to conventional roles and to the relationships such roles imply. Unlike Virginia Woolf's "angel in the house," however, women like Bette Davis's governess do not martyr themselves to lives of sacrifice even though they may suffer and lose heavily. Joan Blondell's secretary is struggling through the Depression; Saunders is demoralized; the governess loses the man she loves and her country as well. Yet they all come to feel that they can have "all this and heaven too" because, paradoxically, they can stand to have less than everything they want. One of the greatest services they perform is teaching men to modify their desires, thus saving them from frustration and failure. The producer has to learn to give up on the glamorous gold diggers in favor of the relatively plain but more deeply suitable secretary; the junior senator has to give up his rosy view of government in order, paradoxically, to save his ideas and his idealism; the duke should have learned, but couldn't, that "it is not given to everyone to have his heart's desire." The governess, who speaks those words to him, flees to America, becomes a French teacher in a girls' school in Manhattan, and marries a fine, intelligent man who loves her but who must pale next to her memory of the duke. She can thrive on less than her "heart's desire."

Girlfriends in any movie might be forgiven for limiting their repertoire to looking pretty and forward to marriage. Even the sweetest ingenue, however, has been known to rescue her role from triteness by amplifying it with the sort of resourcefulness and adaptability the more mature secretaries and governess practiced. Judy Garland in *The Clock* and Cathy O'Donnell in *Detective Story* look like little country girls whom Manhattan would crush and corrupt in a day. In each movie, as a matter of fact, a far more worldly woman stands by for purposes of comparison—Garland's bossy roommate and O'Donnell's sophisticated older sister. Nevertheless, it is the simple girls with the innocent faces who excel at meeting the unexpected and dealing with it maturely. Each, under her circumstances, has only herself to rely on.

In the course of two days—a soldier's forty-eight-hour leave before going overseas—Garland meets and marries a young corporal from Indiana. What makes the story believable is the intensity of their feelings accelerated by the exigencies of the war. However vulnerable she may appear to her roommate, she is a good judge of her situation and of the lonely soldier she meets by chance in Penn Station. Her special role involves showing him the big city and easing away his fear of it. She makes a friend out of frightening New York for him by choosing just those places that represent the comfort of a city's culture: the Central Park zoo; the Metropolitan Museum; a small, elegant restaurant; an Episcopal church. By the end, both are tearing madly in and out of subways and municipal buildings, just like natives of Manhattan, trying to get a marriage license. Although she marries precipitately, her decision suggests courage rather than foolhardiness. The two are obviously suited to each other. It is life that imposes haste on them. Back home in their safe rural nests, they would have courted for years. But the world, the times, the war have chased them to the city. She could hold out for church and orange blossoms when the war is over, but she endures the appalling sixty-second, City Hall ceremony instead, for, like the governess, she has the strength and flexibility to garner the best that this life offers and to accept the instability, tackiness, and uncertainty that life imposes without succumbing to them within herself.

The girlfriend in *Detective Story* discovers that the boy next door not only loves her older sister but has been arrested for embezzling money to afford her expensive tastes. Cathy O'Donnell is infinitely loyal and true; what saves her from having a sticky, cloying effect is the swift efficiency with which she meets this miserable situation. Raised in some clean, distant suburb, she's never been touched by crime and police precincts before, but thrown into a tough urban setting, she knows how to act there. Implicit in her arrival on the scene with all the money she could scrape together are the familiar practicality and good judgment all these women share. She has faith in the boy she loves, understanding in a minute the youthful yearnings, rather than criminal impulses, that made him steal the money. By the staunch fight she puts up for him, persuading his boss as well as one policeman to accept repayment and let him go, she helps him to rein in his desires exactly the way the secretary helps the producer to give up the gold diggers in *Footlight Parade*. Innocent and inexperienced though she is, the girlfriend exercises the quickest and most precise judgment of the main character, the detective McCleod (played by Kirk Douglas), who sees no difference between the psychopathic killer raving in their midst and the shy, romantic embezzler. She even challenges McCleod directly. "Why are you so vicious?" she asks, when everyone else, including his superiors, tiptoe around him, not knowing how to interpret or handle his excesses.

The role of the girlfriend could be uninteresting. (*Boy Meets Girl* satirizes so well the dull, overused role and plot Hollywood's screenwriters feared they'd be perennially stuck with.) *The Clock* and *Detective Story* provide examples, and not solitary ones by any means, of girlfriends who trust themselves and their own feelings enough to act courageously in strange situations and to impart their courage to the men they love. The girlfriend played by Lauren Bacall in *To Have and Have Not* is far more sophisticated than Garland's or O'Donnell's girlfriend. Bacall works harder to make her role look unconventional—she brings humor and panache to her sexual advances; she swaggers around like the guys; she carries the androgynous nickname of Slim; and she does a funny mockery of the pretty, feminine rival—but she is no more, or less, free from squeamishness and fear, meets surprise and danger with the same cool head, believes in and aspires to love and marriage, which commitment, involving risk and resting on strong character, is represented as the final manifestation of each girlfriend's courage, never as a form of displaced suicide. To be a wife, for all of these women, is to have continued opportunities for moral courage.

No better example of a conventional wife—the woman who wants to marry, raise children, and keep house—exists in movies than Mary Bailey (played by Donna Reed) in *It's a Wonderful Life*. The movie itself tests the validity of her role in her husband's life by stressing his frustration with everything in his life, including his domestic "trap." In all the movies discussed here, the women become "centers of interest" partly because they accept limits, that is, see realistically and never expect life to be a fairy tale and are able to teach such acceptance to the men they love. The women's realistic outlook is noteworthy inasmuch as old movies are routinely accused of presenting life as a fairy tale by critics who may confuse fulfillment won by hard work and adjustment with fulfillment won by magic; who may not believe in fulfillment; or who may require amputations, rapes, and toilets before a movie looks realistic to them. In *It's a Wonderful Life,* all the forces of the movie converge to teach George Bailey (played by James Stewart) that his own romantic dreams impede him from feeling fulfilled by a life composed of the very ingredients heroic adventure demands: danger; spontaneity; moral courage; love; and success. The movie implicitly asks an important question about Mary: does she, satisfied simply to marry and raise a family in provincial Bedford Falls, attenuate or enhance George's chances? The movie answers that she enhances them all along. What does she do besides love him truly and bear four healthy children? She takes on George Bailey, knowing he is a dissatisfied, moody man, rejecting the rich man her mother is so excited about, because she has known since childhood that George is made of heroic stuff; she deftly acquires a wreck of a house because, despite its faults, it is affordable, spacious, and charming. Like all the other women already discussed, moreover, she accepts life as a series of problems which often come as rude surprises and need swift solutions. When the villainous Potter threatens to close George's little building and loan business and all the depositors are clamoring for withdrawals, Mary appears at the door with the honeymoon money and so saves the business. It's raining, all their money, save two dollars, is paid out to customers, there will be no honeymoon, George arrives at the leaky, cobwed-streaked wreck late, having had to work extra hard at the office on his wedding day. This is hardly an ideal wedding night or an auspicious beginning for married life for either one, but George has a powerfully understanding friend in his wife; she seized the way to foil Potter and save her husband. She saves the day at the end too. Again the evil Potter threatens the little business. This time, George gives up in despair and goes off to kill himself. While the angel Clarence takes him on a journey through time as if he had never lived, Mary calls everyone she knows, including her rich ex-suiter in Paris, to raise money to save her husband and the business. When George returns from the nightmare of nonexistence, he is ready to treasure life as it is—an uncertain process, a hazardous course, sometimes made fulfilling by warm relationships.

There are many movies of the '30s and '40s about seriously career-minded women, an apt subject for another time (see chapter 4). There are also movies that take a dim view of women, making the best woman the movie has to offer look somehow uninteresting, unintelligent, nasty, or weak, a view that takes firm hold in the '50s. (see chapter 5). Ironically, it was a woman, Clare Booth, who packed a whole play, *The Women,* filmed in 1939, full of antipathy toward women, presenting them in the various guises so rightly alarming to contemporary feminists: helpless; conniving; empty-headed; jealous; idle; disloyal. Most movies of the '30s and '40s, however, conveyed a strong admiration and approval of women, and those that portrayed women filling the most ordinary, conventional roles conveyed special messages about character. The relative drabness of the roles dismisses them from our concern; we don't care much about what the woman as secretary, governess, girlfriend, wife, or mother actually does in the way of chores. We care about what she is and what she does with her mind and heart. Her real work in life involves relationships, for these movies were made at a time when people believed that men and women were ultimately fulfilled by close relationships. In all of these movies, there is a clear desire for marriage, a desire shared by men and women. It is not women alone who desire it, nor is it presented as a way to put a woman "in her place." Relying on a literary tradition that sees marriage as a welcome resolution of a plot that derives its purpose and drive from characters' interpersonal problems, moviemakers of the '30s and '40s so often presented marriage in a spirit of social celebration, suggesting that men and women together can overcome obstacles to achieve personal fulfillment and maturity, thus assuring us that civilization will triumph and orderly life will go on.

The men in these movies show enormous respect for the women they choose, and they choose them as partners, not only as lovers. (Without the partnership, Nick and Nora Charles's marriage, not to mention their *Thin Man* movie plots, would lose all substance.) The screenplays themselves also show enormous respect for the women, casting them with the same spunk and common sense Shakespeare gave to some of his own heroines, like Rosalind, Portia, and Viola. Time and again, the men receive, and accept, guidance and protection from the women. Time and again, the women are called to action and figure out what they must do in scary or lonely situations. Not one of the movies discussed here, incidentally, ends with a kiss at the final fade-out, a gesture so often used as a simplifying statement about a whole story, a relationship and its future, as if to say, here are two people clinging to each other, losing each other in romance, and that's how they'll make it through life. These conventional women are invariably shown as capable of meeting the vicissitudes of life bravely, realistically, and independently.

3.

When Ideology Goes to the Movies

When ideology goes to the movies, no one can see straight anymore. Whatever is really happening up there on the screen must be denied, distorted, even rewritten to suit the party lines. Critics with an ideological bias, particularly some feminist critics, will turn a movie, if not the whole history of the movies, inside out if the party lines require it. I say "party lines" (rather than party line) because ideology is usually made up of several aphorisms, and they often contradict each other, which is part of the system's ingenuity; if one line fails, another will hold up on any given day. For ideologists of all stripes, the truth isn't important; the purpose of argument is not to defend the validity of one's position but to cultivate enemies as proof that the imminent hostility of the fiends forces unity behind a rigid, albeit senseless, set of claims. Ideologists are at war all the time, for that is when they are safest. Offer them a resolution, invite them to see reason, and their whole fabrication, which depends on sustaining the struggle, will collapse, leaving them with nothing to do but face the facts and go make an honest living.

Ideology's essentially martial motive helps to explain the provocative nature of the aphorisms. Some favorite, and famous, party lines of ideological feminists include these:

1. Girls are raised to be slaves to men.
2. Women owe all their problems to men or to their mothers, who raised them to be slaves to men.

3. Conventional family relationships victimize women and aggrandize men.

4. Women conduct much more mature relationships than men do.

5. Women are superior to men in intelligence, character, and morality.

6. Hollywood fostered a degrading image of womanhood but made men look good.

In her monstrously ideological *Popcorn Venus,* Marjorie Rosen fulminates as follows:

> Hollywood would not permit its films to refine or consolidate the image of women, nor, with its conservatism, would it even attempt to educate or offer female alternatives (other than journalism!). On-screen, woman's potential was sloughed aside, and her only sensible outlet was love.
>
> Just as in the twenties Hollywood's moguls appointed themselves guardians of women's morals, so now did they become wardens of their minds. In the MGM universe so carefully ordered by Louis Mayer and Irving Thalberg women were irrelevant, elegant mannequins or drawing-room fops. This emphasis was no accident, stemming from the producers' own attitudes toward feminine social roles.[1]

Rosen's failure to see that Hollywood made women look smart, fascinating, central to the action, rather than "irrelevant, elegant mannequins," and presented them in all kinds of careers other than journalism is not the worst of her faults here, although the evidence of hundreds of movies featuring the wit and wonder of womanhood is enough to cover her whole face with egg. The worst of her faults is the underlying surrender to ideology. She can't mention the strength, independence, and remarkable presence of Hollywood's women played by Mae West, Jean Harlow, Myrna Loy, Bette Davis, Barbara Stanwyck, Katharine Hepburn, and Rosalind Russell because she has to come out showing that Hollywood consistently fostered a degrading image of womanhood. Because such actresses as those above often—though not always—did portray women in relationships with men, Rosen is compelled to distort the truth of how interesting and original they looked in those relationships. What Rosen and her ilk demand for satisfaction is movies in which women have and care principally about top-flight careers and, moreover, are attached to no men. If women show strength of character through family relationships—Jane Darwell in *The Grapes of Wrath;* Olivia de Havilland in *Gone With the Wind;* Katharine Hepburn in *Holiday;* Fay Bainter in *Jezebel;* Sylvia Sydney in *Dead End*—or through originality and enterprise in dealing with life—Bette Davis in *Petrified Forest;* Vivien Leigh in *Gone With the Wind;* Mae West in *I'm No Angel;* Barbara Stanwyck in *Christmas in Connecticut*—Rosen must overlook them all. These movies are honest dramas, whose intention is to show something about human relationships and not to make propaganda.

She must also overlook the fact that men's strength of character, like women's, is, in movies of the '30s and '40s, shown principally through their relationships with women. Clark Gable, king of Hollywood, distinguished himself as an actor in his roles as a man in love. In *Red Dust, It Happened One Night, Gone With the Wind,* and *The Hucksters,* he portrays a man for whom profound, soul-stirring love is the measure of his masculinity. Playing a man ready to stake everything on love brings out the actor's full dignity, integrity, and warmth. The same is true for tough little John Garfield in *Nobody Lives Forever* or feisty James Cagney in *City for Conquest.* Gable played in plenty of all-male war movies and Westerns, but in them he always looks bored and gives perfunctory performances. Even in a war movie as dominated by men and military prowess overseas as *Destination Tokyo,* men's attachment to women back home provides much more than background; it provides the incentive for and suggests a fulfillment beyond victory in Japan. Therefore, Cary Grant is first seen making a call from the ship to his wife; next inquiring of an ordinary sailor about his baby; next writing a letter to his wife; next having assorted warm, personal conversations with subordinate officers; and only after all that, giving a pep talk to the crew. Meanwhile, the rakish renegade played by John Garfield is frowned upon by crew mates for having made a mess of relationships; for not wanting a family; for preferring a literal, sexy doll, which he takes on dates and props up on the seat next to him, to a real woman. The faith in people's being defined, freed, and fulfilled through relationships was such, in fact, that many movies used to resound with this damning refrain: "You don't need a husband (or wife); you're already married to your career (or possessions)! The implication is that people—men and women—not principally interested in relationships are not fully human (see *Craig's Wife, Mildred Pierce, Humoresque, From Here to Eternity*). Hollywood was fascinated with relationships, believed in them. How men and women fared with each other was Hollywood's favorite subject. It wasn't until that fascination faded in the '50s that both men and women really began looking as bad as Rosen claims women looked all along. (Chained to her party lines, she cannot see the illuminating distinctions Molly Haskell draws for us in *From Reverence to Rape*.[2])

Barbara Stanwyck's portrayal of the title character in 1936's *Stella Dallas* has come under special attack and presents us with an especially interesting case of a movie whose meaning, whose very visible evidence, must be distorted in the interests of ideology. Rosen has this to say:

> Stella must be pitied more than admired. For as this grotesque hyperbole of mother love, she has sabotaged her own identity, stifled her fears and dreams, and assuaged her emptiness through a comically vigorous motherhood, which would in the end leave her alone.[3]

For ideological feminists, it is de rigueur to regard Stella Dallas as a failure, to fear the example she provides of a woman who throws herself into a relationship with her daughter. If only these feminists were not so quick to see themselves and their own aspirations in every story, or so quick to regard all literary and cinematic portrayals as personally delivered warnings and recommendations or as political messages, they would allow writers some freedom to write the stories they want to write about people as they see them, instead of criticizing them for the way their individual creations fall short of strict, feminist requirements. Then they might see that the top-flight career or the rejection of men is not the only measure of a woman's success. Feminist reaction to *Personal Best* provides an interesting case in point. Many women were enraged, or agreed to take an enraged position vis-à-vis a movie in which a young woman's first love is another woman, through which love affair she matures and falls in love with a man. The point of the movie is to tell the story of a particular individual's way of developing sexually and emotionally. The enraged position of feminists hinged on the assumption that the point of the movie was to make a political statement against homosexual love. Such objections are in a league with objections to any portrayal of a woman that doesn't meet certain specifications. If it becomes de rigueur to present all women as exemplars, then fiction can no longer be about character, and movies, along with novels and plays, become posters—easy conveyors for propaganda. Clare Booth's *The Women,* though so tightly constructed, so clever and sharp, cannot be reckoned a great play for this very reason: every role serves the author's aim to condemn the whole female sex. Her play hasn't got one really interesting or original character in it.

In Marilyn French's *The Women's Room,* we learn that Val, the novel's paragon of feminism, "was most afraid of . . . ending up like Judy Garland or Stella Dallas." Val goes on to explain:

> "Oh, God! I'll never forget that last scene when her daughter is being married inside the big house with the high iron fence around it and she's standing out there—I can't even remember who it was, I saw it when I was still a girl, and I may not even be remembering it right. But I am remembering it—it made a tremendous impression on me—anyway, maybe it was Barbara Stanwyck. She's standing there and it's cold and raining and she's wearing a *thin little coat* and *shivering,* and the rain is coming down on her poor head and *streaming down her face with the tears,* and she just stands there watching the lights and hearing the music and then she just *drifts away.* How they got us to consent to *our own eradication!* I didn't just feel pity for her; I felt that shock of recognition—you know, when you see what you sense is your own destiny up there on the screen or on the stage."[4] (my italics)

Like Marjorie Rosen, Marilyn French has a perfect right to dislike *Stella Dallas,* but she doesn't have a right to misinform her readers. Both women, moreover, have a perfect right to dislike movies about relationships, but they don't have a right to regard such movies as evidence of a conspiracy to disparage women when, before the '50s, such movies were vehicles for extolling women. In the final scene of the movie that both writers find so offensive, Stella watches her daughter's wedding through a window. It is raining. Rain used to be considered a sign of good luck on a wedding day; maybe it still is. Stella happens to be wearing a handsome tweed coat with an ample fur collar; she is not shivering. The rain dampens but does not stream down. Tears are in her eyes, not streaming down her face, and a beatific smile lights up her face. After the kiss which seals the marriage, she walks slowly for a few paces, visibly moved, and then, as the rain stops, giving way to a beautiful, clear night, she breaks into a full smile, picks up her pace, and marches jauntily off. The scene which she has regarded beyond the window is such a trite one; all the characters in it are far less interesting, generous, or successful than she, for they can live only according to type. That is why they are framed appropriately and forever in that final wedding tableau, while Stella is seen on the move. But the daughter's happy marriage is the final stroke of Stella's success in her relationship with her daughter. Stella herself has refused to conform to any type. She has garnered for herself a life in which she is completely free to be herself, and that has always been more important to her than succeeding as Stephen Dallas's upper-middle-class wife. Once they are separated, she never misses him. He bores her; he is too stuffy. She doesn't want to subdue her hearty enthusiasm, put on airs, act like a lady, so she doesn't. At the same time, she recognizes and respects her young daughter's natural propensity to conventionality. Not bound by convention herself, she has chosen her own way of life, and part of that life is to help her daughter become the perfectly conventional social being she is, by her nature, meant to be.

Olive Prouty wanted to write about women who fulfill themselves in relationships with daughters. That is her subject. Her two best-known works, *Stella Dallas* and *Now Voyager,* are both about women who rise above unhappy childhoods and overcome the deleterious influence of their mothers. Stella Dallas's mother is worn out, discouraged by the drudgery of her working-class life. As played by Marjorie Main, she moves listlessly about, barely audible in conversation, and gives no cheer to her spirited, energetic daughter. But that daughter climbs out of the ghetto, marries into the upper class, and has a daughter of her own. When it soon becomes clear that she and her husband are incompatible, partly because Stella won't "sabotage her own identity," they drift apart, separate, and divorce, leaving Stella alone with her daughter. Charlotte Vale's mother, in *Now Voyager,* by contrast, is an iron-willed, domineering Puritan, whose repressive cruelty eventually drives her daughter to a mental hospital. The final stage of Charlotte's recovery takes place on a cruise where she meets and falls in love with a man who feels duty-bound to remain married to an emotionally disturbed wife and who feels inadequate to help his similarly disturbed younger daughter. That child, Tina, and Charlotte eventually meet, and the story ends as Charlotte becomes, in effect, the mother of this child.

For both Stella Dallas and Charlotte Vale, raising a daughter is a creative endeavor. They are as proud of their creations as Prospero is of his "rich gift," Miranda, whom he regards as a work of art. Olive Prouty is not writing about downtrodden women, victims of men. Her interests lie in the way women, at both ends of the social ladder, suffer from and escape social limitations—the vise of poverty or repression—to forge their own lives. Though both are unlucky in love with men, they don't let that sour their enthusiasm for life. Both women suffer, but it isn't suffering that makes them interesting to Prouty; it's the originality and indomitable vitality with which they overcome suffering. They are neither tragic nor pathetic, neither victims of themselves nor of men or mothers. They suffer because life makes people suffer. Stephen Dallas and Jerry Durrance suffer, too, but in trying to overcome their misery, they must seek the protective shade of convention, which is exactly what Stella and Charlotte don't do. For them, there are other things a woman can do with her life besides marry. It is noteworthy that the movies made from these novels keep playing down Prouty's tear-jerking style and keep emphasizing the women's strength and independence. The movies accentuate the women's nonconformism and originality.

Considering the kind of independent woman Prouty was writing about and the equally independent kind of actress—Barbara Stanwyck and Bette Davis—who portrayed her on the screen, it is somewhat surprising that Marilyn French chooses to attack *Stella*

Dallas. (Wouldn't *Christopher Strong,* in which daring aviator Katharine Hepburn, ruined by an adulterous love affair, commits suicide, have been a better, more valid choice? This is indeed a pathetic story, reeking of double standards and despair. *Anna Karenina* wouldn't be a bad choice either, offering three featured women whose fates are determined by the men in their lives. Or what about Bette Davis's parting trio at Warners, *Deception, June Bride,* and *Beyond the Forest,* all about women of inferior character at the mercy of wishy-washy men? A series like that is enough to make a far lesser light than Davis end her contract. Another superb choice is the decidedly insipid yet inexplicably popular *The Bells of St. Mary's,* in which the sisters, bravely led by Ingrid Bergman, do all the work—teach the children, solve their personal problems, bandage their cuts—while Father Bing Crosby saunters in, croons a tune, and walks off with all the power to hire and fire. The decade of the '50s, moreover, levels at women a "cavalcade of insult" against which French might justifiably have fulminated to her heart's content.) In French's eyes, however, eyes that see "a thin little coat" where a heavy one exists or that see someone drifting away who is actually marching, Stella has no identity, no life, because spending one's time on relationships, especially on any kind of family relationship, doesn't count; that's the way to "our own eradication!"

The Women's Room should, then, offer women all kinds of inspiration for a bright new future. With Val at the helm, women ought to find safe harbor or happy voyages in a fulfillment far beyond anything Stella Dallas or Charlotte Vale envisioned. How disappointing it is, then, to find a group of women with inordinate amounts of free time, cooking, eating, drinking, having love affairs, and railing against men and the Harvard establishment, which happens to be supporting all this leisure, since they are all there on scholarships. If their conversations yielded pearls, that would be one thing, but the great Val, confident, fulfilled woman, dispenses the sort of wisdom one is grateful to oneself for never having credited beyond the age of sixteen: "There's no such thing as a frigid woman; only inept men." "An eighteen-year-old boy is the best lover for a middle-aged woman." And her final gem: "It all comes down to who does the dishes." If it all comes down to who does the dishes, maybe they'd better cut back on all that cooking and eating, and read a book or get a job, but this isn't really the point. The point is that commitment to ideology is so blinding that one ceases to see clearly not just a remembered movie but the very story one is telling. French may think she is telling a story of women who, freed from binding relationships with men, create much better relationships with each other and lead more purposeful lives. It seems to be a given in the story that women are superior to men, that it would be a perfect, peaceful world if women ruled it. Yet the story abounds in failures that women can't fully blame on men, though French may intend one to. Iso, the ubiquitous lesbian, sniffing at the doors of sundry marriages, hoping their collapse will yield her a new female lover, emerges more promiscuous and dishonest than anyone else, and is even caught, in the best French farce manner, hiding her two female lovers from each other, despite the buildup she has had as a woman of integrity as well as an amorous panacea. She does finally pull herself together professionally, moves to London, where she pursues a scholarly career, and lives, as one might have predicted, with a divorceé. Val, the perfect mother for a daughter, brings her up in an atmosphere of open, frank, adult conversation, exposing her instructively to sexual roundelays and drunken flings. She leaves the child to handle situations any idiot can see the girl isn't ready for in the guise of respecting her identity as a capable human being, and one dark night Val receives the daughter's call from Chicago announcing she has been raped. The rapist turns out to be a black boy, at which point the story spins away, like the merry-go-round of *Strangers on a Train,* into ideological madness, with rapist acquitted (men always make judgments that are unfair to women) and with Val counselling forgiveness of the rapist (white men make black boys want to rape white women). It never occurs to Val that Lollie Dallas never got raped, maybe because her mother took care of her and taught her not to walk home unescorted late at night on city streets. Care is precisely what Val doesn't give her daughter. There aren't even the usual questions or consoling remarks when the daughter calls with her ghastly news. This perfect mother's first and last concern is with how they're going to beat the system in court. After the rape, and subsequent trial, the best Val can do is to send her poor daughter away to a female commune, when common sense might suggest holding the child close and driving the demons away with mother love. Finally, despite their Harvard scholarships and superior brains, these women don't ever sound very original, intelligent, or even motivated. When they aren't cooking, eating, or making love, they're in Harvard Square passing out leaflets or swapping gripes at the Women's Center. It's hard to imagine top-flight careers resulting from such meager ambitions and efforts. (Suddenly, ending up like Judy Garland doesn't look half bad!) Even listening to one of the villainous oppressors lecture on Chaucer or constitutional history might prove a more worthwhile use of their time (and such endeavor won't, under normal circumstances, come down to dishes).

The movie of *The Women's Room* departs from the book on precisely the issue of motherhood; the result is a story that, while still awash in hostility toward men, benefits from some ideological housecleaning. Two of the main characters, Val (played by Colleen Dewhurst) and the novice Mira (played by Lee Remick), have children. In the book, Mira abandons her two sons to go off and find herself on her scholarship to Harvard; in the movie, she makes a suicide attempt, after which her nasty, philandering husband wins custody of the boys. Thus abandoned, she finds her way to Cambridge. In the book, Val's daughter is raped in Chicago; in the movie, Val's daughter doesn't go to Chicago, nor is she raped. In the book, the end is bleak for all in this cruel world where men rule and women suffer. In the movie, Mira becomes a professor of English at Harvard, a perfect—oh, God! here it comes—role model for Val's daughter, who sits contentedly in Mira's class. Somewhat freed from the exigencies of ideology, the relationships among the women have a truer ring in the movie than they do in the book because people's behavior and destinies in the movie are motivated by their characters, by their relative capacities to confront life and each other, rather than by their ideology. What the movie does, in effect, is to give the women definite identities, so that we can see so clearly how the book's overweaning ideology, by robbing people of the right—or delivering them from the need—to think for themselves, robs people of character, too. Here is some true sabotage of identity for Marjorie Rosen to look into. Buttressed by consistently strong performances, with the outstandingly individual Dewhurst and Remick in the lead, the movie makes sharply delineated individuals out of French's amorphous female aggregation. Great movie stars and great novelists have exactly this in common: they can make ordinary people enchantingly original and their lives strikingly important.

Val says, "It all comes down to who does the dishes," but the novel and movie both show otherwise. Even in a story that believes and asserts that liberation is freedom from family ties, it still all comes down to how much a person can love someone else, how much people can care for each other. Ideological feminists must revile such love, which poses a threat to the self-spawned, self-seeking ideal who, tied to no one, can proudly proclaim, "I don't need anybody; I have myself." That is why they can't see the strength of Stella Dallas or Charlotte Vale. Nor can they see the strength of those extraordinarily powerful women who portrayed them on screen. Bette Davis and Barbara Stanwyck consistently played women involved in close relationships, some of which succeeded, some of which failed. That was Hollywood's great subject. Feminists may justifiably say they don't like the subject, but to insist that the dramatization of that subject eradicates or sabotages women's identities is plain distortion.

Speaking of those two great actresses prompts an aside. At the 1986 Golden Globe Awards ceremony, all the young actresses who made presentations appeared at the podium looking like floosies: too much make-up; hair suggestively tousled; breasts peeping slyly from slinky gowns. Bette Davis and Barbara Stanwyck also appeared, one to make a presentation, the other to receive an award. Davis and Stanwyck were practically the only women who looked as if they had any dignity and self-esteem, whose very presence, never mind their elegant attire, evoked a sense of strong character which unfolded to our memories, dissolve upon dissolve, the cast of vivacious women they have created for our own self-esteem. What disheartening confusion young women must feel that they clamor to be regarded as people, not sex objects, and yet make vulgar, self-denigrating displays of their bodies.

Marjorie Rosen must see every movie as an insulting portrayal of women in order to shore up her claim that Hollywood has played a very nasty trick on little girls in the name of entertainment. Marilyn French, too, must present a consistently negative picture of women's lives—in and out of movies—because such a picture gives credence and purpose to the party lines. French shows life as hard, unfair, and disillusioning for all her characters, weak and strong alike, which is a violation of common sense as well as of her characters themselves. It sends a confusing message out to all those young, hopeful women ready to take the world by storm, as silly and useless to modern womanhood in its way as the message of *Total Woman* is in its way. Olive Prouty, not bound by ideology, is free to concentrate on her characters as real people. She shows life as hard and imperfect for all her characters, but rewarding in some way for those who can struggle and love. When people really care about each other, one may suppose that the dishes will get done somehow.

4.

Labor's Pleasures: Professional Couples in the Movies

The movies of the 1940s abound in professional men and women: two-career families; career teams; and competitive colleagues. The stories' focus remains very much on personal relationships, but in many movies what makes people attractive and exciting to each other is the career, which becomes a new means for bringing out character, just as the workplace becomes a new setting for the business of personal life. In many instances, the division between the office and home melts; the office becomes home. Such changes in the emphasis on careers and in the setting for personal relationships depend on women's joining the professional ranks. As soon as women do join, careers themselves—what people actually do in a day's work—suddenly become interesting dramatic subjects and, moreover, suggest other, related subjects, like the way careers make individuals themselves interesting, the problems couples who work together face, and the conflicts careers engender when they absorb too much of a person's attention.

Before women came into the office in movies, the drama took place away from the office, and the man's profession, however important and fulfilling to both men and women, seemed negligible nonetheless and lingered in the background of their lives. Clark Gable dashes in and out of the office once in *It Happened One Night*, a shot, more than a full scene, one easily forgets, for the real story is set in the bus, the car, and assorted fields and motel rooms—apt settings for romance. Henry Fonda garners a scene at the office in

Jezebel, but his impatient fiancée does all she can to get him out of the bank, and, indeed, the rest of the action is located in one or another of the movie's gracious houses. Even in *Dark Victory*, where George Brent's profession is central to his appeal as a lover in the mind of his grateful patient, we see him once giving a physical that is photographed in those caressing close-ups we know foretell love, and twice hurrying out of surgical attire, but otherwise in various social and domestic settings.

When women joined men professionally at the office, careers in general—it didn't matter if it was a man's or a woman's since men and women pursued the same careers—acquired substance in movies. (The biographical picture constitutes a kind of exception because it does concern a person's career, but the career in such a movie has historical rather than dramatic importance.) Now it was possible to see what men other than boxers, servicemen, and gangsters actually did during the day. Part of what they did, inevitably, was to fall in love with their female co-workers, but they also worked diligently enough on professional projects to give us an idea of what kind of work they did and how they felt about it. It is true that in all these movies life in general and life at work in particular are stylized and glamorized, omitting with swift editorial finesse the diurnal tedium someone like Andy Warhol can't bear to cut from his movies; showing us only those aspects of each career that look interesting and that invite dramatic possibilities. By advancing the cause of relationships at the same time, these movies about careers suggest that relationships are a boon to the careers themselves.

The '40s movies about professional men and women are both casual and complimentary about professional women in the sense that the women require and receive no excuses or apologies to account for their presence—they are simply there, respected for the quality of their work, expected to keep up with if not to set the pace. The women are not in the least self-conscious or insecure about their positions, and the men accept them without nasty cracks or vulgar overtures. Within the movies themselves, no one makes any special mention or takes any special notice of the fact that Myrna Loy, for instance, is a pilot in *Too Hot to Handle* and a judge in *The Bachelor and the Bobby Soxer*, or that Constance Bennett is a lawyer in *Smart Woman*. Like the men, the women are attired simply, relying on character and ability, never on good looks, money, or beautiful clothes, to make their mark in both profession and relationship.

While it is true that, in these movies, a career enhances a woman's attactiveness and also that a woman's having a career enhances her relationship with a man, making it incontestably a relationship of equals, it is also true that careers sometimes interfere with the possibility of a relationship and often come into open conflict with a relationship. Working together is part of what draws men and women together, even though it also serves sometimes as the source of their arguments and hostility. Such movies, then, show us what Hollywood had to say about professional women, but, appropriately enlarging the scope of their subject, they go on to explore the problems of professional people, who tend to fall in love with their work, to work compulsively, to neglect people, to mix up love and work in improper ways, and who find sometimes that one life won't grant both a great career and a great love.

His Girl Friday alerts us to the attractiveness inherent in Rosalind Russell as journalist at the first fade-in. She deposits her terribly timid, square, and somewhat obtuse fiancé (played by Ralph Bellamy) on a bench and breezes confidently past reporters and stenographers toward the office of her daring, witty, shrewd ex-husband (played by Cary Grant). In that shot, she traverses the distance between two lives: as the conventional wife of a reliable insurance salesman at home in Albany (since Henry James started beating on upstate New York in *Daisy Miller*, the region has been fair game for anyone in search of a dull setting); as the wife and partner of a high-powered newspaper editor at home on Manhattan's streets, in courthouses, jails, telephone booths—wherever there is disturbance. The movie itself, unable to abide the thought of a vibrant, intelligent, capable woman's burying herself under a picket fence in Albany, winds its plot any way it can to keep her working with her ex-husband. Even her fiancé joins in, changing their departure time to make room for her crucial interview of the murder suspect. She thinks she seeks a quiet, ordinary life, but, when caught with a story she alone must write for the newspaper, her joyful acceleration, her hightened efficiency, her complete pleasure in getting a first-rate article out belie her mundane aspirations. As the movie's end suggests, there is no perfection to be had. Life with Ralph Bellamy would offer infinite consideration, security, and boredom. He is a very sweet, gentle man. Life with Cary Grant offers rough neglect, continual upset, and excitement. He is a somewhat boorish man. The choice isn't simply between boredom and excitement, though, or even between consideration and neglect. Implicit in the choice of a man is a recognition of the personal importance of a career to a man, to a woman. Having been set afire by a story herself, she may now be able to understand why the man she is about to remarry gets so passionately involved in his work that he forgets about her. Didn't she forget all about her fiancé, who'd been waiting for the duration of the movie to take her to Grand Central Station? Although her having divorced him once may make the editor try to be a little careful and considerate in future, there isn't much hope for reform in the closing fade-out: he barges through the door, ahead of her, leaving her to struggle with the bursting briefcase. What really matters, though, is that they have fun working together, that they truly know each other, and that they can be themselves with each other. They won't have much of a conventional home life, and she may have to forefeit her honeymoon this time too, but their careers don't have to be regarded as competing with other interests. They can be regarded as satisfying them, as incorporating those other interests once it is clear that the characters actually come to life for and are drawn to each other through their careers.

How Rosalind Russell might have languished in Albany is dramatized in *You Belong to Me*, where Henry Fonda, as an idle millionaire, has fallen in love with and married Barbara Stanwyck, the doctor who rescued and treated him after a skiing accident. Every morning she leaves their posh mansion and goes off to work in her plain office, and every day her rich husband mopes around the estate watching his servants get work done. While he is jealous of her male patients, he never specifically resents her career, for it is precisely her energy and competence that make her so attractive to him. The solution is very simple: he must find a career too, and, in the true New Deal spirit, he must do something with his millions to create many jobs, not just one for himself. The animated look, the brightened features with which he greets her at the end, when he has bought a near-bankrupt hospital where he will be the chief administrator and she will be chief of staff, say so much about the emotional thirsts that are quenched by careers and about the role of careers in enhancing a relationship.

You Belong to Me—the title is annoyingly stupid and inaccurate, just like the title *His Girl Friday*; both imply an unequal relationship, when the stories pointedly proclaim the success of teamwork—is one of many movies in which a man spends some time playing impressed spectator to an accomplished woman, a woman whose drive, poise, and expertise attract him to her and, moreover, to the possibilities of leading an energetic life himself. This is the role that Joseph Cotten finds himself playing in *The Farmer's Daughter* vis-à-vis Loretta Young's housemaid. He has inherited an old family name, a huge house, great wealth, and a Senate seat in Washington; she is a bright young woman from a Swedish-American farming family, whose nursing school money was swindled away from her on her way to the big city. Brave and resourceful, she stays in the city and finds herself a job as a domestic servant in that huge house rather than go crying home penniless. Contact with the senator and all the political people who appear at the house for meetings and parties sparks her curiosity. Before long, she is herself fully involved in politics and running for a Congressional seat in the opposing party. Despite her opposition, the senator finds her irresistible, wants her to win, ultimately teaches her how to campaign because everything she takes an interest in becomes interesting to him. Her very receptivity to learning carries a charge that his teaching lacks. Prone to passivity and lethargy, he is awakened to the thrill of the position he already holds by this young immigrant hopeful. And true to the message that Hollywood seemed bound to convey about shared professional life, at the end of the movie, when she has won both her seat in Congress and the senator for a husband, the two arrive at Washington's Capitol, where he picks up his bride and carries her across the threshold of their new home: the office is home.

The vivacity with which professional women are endowed indicates Hollywood's favorable attitude toward, even fascination with, them. In movies where careers are not shared but both men and women have them, it is often the women who become the centers of attention where both the story and the men in the story are concerned. That is true in two Bette Davis vehicles, *Old Acquaintance* and *The Great Lie*. In the former, Bette Davis is a serious novelist whose budding success spurs her jealous friend from childhood, played by Miriam Hopkins, to become a writer too, albeit a writer of formulaic romance novels. Miriam Hopkins has an extremely pleasant, sweet husband who undoubtedly has a career of his own, but we hear nothing of it. Rather, the movie focuses on the women, promoting the serious artist and ridiculing the cheap imitator. The husband finds himself repelled by his wife, whose fierce competitiveness, vanity, and zest for fame leave no room for relationships, and drawn to her friend, whose scruples and tender heart will not permit her to "steal" her friend's husband, even though their marriage has died on its own. So both women lose where love and marriage are concerned. Miriam Hopkins is something of a villain in this movie; we are invited to think that she heartlessly abandons husband and child to concentrate on a worthless career. But Bette Davis loses not only her friend's husband but other men too. Somehow, relationships keep failing, although she becomes a huge success artistically, for some careers, especially artistic careers, take time that one can't share. (A notable exception is acting, to which Hollywood responded with numerous outstanding theatrical couples playing and battling their way through life. More of them later.) When a career demands most of one's time and thought, as it does for Bette Davis in *Old Acquaintance*, one misses chances for love. (Seven years later, in *All About Eve*, a sad, anxious Margo Channing, also played by Bette Davis, will talk directly to this point of the way pursuit and achievement of greatness in a career preclude the chances for a strong relationship, certainly before middle age.) Life doesn't offer complete fulfillment to the novelist, but the movie certainly doesn't blame or compassionate her for that. There is no suggestion that without marriage she is a failure. On the contrary, her unconventional life is presented as one intriguing, valid, and satisfying possibility among several from which honest, intelligent, and talented people may choose. Her extramarital affairs lend her a certain appealing worldliness and maturity in contrast to the pinched provinciality of her friend. She is presented, moreover, as a better mother and example to the romance writer's daughter than the legitimate and priggishly correct mother.

The woman Mary Astor plays in *The Great Lie* receives the same sort of approval as Bette Davis's novelist in *Old Acquaintance*.

A famous concert pianist, Mary Astor toys with the ideas of marriage and motherhood, but she really doesn't have time for either and gives up both, leaving the man free to marry Bette Davis. Even though Davis ends up with George Brent and the baby, it is the pianist who stands out. She's not a nice person; in fact, she's a trouble-making prima donna, but when she enters a scene, one is tickled by the vitality behind her selfishness and colossal nerve and the humor behind her impudently assertive style. As George Brent says, in trying to assuage his wife's jealous fears, "Any man would find her (the pianist) exciting," but he feels well out of marriage with her. He is one of the few men involved with a dynamic professional woman in '40s movies who actually pressures her to give up her career for him without realizing, as the other men do, that her passion for her career is part of what makes her so exciting. That a woman who chooses a career over marriage has second thoughts, tries to break up another woman's marriage, and threatens to "steal" the baby should win a movie's implicit approval by charming us with her pluck says so much about the attitudes prevalent in the '40s. Those "unsavory" acts would define her total character in a '50s movie, but in *The Great Lie* they are handsomely outweighed by her admirable talent, independence, and sophistication. One other interesting feature of this movie is the handling of George Brent's career as a daring pilot. He does get a few chances to land small planes on Davis's lawn, but otherwise he carries out what must be pretty important exploratory missions for the government offscreen, while Mary Astor pounds away at Tchaikovsky's First right before our eyes. For when men and women have separate careers, pursuing different professions, the movies tend to concentrate on the woman's career, making both the woman and the career look admirable and delightful.

There are many movies about shared careers—*His Girl Friday* is one example already discussed—which deal directly with the fun couples can have working as a team, with the way twenty-four-hour days together heighten people's awareness of each other's needs and deepen their sensitivities to each other's vulnerability. In movies like *It's Love I'm After* and *To Be or Not to Be*, both about theatrical couples, the leading man and woman have all kinds of problems with each other, but their relationship is enhanced by the time they spend on stage together because the acting itself—the being somebody else with each other—ultimately compels them to define their real selves. Each knows who he or she really is beneath the costume and make-up because the other is waiting, also underneath the costume and make-up, to confront the real person. It may be hard for someone not involved in theater to understand the thrill of discovery such a couple feels each time they meet each other and get to be themselves again. Even if they meet to fight—and that's largely what happens between Bette Davis and Leslie Howard in *It's Love I'm After*—they fight joyfully, relishing the use of their own words, thinking up their own plots with gusto. Knowing a person through his or her disguises becomes an affirmation of one's own self and the true self in the person one recognizes and loves. They can't fool each other, which means two things: they have to be honest with each other, which is the emphasis of *It's Love I'm After*, and they can act as a team in perfect coordination to fool everybody else, which is the emphasis of *To Be or Not to Be*. (There are theatrical stories about catastrophe, too, a subject that deserves treatment in its own right, in which acting serves neurotic needs, as it does for Hamlet, creates confusion about who one is, as it does for Margo Channing in *All About Eve*, or occasions the loss rather than the recovery of self, as it does for the actor in *A Double Life*. In such stories, acting has nothing to do with having fun at work and becomes eventually intolerable to each actor. Another kind of theatrical couple is presented in 1954's *A Star Is Born*, this version surpassing the original because of the sharpened delineation of the fading actor's motivation: yearning for his own rebirth, he hopes to achieve it by living through the gifted singer's career. Thus, her career becomes necessarily both a triumph for him and a reminder of his failure, eventually making her professional life intolerable to both. Their greatest scene may well be their last, in which we see two people whose love, though true, is founded precariously on a subtle interplay of sympathies and generosities that finally force them to be secretive and false with each other. At the end, they are acting, fooling each other, unable to find each other, and not wanting to be found, beneath the disguises. For a further discussion, see chapter 8.)

The opening scene of *It's Love I'm After* shows us that the couple playing the death scene of *Romeo and Juliet,* while engaged in acting, know who they really are, for *sotto voce* they are quarreling. As soon as the curtain falls, they leap up and accost each other in a rapture of insults. Their fights keep them on an even keel, protecting them from the risks theatrical flesh is heir to, like losing oneself in one's parts, falling in love with oneself, and identifying with the adulatory image adoring fans fashion out of one's performances. In this movie, the man is particularly at risk, and the woman who knows him so well saves him. When Leslie Howard has got himself utterly enmeshed in an offstage theatrical plot to persuade dizzy Olivia de Havilland that he is not worth her infatuation, he himself succumbs to it even though he has had the discernment to ask her whether she loves him or the parts he plays. At this dangerous juncture, Bette Davis, theatrical partner and lover, appears on the scene. Her mere presence is almost enough to restore her man to his senses, but she delivers some shrewd observations that show him, and us, the true value of a shared career. They love acting and make a wonderful team on stage, but they are not the parts they play. He especially needs her to remind him who he is, and she does so by painting a picture for him of marriage with the doting de Havilland, who "won't fight" and "won't give him an out". "Love for breakfast, love for lunch, and love for dinner." What else could happen to him in such a marriage, she is saying, but that he should have to become an actor in his private life? (No wonder he groans "Oh, horrible!" in response.) She doesn't need to add that with her he can relax after a hard night on stage, have a good row, be as obnoxious as he pleases.

The theatrical couple of *To Be or Not to Be,* played by Jack Benny and Carole Lombard, happen to be very poor players on stage, even though they are stars in their native Warsaw. (As a suitably unimpressed Nazi says, "What he [Benny] did to Shakespeare, we are now doing to Poland." Benny's rendition of a mere two of Hamlet's lines is enough to bear out the Nazi's evaluation; luckily we are spared Lombard's Ophelia.) Nevertheless, they find their true calling as actors offstage playing to outwit the Nazis. They are acting for their lives, and once they commit themselves to this new career, the usual actors' weaknesses like vanity, jealousy, and the need to be pampered and reassured, so characteristic of their behavior before Hitler's invasion, fall away, rendering them poised and flawless performers. Each carries off solo impersonations, and finally they are brought face to face, he as the sinister spy, Professor Siletsky, whom Benny has actually just murdered, and she as the beautiful spy who is betraying her country and her husband by her alliance with Siletsky. The confrontation comes as a surprise to them, and they must play the scene without benefit of rehearsal or even of script. Their improvisation is brilliant, doubly so because they are acting toward each other as both the Nazi spies and as the real theatrical and married couple whose lives they must save. The enthusiasm, skill, and intelligence with which they succeed at their new career matures their relationship. Their days of playing with infidelity, petty jealousy, and injured sensibilities are over. Now they meet as loving adults whose excellent team-work serves a real purpose on the terrifying stage of Hitler's tyranny. They are rotten Shakespearean actors, but they have learned this much from the plays: the world's stage often demands the highest artistry.

In some movies, whether couples share a career or have separate careers, the professional life comes into open conflict with the relationship, and the story turns on the way people can run them-selves aground when careers mean too much to them. *City for Conquest, Woman of the Year,* and *I Can Get It for You Wholesale* deal with the dark, potentially tragic underside of career-minded peo-ple. All, therefore, are about excessive ambition. A woman is the main character in each story, and even though she suffers from what could be a fatal flaw and wounds those who love her, she is nevertheless endowed with the vitality and charm that make Ros-alind Russell's journalist, Barbara Stanwyck's doctor, and Mary Astor's pianist attractive. In other words, though they may be chastened, women are not punished, that is, stripped of their careers and sent home, for their ambitions, even when they grow beyond control. (If they refuse to be chastened, like the romance writer of *Old Acquaintance* or the villainous Eve Harrington of *All About Eve,* then they are punished to the extent that they are roundly detested by everyone in the movie and audience. They certainly don't lose their careers, though.)

City for Conquest concerns the ambitions of four people, three men and one woman. Only one, the even-tempered composer played by Arthur Kennedy, has a healthy ambition, and he becomes the greatest professional success. (A healthy ambition must be regarded here, as it has been since ancient times, as one that corresponds to the individual's capacities and that will not endanger his relationships with people.) The main plot of the movie concerns the desire of a young woman (played by Ann Sheridan) to become a professional dancer of the sort Ginger Rogers played, so she needs a partner. A very unpleasant dancer, played by Anthony Quinn, arrives to satisfy her desire. But it isn't simply the dancing she craves; she wants fame and social advancement, so she builds a very successful career with her sleazy partner and abandons the man she really loves, played by James Cagney, because his sights are too low, his prospects too dim. Her rejection stirs in him a desire to prove himself to her, so he becomes a boxer. Both Sheridan and Cagney are harmed by their careers: she is abused and degraded by her dancing partner, and he is blinded in a fight. This movie does not hesitate to make judgments about the relative value of careers, rating the artistic career above all others, as did *Old Acquaintance,* granting the composer a serene rise to fame at Carnegie Hall, while his boxing brother and the dancing girl struggle and fail in sordid settings. *City for Conquest* also rates a close tie between a man and a woman above either one's career, except in the case of the composer. At the end, the blind James Cagney stands at his deserted newsstand on a foggy night listening to his brother's Carnegie debut on a little radio. The humbled Ann Sheridan appears, and even though his sights are even lower than when she scorned him before, she now cherishes the purity of his love for her. It is a bittersweet ending, reminiscent of Pip and Estella's reunion in the ruined garden on that misty evening, with the same closing sense of love's being the only warm shelter in a world that continually tempts us into its cold depths.

Woman of the Year treats the same problem of an ambitious woman who, by her excesses, harms the man who loves her. The movie features two writers, played by Katharine Hepburn and Spencer Tracy, who work for the same newspaper. He is simply a reputable, contented sportswriter; she is "the second dame in the country next to Mrs. Roosevelt." She may work for a newspaper, but her reputation rests on so much more than a career in journalism, and she lets everyone know it and feel it. She is a dynamo: internationally recognized; politically influential; linguistically at home the world over. (Her catalog of credentials comes close to comprising a parody of the accomplished woman, similar to the all but royal qualifications that drape Sidney Poitier almost three decades later in *Guess Who's Coming to Dinner?*) Aside from their obvious attractiveness to each other, these two seem ill-suited for marriage. Though he is fascinated by her arch demeanor and subtle, intellectual sexiness, he is bound to suffer at her hands. Once married, she has very little time for him—the career always comes first—and she has very little respect for marriage. She treats him almost as a kept man, prancing in late from the office with her male secretary in tow, with whom she settles down to complete the day's business while her husband goes sadly off to the kitchen to cook. In a revealing conversation with her aunt, the stunning professional woman she has emulated all her life, calling her "my woman of the century," she expresses disappointment at her aunt's impending marriage: "I always thought you were above marriage." The aunt never felt above marriage; like the novelist in *Old Acquaintance,* the pianist in *The Great Lie,* and the composer in *City for Conquest,* bent on her career, she missed chances for relationships until middle age and, as she explains to her niece, eventually found success tiresome when there was no one to share it with.

To save herself from the degradation she associates with marriage, Katharine Hepburn's journalist degrades her husband. He tolerates everything but her exploitation of a little immigrant she has adopted. Swept away on the tide of her own importance, she callously leaves the child without a babysitter to go off and be named "woman of the year." At this, her husband skips his wife's great moment, returns the child to the agency, and moves out. Now she must confront the choice between an undisturbed pursuit of her career and the loneliness of life without a close relationship. Given to extremes, she tries to persuade herself that she really wants to be a full-time housewife. Neither the movie nor her husband will let her get away with that, however. Her husband asks her, "Why can't you be Tess Harding Craig?" rather than Tess Harding, career woman, or Mrs. Craig, housewife. The movie ends with the two reconciled and presumably with her understanding and respecting his steady capacity to balance love and work. The credibility of this ending is another matter. The stars' compatibility may make the ending plausible, but it's more likely that Tess Harding met the right man too soon and couldn't really cherish him until middle age, after a surfeit of lonely successes will have softened her. Unlike Rosalind Russell's journalist, who is easily friendly with people and secure about herself as an independent woman, Hepburn's Tess Harding is uncomfortable in close relationships, competitive with colleagues, achieving her sense of independence by subordinating others to her. Tess Harding's aunt, the novelist of *Old Acquaintance,* the pianist of *The Great Lie,* Margo Channing of *All About Eve,* and the composer of *City for Conquest,* all great professional successes, give up or miss chances for love in youth. These movies' recognition of the limitations life imposes, even on the great, seems more credible than the hasty happiness served up to Tess and Sam at *Woman of the Year*'s close.

I Can Get It for You Wholesale states the same problem: excessive interest in a career can make people hard and heartless in relationships. We see it in the top designer, played by George Sanders, a man who expresses explicitly his refusal to waste time on people's emotions. For him the career is what it is in so many '50s movies: a stern cultivation of ruthlessness varnished by a smooth, even graceful, exterior—a willful denial of the personality, especially its exuberant, imaginative manifestations, rather than the fulfillment of it. But in this movie, such a character looks cruel, nearly villainous (more like the mean, fat cats of earlier movies) rather than extraordinarily competent, as he will look in later '50s movies. The young woman played by Susan Hayward has a choice: she can ally herself with the top designer (Sanders), thus soaring to the top herself and coincidentally ruining financially the man she loves; or she can temper her ambitions and work with the man she loves, achieving professional heights eventually but not immediately. As in *Woman of the Year,* the career woman played by Susan Hayward possesses energy and impatience for success that make her special, just as such qualities make a man special, but they are dangerous sometimes, like wild weather, riding on a surge of inner savagery. Both the journalist of *Woman of the Year* and the designer rage out of control. They do and say preposterous things to wound their men, but both learn in good time to temper their ambitions so they won't have to lose out on love. The happy ending of *I Can Get It for You Wholesale* seems quite believable, because the designer is not completely hardened but is chastened by her struggle to the top. She and her business partner have been professional equals who struggled together before her ambitions skyrocketed, so they have a safe past to rest on (unlike the couple in *Woman of the Year*). And there is the sage influence of a loving employee, played by Sam Jaffe, who encourages the couple to save their relationship. In the kindest tone, he declares, "Love is a mess!" What better way could he find to convey his understanding of their quandary? When you yearn for professional success, love is such an inconvenience. Yet he knows it's all we have to save us from deserted, foggy streets, empty apartments, or icily efficient business partners. Working with the man she loves, the designer will share the fun, intimacy, and excitement enjoyed by the couples of other movies discussed here, notably *His Girl Friday, You Belong to Me, The Farmer's Daughter,* and *To Be or Not to Be.*

Movies of the '40s smile upon professional women and worry only about exaggerated ambitions, which worry writers have had about men and women for centuries. These movies prefer professional people—men *and* women—to find lasting love, too, but that is not a requirement for approval. Great talent, like the novelist's, the pianist's, and the composer's, is obviously valid in itself, as is strength of character. Such movies applaud courage and enterprise in their characters whether they succeed in love or not. Scarlett O'Hara may have lived in the 1860s, but despite her emotional and moral childishness, her agile adaptability and ready skill in business are consistent with the irresistible appeal of capable professional women to audiences of the 1940s, as well as with the admiring regard of men for such women within '40s movies. Scarlett defies all traditions of Southern femininity, but she's the one men find attractive. "I've always admired your spirit," Rhett says to her, and he could just as easily be speaking to a woman of the '40s, to his co-star Myrna Loy as the pilot in *Too Hot to Handle,* for instance. The respect granted as mediocre a movie as *Kitty Foyle* confirms Hollywood's interest in vigorously independent men and women. Kitty herself is enterprising and successful at business, "a real Main Liner," according to her working-class father, meaning someone who laid the railroad tracks rather than someone like Wyn (Dennis Morgan's part), who merely lives on the right side of them. Wyn is weak, a failure at work, a victim of inherited wealth, which has made him soft and feckless in contrast to the hard-working Jewish doctor Kitty eventually marries, who has become rich and successful by the same kind of vigor and independence that define Kitty.

Only the appeal of such characters can explain Ginger Rogers's Oscar for an unremittingly flat performance in a year (1940) when Katharine Hepburn sparkled as a true Main Liner, a wealthy Philadelphia socialite, in *The Philadelphia Story*. The movies of the '40s do not worry about professional women undermining, threatening, or competing with men. (These are worries for later decades.) If there is any harm in a woman's career, it is likely to affect her most, but even then not disastrously.

Couples who work, especially those who work together, are generally portrayed as having a richer, more intimate knowledge of each other for knowing about each other's passional fires, creative forces, and failings as they are manifested beyond the strict bounds of their personal relationships. These elements affect their personal relationship, of course, and in most instances favorably. Such couples are also portrayed as confronting the world and each other with great energy, so that their relationships as well as their careers are perennially infused with a sense of action. These people have what it takes to fight depressions and win wars. In their optimistic view, '40s movies see in professional people human beings who accomplish great things, and in the professional couple joyful examples of people who, spurred by the power of love, accomplish great things together.

Part II:

In The Doldrums

5.

Blank and Pitiless as the Sun:
Movies of the '50s

Nowhere since the nineteenth-century novel have men and women looked as good as they do in movies of the '30s and '40s. No matter what their moral make-up, the leading characters have presence. They are full of drive and desires, they are dynamic and passionate, they have a great deal to say for themselves, and what they say goes far to justify what they are as people and what they do with their lives. In those movies, men and women are shown largely in relation to each other, speaking, arguing, joking, teasing, admiring, scolding, seducing—always avidly verbal. Though the characters may have private dreams, ambitions, and occupations, the drama focuses on relationships, a felicitous union, for drama craves the interaction between people that is manifested by personal conversations. It is also true that during the '30s and '40s, the decades of the Depression and World War II, relationships for many, if not most, Americans were the best life had to offer. At work, if one was lucky enough to have a job, one struggled to make money and rejoiced if one could make ends meet. At war, one endured separation, uncertainty, fear of death and rejoiced if one survived. Relationships, especially the permanent one implied by love between a man and a woman, but other close ties too, like friendships, sweetened, warmed, and ordered a world that was otherwise bitter, chill, and mad. To some extent, the movies do reflect, if not the actual relationships real people had, their great interest and faith in the close, lasting ties they wished to have.

The movies of the '50s, by contrast, show a change in attitude toward men and women and a shift away from the emphasis on relationships. Men and women are treated ambiguously, which is not to say they are interpreted with greater psychological complexity than before. Here ambiguity takes the form of cloudiness in the attitude toward the characters; one cannot be sure what to think of them. This is different from a cloudiness in the characters themselves, which one readily grasps, for example, with the protagonists of *Double Indemnity* or *The Maltese Falcon,* where ambiguity results from mixed motives rather than from lack of definition as a person. Characters in '50s movies seem to have lost that presence that made such ordinary people as James Cagney in *Public Enemy,* Clark Gable in *It Happened One Night,* Bette Davis in *Dark Victory,* and Olivia de Havilland in *To Each His Own* seem so important, so brave, so gloriously alive. Behind so many movies of the '30s and '40s are screenwriters who love their created characters; behind many movies of the '50s are screenwriters who are dissatisfied with their created characters. (The HUAC and later McCarthy hearings undoubtedly dampened moviemakers' spirits and invited literary cowardice. The '50s show so few daring characters, as if there were a general reluctance to show force, originality, controversy. The closest approximations to originality are sometimes interesting but usually unhappy, neutoric types.) The best of them are men, played by Marlon Brando, Montgomery Clift, and James Dean. These actors play men who are confused and inarticulate, drained of the quick wit, interest in life, and burning motivation that distinguished and justified the four mentioned above. These three men of the '50s are no foil to the bitter, chill, mad world; it has crept into their souls. Although their movies involve them in relationships with women, these relationships are not central to the stories. The men and their alienation are central.

Women were not written out of movies in the '50s. (The near-exclusion of women from movies other than Westerns and war movies, from which they were often absent, occurred later, in such dramas as *Midnight Cowboy, Easy Rider, Butch Cassidy and the Sundance Kid, The Sting, The French Connection,* but *The Wild One* of 1954 was the harbinger. When dramas returned from the subject of alienation to the subject of relationships, they were largely about relationships between men seeking the solace and security of a mirror image. It's back to the raft with Huck and Jim or off fishing with any number of Hemingway's "boys." Moody, introspective, disaffected by women, the men turn back, hoping to find the youthful idyll of boyhood adventure. That is what is shown over and over in movies of the '60s and '70s, such as those mentioned above, and in the "buddy" movies of the '80s.) While Brando, Clift, and Dean, in *On the Waterfront, From Here to Eternity,* and *Rebel Without a Cause* respectively, played out adolescent versions of heartache and sacrifice, formerly the specialty of women's pictures, or of moral malaise, formerly the specialty of *film noir,* Marilyn Monroe, Jane Russell, Doris Day, June Allyson, Jayne Mansfield, and even Lauren Bacall (one of the few worldly women of the '40s to join this crowd of deflowered ingenues) were rising to questionable fame as helplessly, hopelessly feminine "girls," all fluff and jello, waiting for some rich man to rescue them from careers and the independence they imply.

Part of what may account for the regression in both men and women as dramatic characters is that, after the war, careers—not merely jobs—became more important, and it was men who pursued those careers. In response to the possibility of great wealth, men invested emotionally in their careers and brought home the security of prosperity rather than the security of personal attachments. Careers for high stakes in large organizations, moreover, emphasize the discrepancy between a man's and a woman's earning power. When the salary was small, as salaries were for most people during the '30s and '40s, it was possible for a couple to feel they shared in its earning even if only the man was employed, and to feel, too, that the earning was done for the home and the relationships it housed. In the '50s movies, men often have absorbing careers that compete with relationships. Men with serious, executive-type careers were cigar-chomping "fat cats" before the '50's— often played by Edward Arnold, Walter Connolly, and Sidney Greenstreet, all lending a somewhat sinister interpretation to the role. In the brilliant opening of *The Best Years of Our Lives,* just such a fat cat has easy access to the commercial airlines, while returning soldier Dana Andrews is summarily dismissed at the ticket counter and has to make it home on an old war plane. That small scene conveys a familiar attitude toward rich, overprivileged businessmen and simultaneously offers a forecast of their expanded power. For by the '50s, they've become young, trim, and respectable. See William Holden in *Executive Suite,* Richard Widmark in

The Cobweb, Gregory Peck in *The Man in the Grey Flannel Suit,* and Paul Newman in *The Young Philadelphians.* June Allyson, Gloria Graham, Jennifer Jones, and Barbara Rush, respectively, stay home, completely separated from their husbands' work and workplace.

Molly Haskell has suggested, in her excellent study *From Reverence to Rape,* that there is something punitive about the portrayal of women in '50s movies. Having succeeded in the working world during the war, women, Haskell contends, had to be put firmly back in their place afterwards. Of course they weren't put back into the mature partnership they had achieved with men in movies of the '30s and '40s; they were put into the background, back into boys' adolescent fantasies of voluptuous yet virginal playgirls. After two decades of grown men and women marching bravely through life together, it is telling that the decade of the '50s ends with men lusting after a largely recumbent Baby Doll and Lolita.

In certain movies typical of the '50s, men and women don't get along very well, they aren't very close to each other, they behave awfully childishly with each other, and they are not evenly matched. Men are at the center of the action but not in control of it, even when they may have fantastically high salaries. These movies give us women hanging around in various poses, playing if not being dumb, waiting for men who have high-powered jobs to notice them. They are sexy without subtlety or wit. Where Mae West and Jean Harlow used their blonde bombshell image consciously to ridicule men's most childish, simple-minded views of sex—pink skin, blonde hair, big breasts—only to clobber them, to everyone's amusement, with their own absurd notions, thus emerging as burlesqued, rhinestoned versions of Shakespeare's snappy, comic heroines, the women of so many '50s movies suppress any intelligence they may have as if they are trying to conform to those childish views. They are trying, too, to live up to the cheap, poster-like cinematography that gave rise to the loud, overpainted advertisements, with stupid grins and silly struts, that abound on television.

While Brando, Clift, and Dean movies about alienated men were inherently sympathetic to them and evoked waves, if not floods of identification in the audiences, the movies that concerned women were hostile to them, shooting right into the cleavage (see *The Outlaw*), tracking the jiggling flesh (see any Marilyn Monroe or Jayne Mansfield movie), zooming into the maiden bed (see *Pillow Talk*), photographing women as if they were helpless, laughable victims of an unwieldy, even unnatural anatomy. Katharine Hepburn comes through slim, athletic, and upright in 1952's *Pat and Mike,* but the majority of '50s women, the camera leeringly hints, are about to strip, beg, and roll over.

Even the sleeker types, like Grace Kelly and Kim Novak, portrayed women with icily refined airs which merely mask the dumb blonde, the airhead, the mantrap underneath. Alfred Hitchcock's misanthropy, well disguised to the end of the '40s, had a field day in the '50's. In *Notorious* of 1946, Ingrid Bergman and Cary Grant have depth and force as characters—they drive the plot; it doesn't drive them. Furthermore, despite their personal wrangles and misunderstandings, their love is very important, and we become as much involved in the resolution of their relationship as in their defeat of the villains. In both *Rear Window* (1954) and *Vertigo* (1958), changes are apparent. The characters are at the mercy of the plot. The women, not merely lacking Ingrid Bergman's natural sincerity and openness about feelings, are pointedly deceitful with the men they love, Grace Kelly putting on silly, little flirtatious shows and Kim Novak literally disguising her identity. Where the act Bergman has to put on in *Notorious* pains her, Kelly and Novak thrive on their wiles in *Rear Window* and *Vertigo.* Clothes have become terribly important, not just in the usual Hollywood way of giving us something glamorous to look at. Kelly and Novak don't wear clothes; they model them, a point eventually connected to the women's intellectual and emotional shortcomings in the movies. Indeed, they can't afford to do a movie in one suit, like Rosalind Russell in *His Girl Friday,* because they haven't got the character, the wit, or the intelligence to carry it off. James Stewart, the male lead in both of these '50s Hitchcock vehicles, doesn't fare any better than the female leads. Cast in earlier decades variously as a man of action, integrity, artistic ability, and emotional range, here he is handicapped, helpless, and dull, ending up with women who have successfully entrapped him. Wit and honesty, such as they are in these movies, have been relegated to the supporting women—Thelma Ritter and Barbara Bel Geddes respectively. Pointedly unattractive and unmarriageable, they have the movies' character and good lines. As we are more likely to notice Kelly's and Novak's costumes than their characters, so, when they speak, we hear their phony, elocution-class English rather than anything they may have to say.

How to Marry a Millionaire (1953), *A Woman's World* (1954), and *Designing Woman* (1957) are three movies representative of a new look and attitude. Vulgar and insulting, while pretending it's all in good fun, they throw into sharp relief the diminished presence of both men and women and the dissolution of their partnership. The decades of the '20s, '30s, and '40s have their vacuous, entertaining trifles, short on dramatic content, long on good musical numbers and talent, that, despite their dependence on fantasy plots, never yield on the issue of strong character. These movies of the '50s, however, offer an insidious reversal: they are long on content, giving us elaborate plots and even taking on subjects as if they were "issues," and short on character. Because the people rather than the plots have become vacuous, such movies neither move nor entertain us, even though that's their ostensible motive. The newly disenchanted moviemakers, not ready to be honestly critical of their subjects, hypocritically cast them in the lead and give them happy endings, only to betray them by making them look like imbeciles.

The title of *How to Marry a Millionaire* tells us almost everything we need to know: men have become rich; rich men are desirable; women want to be rich too; the way to become rich is to lure a man into marriage. The cast tells us the rest: Marilyn Monroe (breasts); Betty Grable (legs); Lauren Bacall (brains, supposedly). The men, including William Powell, have not even these distinguishing anatomical features; they don't need any, for they are millionaires. Each woman is matched up with a rich man at movie's end. One can hardly remember, nor does it really matter, who ends up with whom. Lauren Bacall draws William Powell, as a matter of fact, but not on the strength of what they are in this movie; they draw instead on the characters they used to have in their movies of the '40s, when they had wit, charm, and individuality. Here, she is a pretty face and figure, while he is a moneybags with lines as unmemorable as everyone else's. This movie proves that a gold digger's story in which everyone sincerely believes in the big money and wins it, and in which no one believes in anything else, caves in morally, emotionally, and dramatically.

"The center cannot hold," of course; the whole cast is virtually washed away. There may be three marriages at the end, but there are also six people with no identities. Thanks to the focus on female anatomical parts and male monetary possessions, the people have become props.

A Woman's World also concerns three relationships and, while drawing similarly unpropitious conclusions about the stature of men and women, does leave them the dignity of some character. The chief executive of a New York-based company (played by Clifton Webb) has a top position to fill. He has narrowed his choice to three men (played by Cornell Wilde, Fred MacMurray, and Van Heflin). The choice is very serious business because the executive's is, after all, a very big business. To make sure of his man, he invites all three, simultaneously, to spend a week of interviews and social gatherings in New York with their wives (played by June Allyson, Lauren Bacall, and Arlene Dahl).

The movie's screenplay is essentially confusing. If the movie were simply a mystery, focusing our attention on who will get the job, we would be mystified but not exactly confused, for, as with any mystery, we should trustfully expect a rational solution. In such a case, one of the couples must prove to have a superior relationship or one of the wives must prove to be a tremendous asset to her husband, both suppositions meeting some sort of rationale that will be easy for us to grasp, and all we should have to do is to wait for Clifton Webb to make his choice. As it happens, however, all three couples, as well as all six characters—and it's noteworthy that each has something of a distinguishable charac-ter—keep throwing us off balance. Each man, in his way, seems qualified for the job. Each has a style of intelligence, knowledge about the business, and ambition. At the same time, each man has a serious problem with his wife where the job is concerned. So, each man could be the right choice, but each woman could be a liability.

June Allyson, as Cornell Wilde's wife, is the darling of the party. In the context of this movie that means she's incredibly stupid and gauche, emitting faux pas and belches at dinner, inca-pable of buying clothes that fit, appearing generally retarded—or is it just that Wilde has brought his preschool daughter instead of his wife by mistake, we may fleetingly wonder; but, no, it is his wife, indeed, as the two hop licitly and virtuously into their twin beds at the hotel. They love each other very much, which means she constantly makes a fool of herself in public, which means, in turn, that she is sweet and honest (unlike smart women, who are sly and deceitful—more later), and her husband always protects her and stands by her, which comes to mean they have an ideal marriage. In her own cute, addle-pated way, she wants him to want the job, but hopes he won't get it so she won't have to live in great big, scary New York City.

Lauren Bacall, as Fred MacMurray's wife, is an intelligent, sophisticated woman, easily the most attractive individual if one is looking for a woman who has maturity and can therefore be an asset to her husband. She knows how to behave herself in public; she is polite, understated, discreet. Furthermore, she and her husband have real, grown-up conversations in private. She loves her husband and fears, justifiably, that this big job will strain further a relationship that already suffers from neglect. Her husband is very ill with ulcers, from overwork presumably, and she thinks he should rein in the ambitions that are killing him and work with her instead on a healing relationship that would restore them both. These two are troubled, but, in a way reminiscent of the sort of adult partnerships movies of the '30s and '40s show us, these two people sound like fully believable, independent people who know how to have conversations that might help them resolve problems. Yet this couple is relegated to third place in the movie, fades in importance, and Fate resolves their problems for them, denying them a chance to use their own initiative and judgment.

Arlene Dahl, as Van Heflin's wife, is the movie's one truly ambitious woman. Her husband wants the job, as do the other two men, and she wants him to have it but, as it transpires, she is more intensely eager for the job than he is. She is ever alert to the competitive aspects of the situation and moves aggressively, albeit enticingly, to advance his chances. She is the kind of woman, full of energy and schemes, frustrated by woman's lot, who seeks fulfillment by living through her husband's career. The movie suggests that such a woman is evil, a killer and a tramp—after all, doesn't she offer her ample body to the chief executive, in trade as it were? This woman bears, in addition to her weighty physical endowments, all the faults Clare Booth distributed liberally among a hive of execrable women: she is catty, common, and faithless; she thinks little of men and despises women. (In Dahl's '40s movies, her smooth roundness and rich coloring are graced rather than shamed by the camera, making her look pretty and pleasing, a little like Renoir's paintings of women.) As she becomes overtly aggressive, her husband withdraws from her, becoming subdued and aloof. Unlike Macbeth, this husband will not be aroused by the exciting incitements of his wife.

The way this movie treats energy and drive is quite disturbing. Those qualities, so fresh and charming in the '30s and '40s, appear silly or dangerous in the '50s. June Allyson and Cornell Wilde have plenty of energy, but they're like enthusiastic children; Arlene Dahl is bursting, but she's a false, manipulative woman. It's not exactly subtlety that the movie seems to advocate, although the ambiguity of its final message may resemble subtlety. Rather, if Clifton Webb himself is the model of a successful man, the movie is looking for a degree of self-effacement, a willed suppression of emotion in the interests of brilliant business. Like the dapper William Powell of *How to Marry a Millionaire,* the dapper Clifton Webb succeeds in shedding those lovable traits of crustiness and suave humor that made him special, that made him an energetic character in earlier movies, and his lines, so didactic and dull, ably assist in the process.

If, therefore, instead of looking at the couples, we had looked at Clifton Webb, we should have guessed right away who his man was: the man least attached to his wife; the man whose marriage was a failure—Van Heflin. When it appears to her that her husband will not get the job, Arlene Dahl takes off, leaving Van Heflin free, the only man not handicapped by a woman. The least aggressive, least emotional, least attached man wins. The height of ambiguity—again in the sense used earlier to mean lack of definition resulting in a cloudiness of attitude—comes when Clifton Webb closes the movie by repeating what must be one of his slogans: "It's a great big woman's world because there are men in it!" What can this baffling statement mean in the light of the choice he has just made? How can it be a woman's world if the one woman who wanted a slice of it is now getting nothing? How can it be a woman's world if one man is making the choice and one newly unattached man wins the prize? And why does the presence of men assure women's possession of the world when the two women who prize their marriages over their husband's careers have to wait on the chief executive's decisions to know their fates? If the statement means anything, the meaning can lie only in the confusion it generates. There is rampant confusion throughout this movie: about what counts in life; about how men and women can get along with each other; about how they will stay close to each other in a corporate world that values impersonality; and about how they will share the benefits of a job that has turned into a career that competes for time and love with relationships.

The movie answers none of the questions it raises, leaving us to conclude that, Clifton Webb's prosing notwithstanding, it is neither a woman's nor a man's world. The world is too much with and for everyone. The characters who struggled against the Depression and the war in the movies of the '30s and '40s seemed large enough to conquer the world. It couldn't destroy them. Even if they died, like Tommy of *Public Enemy* or Judith Traherne of *Dark Victory,* they triumphed in our eyes by the sheer ecstasy with which they lived. Neither technicolor nor cinemascope can magnify the characters of *A Woman's World* sufficiently to make them feel they own the world. The technology, in fact, magnifies their weaknesses and enlarges the space between people, and that space, deplored by all directors who excelled at working on drama with good actors, expresses, perhaps unintentionally but nonetheless aptly, the characters' real fears of the world's emptiness.

Lauren Bacall, who fared rather better in *A Woman's World* than she did in *How to Marry a Millionaire,* regaining, if nothing else, the status of a thinking adult, sinks to embarrassing depths in *Designing Woman* and takes the rather rigid but appealingly mature actor, Gregory Peck, right down with her. The title, with its painful pun, already makes an unfriendly comment, calling into question the validity of her career and her character. Playing a career woman, Bacall may be forgiven for lacking the profound integrity and independence of journalist Rosalind Russell in *His Girl Friday,* novelist Bette Davis in *Old Acquaintance,* or doctor Barbara Stanwyck in *You Belong to Me,* but not for lacking the simple honesty of designer Susan Hayward in *I Can Get It for You Wholesale,* a movie that makes its characters confront sensibly and even sensitively the conflicting demands of love and ambition. The designer of *Designing Woman* is, we must remember, "designing," a wily schemer, like Grace Kelly's fashion plate of *Rear Window*.

Bacall and Gregory Peck meet and marry within a couple of days, which, without war's imposing the urgent need to keep up familiar, life-affirming rituals (as it does in *The More the Merrier* and *The Clock*), seems idiotic. This two-career couple plays at being sophisticated professionals who work in Manhattan and take airplanes to conferences—something, we must remember, that looked very snazzy in the twilight years of trains and ocean liners— but the real drama focuses prudishly on, of all things, their chastity. Why should Gregory Peck have to hide the fact that he had a girlfriend before he met his designing woman? Why should Lauren Bacall worry about being compromised because she's seen talking to another man? And why, if she doesn't like her husband's having the boys slobbering around for all-night card games, can't she just tell him so instead of plotting her own little sideshow? If this is supposed to be even a faint echo of Lubitsch-style bedroom farce, it won't work because in such farce the fun derives from sexiness, not from chastity. (Similarly, Bergman and Grant, so sensitive and honest in *Notorious* are ludicrous and decidedly overage guardians of their chastity for their 1958 reunion in *Indiscreet*.) For Lauren Bacall to be playing the very conniving, eyelash-batting schemer with the straitlaced soul she ridiculed so charmingly in *To Have and Have Not* is quite a come-down. It's one thing for Doris Day to ward off middle age by reclaiming her virginity; we can let that pass. But when Lauren Bacall, without Day's freckles, tomboyish stance, and shallow expression to validate her chosen role, takes the same route, and, worse yet, when Bette Davis, after a beautiful career devoted to making any kind of woman's life look exciting and singular—even her sniveling Maryland socialite tells "a great lie"—plays the same kind of coy dope in *June Bride,* and, even worse yet, when men with intelligence and urbanity, like William Powell, Robert Montgomery, and Gregory Peck, actually pursue these "girls" without once suggesting that they'd prefer grown-up, independent women, we know that men and women of the '50s have gone down the chute.

Molly Haskell may be right in seeing the presentation of women in '50s movies as men's way of punishing them for having become worldly and independent during the war.[1] Men take such a beating too, especially in movies about relationships between men and women. Men look just as vacuous and immature as women. Despite their wealth, which seems to permit them a somewhat patronizing attitude toward what has become "the little woman," they do nothing to encourage an adult or even an interesting relationship with women.

Very little happened in movies between the '50s and the early '80s to inspire hope for improved relations between men and women. The movies about promiscuity that's supposed to be fun but keeps going sour, like *Darling* of 1965 and *Alfie* of 1966, ushered in the movies of the '70s. Characters slosh around in a swamp of personal failure—men and women pathetically lonely by themselves, even more lonely with each other. In such movies, the screenwriters and directors take a disheartened yet sympathetic attitude toward the characters, making us pity their plight rather than censure their stupidity. In the kind of movie from the '50s discussed in this chapter, however, screenwriters and directors seem sympathetic to neither men nor women; rather, they are critical without expectations—that is, contemptuous. (The very camera is cruel, foregoing the silvery, lyrical close-up in favor of the harsh exposure in garish technicolor.) The result is a movie like the three discussed here which humiliates and cheapens people in a nihilistic way. There is a hint of satire's tone in the critical edge, but none of satire's purposeful suggestions and implied respect to indicate, for our benefit, exactly how these characters are erring and how they should reform. The characters seem intrinsically foolish, yet the screenplay cheats by steering them toward the comic rewards of an ending traditionally reserved for characters who have mastered their folly, grown wise, and merited happiness. We are cheated as much as the characters, for we are finally asked to feel happy about people who haven't the human stuff in them to feel anything. The scripts themselves lack the courage to make strong characters, however reprehensible, and then properly shoot them down if that's what they deserve.

The 1956 remake of *The Women*, now ambiguously retitled *The Opposite Sex*, seems the perfect choice for this cowardly yet misanthropic decade: when given a chance to tear people apart, a chance Clare Booth's play provides with abandon, the script extracts the venom, dilutes the punch, and leaves us once more with a grinning June Allyson. This is not to say that the decade of the '50s lacked all greatness or courage. The leading directors of serious actors never yielded to poor taste or falseness or cowardice. Adhering to fine literature or stories that had been filmed before, George Cukor (*A Star is Born*, 1954), Elia Kazan (*A Streetcar Named Desire*, 1951), George Stevens (*A Place in the Sun*, 1951), William Wyler (*Detective Story*, 1951; *Roman Holiday*, 1953), and Fred Zinnemann (*From Here to Eternity*, 1953) drew their customary, superb performances from every actor and dealt honestly and compassionately with some of the very problems that movies with a representative '50s look merely flirted with. Nevertheless, it seems that, their imaginations shell-shocked by HUAC first and later by Joseph McCarthy, by the enforced decline of the studios, and by the studios' demoralizing decision to fight the foe called television with gadgets and gimmicks rather than with great writing, moviemakers no longer saw anything in men and women, or possibly in the medium itself, to celebrate. The movies of the '30s and '40s are, after all, a celebration of human vitality. The movies of the '50s are a derisive display of human frailty.

6.

Loners, Lovers, and Lawbreakers:
Whatever Happened to the Men?

As James Cagney's Tommy Powers slips into the rain-drenched gutter, clutching his bullet-ridden stomach, he mutters, "I ain't so tough." Eighteen years later, Cagney's Cody Jarrett climbs to the top of a gas tank, oblivious to the bullets seeking their home in his body, and shouts, " 'Made it, Ma. 'Top of the world.' " as the tank explodes. In both movies, the criminal's last words are ironic, for throughout *Public Enemy*, Tommy has been nothing if not tough. His last words, which mark the first time he has felt vulnerable in his whole life, don't define the scrappy, resourceful, charismatic little guy, whom everybody except his dull, pious brother loves; rather, they define the cast of helpless, passive, despairing people who surround him, who draw strength from his dauntless rebellion against a system that has failed millions and left them in the lurch, jobless and hungry. Cody Jarrett of *White Heat*, however, has been a dangerous and pathetic psychotic—a criminal because he couldn't be anything else. His last words only underline his delusions of grandeur, his absurd view of himself as a great person, when he's only been a rotten little apple at the bottom of the barrel all along, unable to command anyone's loyalty except his similarly deluded mother's.

These movies are superficially similar—both offer the excitements of action-packed crime dramas, and Cagney gives both roles everything he's got—but they tell significantly different stories, and in their differences we can trace an emergent pattern in Hollywood's changing view of men from the troubled times of the Depression to the troubled times of the Cold War. For all his

70

criminality, Tommy Powers stands out in his community as a fiercely purposeful and courageous man. He is a leader unwilling to brook defeat in the prime of his enterprising, self-sufficient youth. Between him and the deranged Cody Jarrett fall Humphrey Bogart's Duke Mantee and Henry Fonda's Tom Joad, two law-breakers whose alienation from society commands respect and whose courage to stand up and make some mark on the world commands a following. They have the power to transform their poor, worthless selves into legendary figures. Mantee is much more aware of the importance of image than Joad, but both answer the need of hungry folk, in sandy and dust-blown regions, for human vitality, for extraordinary prowess, for some watering of the imaginative life. In *The Petrified Forest*, Gaby's grandfather can't contain his enthusiasm over Mantee's arrival. The sonorous bulletins of Mantee's whereabouts that come over the radio only heighten the grandfather's pleasure in the presence of the only greatness he has ever seen. Tom Joad's last speech to his mother is positively messianic, and the last shot of him, a solitary figure mounting a steep hill against a broad, clear sky, drives the message of his lonely greatness home. Tommy, Duke, Tom—all three are bad men in the eyes of the law, of course, but they have something of heroic mettle to them; in the eyes of people who know them, they represent an undeniable and inspiriting positive force. Indeed, though they are loners in the sense that they are unafraid to strike out independently, they remain in touch with people and know exactly how to meet their needs. Even Duke Mantee, whose glowering, scowling looks vaguely anticipate Cody Jarrett's mad antics, grants the failed intellectual his wish, takes seriously the girl with whom he has a rendezvous, and appreciates the grandfather's admiration.

In Cody Jarrett, we see the criminal who thinks he resembles men like Tommy but who lacks their character and originality, as seen repeatedly in Cody's craving for someone to depend on. Though he is married, his best girl is still his mother, who takes him on her lap when he has migraines, who strokes his head, who coaches him in how to be a big bad man. It is easy for the police plant, played by Edmund O'Brien, to ensnare him simply by befriending him and acting toward him in the capacity of an older brother who also soothes him through his migraines and helps him plot his prison escapes so he can be a big bad man once more.

71

Being simultaneously alienated and dependent comprises the qualities of Hollywood's lawbreakers who succeed Cody Jarrett. Though they are not necessarily extravagantly aberrational like Cody, they share his childishness. What is especially interesting to notice, though, is that the childishness of Cody looks repellent, whereas the childishness of those who follow, like Dustin Hoffman and Jon Voight in *Midnight Cowboy*, or of Paul Newman and Robert Redford in *Butch Cassidy and the Sundance Kid* (not to mention Ryan and Tatum O'Neal in *Paper Moon*), looks endearing. From Tommy Powers, who cuffs his mother affectionately on the chin, as if she were his child, to Cody Jarrett, who sits on his mother's lap, the movies' lawbreaking course goes back and back to find at the source pairs of adorable little boys.

A sweep of the decades gives us just this: a reflux from manhood to boyhood. Although every one of the more recent lawbreakers is involved in serious criminal business, they all seem to us too young to take full responsibility for their actions because they seem to be playing. What matters to them is never the justness of their cause— Tommy Powers, Duke Mantee, Tom Joad, and also Little Caesar, have reasons for their actions that can never legitimate them, of course, but that do say something to their followers about fighting for the dignity of manhood. They are, therefore, rebels with a cause. What matters to the more recent criminals instead is their freedom to find themselves, to be themselves, to romp forever in playgrounds, innocent no matter what they do. (*Bonnie and Clyde*, too, emphasizes the childish charm with which the couple assert the innocent view they have of themselves. See chapter 11.) *The Sting* probably captures and rewards the boyishness of such aspirations best of all movies by sending the happy pals off, after their scam, united and smiling; *Butch Cassidy and the Sundance Kid* comes close in its sunny portrayal of childhood friendship, prolonged through criminal freedom, as an ideal and culminating relationship. *Midnight Cowboy*, though ending in the death of Ratso Rizzo, also ends in the strong affirmation of close friendship, as does *Paper Moon*, in which a little girl maneuvers her surrogate father/lover into the role of best friend (and sometimes, when she's feeling especially bossy, into the role of son) as the two go rollicking off, at the end, to an eternity of criminal bliss.

A similar reversion to childhood shows up in movies whose

main characters are loners. The Westerns used to provide a stable home for those men whose loneliness signifies something stalwart and civilized. The actors who played these loners—John Wayne, Gary Cooper, James Stewart, Henry Fonda, Joel McCrea, Alan Ladd—attach to the role an inherent superiority, not of intellectual training, which they scorn as a craven, worthless East Coast tradition, more European than truly American, but of natural decency and self-assurance, which frees them to be nonconformists in an intrinsically American sense. They become identified with something called the heartland, the innocent setting for characters who naturally know right from wrong and who have the strength to be "rugged individuals." These are the men who by raising their lone voices tame mobs; who are enviably even-tempered and sound of judgment; who dislike shoot-outs but, when pressed, invariably turn out to be unbeatable. (See Stewart in *Destry Rides Again*, and Ladd in his Westerns like *Shane*, but also in a movie like *The Blue Dahlia*, where he navigates the dusky plot, ever clear and defined himself, an unusual feat for a *film noir* protagonist.) They always know exactly who they are and what is right. They trust themselves and their actions to practical knowledge and horse sense. Their very aloofness enhances the just image by which they seek to be known, but, like their lawbreaking contemporaries, they are hardly indifferent to other people. The loner may not have much time for women, but they generally regard him as a most desirable lover, and after proving himself an elegant dancer—something else the loner turns out to be when pressed—he usually draws an especially fine bride (see Fonda in *My Darling Clementine*). Neither the lawbreaker nor the loner necessarily ends up married, but both are presented as wanting to do right by women and children. (Cagney's grapefruit in Mae Clarke's face notwithstanding! His love for Jean Harlow and his generosity to his mother more than make up for that cruel reaction to Clarke's nagging.) The picture of a man alone in Westerns suggests to our imaginations his fearlessness of unknown lands as well as his romantic love for wild nature, qualities that connect him to trailblazing leadership. The names alone of John Wayne's movies conjure up just such a picture: *The Big Trail*; *The Loney Trail*; *The Sagebrush Trail*; *The Oregon Trail*; *Straight Ahead*; *Riders of Destiny*; *Tall in the Saddle*. Gary Cooper is Wild Bill Hickok in *The Plainsman*, Henry Fonda blazes *The Trail of the Lonesome Pine*, and Joel McCrea wears the most prominent of *Four Faces West*. The loner of Westerns is a tough man with a big heart and a clear destination, who, as he goes riding off across prairies, is not meant to strike us as antisocial. That lonely ride is a tribute to his resilience, and we are meant to recognize in that familiar composition of man and beast and vast space the natural harmony that ensues when an unassuming, just man withstands the rigors of a man's life.

The lawbreaker and the loner, as presented in movies before and during World War II, are two kinds of nonconformists: the urban rebel who fights for his rights against a system he perceives to be corrupt and devouring; and the rural individualist who fights to establish a framework of law and order so that the land will be safe for loners. The loners who emerge after World War II have moved to the city where, unlike the law-enforcing loners of Westerns, they live on the peripheries of crime, not drawn to it by conviction, like Tommy or Duke, but sucked in by their weakness. In fact, they live on the peripheries of all areas of life, never wholly involved anywhere or with anyone. Their loneliness doesn't suggest strength but disaffection. Their bashful, abortive attempts at relationships with women remove all doubt that the loners played by Montgomery Clift (*A Place in the Sun*), William Holden (*Sunset Boulevard; Stalag 17*), and Gene Hackman (*The Conversation*) are troubled teenagers no matter what their real age, level of sophistication, or professional success. At heart, all of them resemble James Dean, torn by conflicting pressures of hateful parents, neurotic girlfriend, and drag-racing schoolmates. Uncertain, unloving, maladjusted, these loners often affront life with a facile cynicism that just as often veils an intensely cherished and childish dream life.

Montgomery Clift's George Eastman sees in the beautiful, rich Angela (played by Elizabeth Taylor) the embodiment of his ideal view of happiness. During his scenes with her, he responds awkwardly to her sweet, warm mothering. ("Tell Mama all," she murmurs in their first love scene.) William Holden distinguishes himself as an actor when he plays the cold, removed character, close to and satisfied with no one; smart and talented but lacking the faith and perseverance to succeed—a role he was evidently made for. (While Holden plays this alienated, disgruntled character perfectly, he is never credible as a conventional lover, looking clumsy in his debut with Barbara Stanwyck in *Golden Boy*; embarrassed in such silly fare as *The Moon is Blue*; and downright insincere with Jennifer Jones in *Love is a Many-Splendored Thing*.) In *Sunset Boulevard*, however, he excels as the writer shunted between two contrasting women, the once-great actress and the modest screenplay writer. From their separate stations, each woman supports him in some way, each showing a vitality and enthusiasm for life, a belief in struggling to create something, while he is largely brooding and passive, all that potential evaporating before our eyes in clouds of complaint that turn out, ironically, to be his one great screenplay, brought to us from beyond the grave. He plays the same sort of loner in *Stalag 17*, where his moody arrogance throws into relief the good nature of the other G.I.'s. His keen intelligence empowers him to emerge heroic at relatively little cost, yet he himself jumps to stress his selfish motives lest anyone suspect him of being noble. Like an embarrassed grade-school kid, he doesn't want to be linked with all that "mushy stuff" like love of country, love of one's fellows, or love of moral action, and he isn't. One is grateful to him, in this movie, for outwitting the traitor and for engineering the escape, but one doesn't love or respect him as one does young James Stewart of *Destry Rides Again* or old James Stewart of *Bend in the River* for taking on and demolishing the villains single-handedly because he knows what is right and feels some sense of attachment and obligation to the rest of the population. Holden's acute skepticism, so coolly conveyed by suspicious smirks and grimaces, renders him a perfect satirical actor, precisely the sort he became toward the end of his career, looking so natural in *Network* and *S.O.B.* When he suppresses his sardonic air, intelligence seems to drain from his face, leaving him looking sappy. But his supreme detachment, best shown in *S.O.B.*, where he catches the swooning fan in the supermarket, casually drapes her over his shopping cart, and moves on past the apples and pears with airy aplomb, suits him perfectly.

The most interesting of recent loners is Harry Caul, played by Gene Hackman in *The Conversation*. The electronics expert comprises within himself the perfect metaphor for what he calls "the lonely and anonymous" individual. Like a little boy, he creates a vast secret life dominated by an apparatus of gadgetry, and, again like a little boy, looks up from his workbench every so often, frightened, in his deserted office or his deserted apartment, by the absence of other people. At such times, he seeks out his affectionate girlfriend, played by Teri Garr, but her very affection weighs on him, demanding exactly what he cannot give: a personal conversation. He experiences only the "side effects" of love, like jealousy, suspicion, possessiveness.

Tortured as he is by loneliness that no companion can assauge, Harry tries so hard to be a stalwart loner, but he doesn't have the Western heroes' courage to be alone or their sense of attachment to and responsibility for other people, from which they draw so much of their courage. "I have nothing to do with human nature," states Harry Caul, running to the shelter of his tape decks, telephone, and saxaphone—the props and hobbies that keep him self-sufficient and preoccupied. "I don't need anyone," he says when he is most afraid of being alone. Yet he goes to confession, where his mumbled catalog of venial sins—he hasn't confessed in three months; he stole newspapers; he feels guilty for eavesdropping—betrays his scant spiritual growth and his reluctance to speak personally, truly opening his heart. Unwilling to face his needs, and unable to articulate them, Harry Caul is afraid of his own humanity, which sentences him to a life of feelings. He longs to merge with his machinery on the one hand—and so to be emotionally frozen—and, on the other, to have a conversation with a woman who equals his ideal, the Virgin Mother, of whom he has a little statue in his apartment. It is ironic that he finds an outlet for that stifled passion whimpering for a mother within the machinery, where he captures the conversation of the adulterous lovers, whose words of simple intimacy and emotion fascinate and move him. "Their conversation makes me feel something," he says, and his interest in them follows him into his dreams, where he meets and has his own conversation with the woman. For the first, and only, time in the movie, he speaks personally, but the conversation he initiates is full of childhood sorrows he has harbored for years: his illnesses; his near-drowning; his thoughts on death. His discovery that the woman is not the Mary he seeks, not even the innocent victim of her husband's murderous plot, but instead an adulterous murderer herself, is a bruising blow for this man. Racked by suspicion, professionally suspect himself, and threatened by the clients about whom he knows too much, he learns from this affair only that no woman can be trusted, nor any man either. In wrecking his apartment in search of the bug he is sure his enemies have planted there, he finally smashes his statue of Mary in a rage of disappointment. At the end, his life, like his apartment, is a shambles, and as he sits playing his saxophone into the ruined vacancy, waiting for his enemies to strike, he is not substantially different from lonely, unfulfilled Montgomery Clift going off to the electric chair or William Holden floating face down in the swimming pool.

If loners, even the strong loners of Westerns, don't distinguish themselves as lovers, we cannot be too disappointed. If they do, it's a bonus rather than an expected benefit. But screen lovers, in movies about men ardently pursuing women, show us the same distressing trend over the years from mature men with stature gained from confidence in their feelings to boys preoccupied with their physical urges, prowess, and sensations. Such a trend *is* a disappointment.

Three actors stand out as great screen lovers: the virile Clark Gable; the sexy Charles Boyer; and the witty Cary Grant. These three are special because they did their best work on screen as lovers. Each brought forth a kind of lover that has the same impact as a great literary character: original; believable; recognized and accepted as part of the population even though he is but imaginary. Gable in *Gone With the Wind*, Boyer in *All This and Heaven Too*, and Cary Grant in *The Philadelphia Story* are lovers because they feel love. Perhaps because of the restrictions imposed by the Production Code, these actors felt forced to cultivate many ways of expressing love, but in being so forced—if that's what lies behind the richness of their performances—they convey a tremendous range of feeling by their ways of speaking, their facial expressions (especially the use of the eyes for Boyer and Grant), and their ways of moving, rather than just by bodily contact with a woman. The range they convey has the effect of enhancing the importance of love itself, as if each actor were saying love is worth all my efforts to portray it truly as it gladdens or grieves, excites or cloys.

In every scene, Gable as Rhett Butler expresses his simple pleasure in being a strong man. Whether he is grinning at Scarlett, teasing her about her love for Ashley, waltzing with her, comforting her after a nightmare, holding her face in his large hands, or sweeping her up the stairs, he is a man at home with himself physically, who infuses every emotion he expresses with a sense of his male presence (which is precisely what offends, or frightens, the young Scarlett too immature to appreciate him). His ease in dealing with women extends to his friendliness toward Mammy, his intimate conversations with Melanie, and his warm, maternal feelings toward his daughter. Confident in the harmony of his body and soul, Gable's lover is always completely forthcoming about his feelings.

Only once, in *All This and Heaven Too,* does Charles Boyer go beyond the formal handshake to kiss the governess's hand. Otherwise, Boyer achieves every effect of a man deeply and, as the movie progresses, ever more deeply in love by use of his face and voice. Nothing could suit better, of course, a story of thwarted love than such restraint, but the restraint spurs the character (just as it does the actor) to find "legal" ways of expressing himself. Boyer's French accent, his mellifluous voice, and the large, velvet eyes against the intensely white face, eyes that seem melting with desire, combine to create the sexy lover without his having to be near the woman he loves. Gazing at her across a space, which he does before the camera alone, accomplishes all he needs to, just as Garbo achieved some of her greatest effects as a lover by the way she reacted to objects that stood for her lover: a bouquet of flowers; a letter; a telephone. (see Charlges Affron, *Star Acting,* New York: E. F. Dutton, 1977.) Boyer's parting look, across a room at Bette Davis, a look full of love and longing, opens a window on his steadily flaming passion.

What Cary Grant projects best is a man for whom love is sophisticated fun. In *Notorious,* he plays a man temporarily confused and disturbed by love, but even in this movie, some memorable scenes are those in which he imbues love with the humor of amusingly sexy jokes: he guards Ingrid Bergman from the chill night air by tying a little silk scarf around her bare midriff while his eyes dance with merriment; they kiss in slow, graceful stages, like a minuet, while he is gathering information from his answering service on the telephone. It is in his role as C. K. Dexter Haven, however, that he shines with refined wit. His sense of humor singles him out as the most mature of all Tracy Lord's "suitors." He can be sober without being self-righteous like her fiancé; he can be amusing without being reckless like Mike Connor (played by

James Stewart). His quick wit, offset by words of wisdom, allows Grant to emerge on screen as a man who feels deeply enough always to have something original to say, something that may be infuriating but that bears nevertheless the weight of his warmth, charm, and intelligence. Add to that his wide-eyed, mock ingenuousness, from which he flows into easy tenderness, and Tracy would be a fool to pass him up. Cary Grant in *The Philadelphia Story* and also, at break-neck speed, in *His Girl Friday,* by his physical agility, his swift, humorous repartee, and his various looks of bemused surprise, lets women know that they are central in his life, worth his most persistent, intelligent, and entertaining efforts to win them.

For all three of these great screen lovers, love means a deep attachment to a woman. In their best roles, the men, whatever their individual styles, demonstrate an interest in the women's characters and admire especially women of unusual strength, skill, and intelligence with whom they can share a partnership. There are three contemporary actors who are roughly—very roughly—comparable to Gable, Boyer, and Grant respectively in the styles they have adopted as screen lovers. Yet what we notice immediately on seeing the virile Jack Nicholson of *Carnal Knowledge,* the sexy Warren Beatty of *Heaven Can Wait,* and the witty Woody Allen of *Annie Hall* is that the big men who loved so deeply have been replaced by little guys, whose very littleness is emphasized, by contrast with the men played by James Cagney, Edward G. Robinson, Claude Rains, and even wee Mickey Rooney, who made up in energetic presence for what they lacked in height. For the more recent little guys are small in size and character, lacking finesse—they seem to run around in sneakers all the time—and full of boyish impatience. Their conception of love has more strictly to do with sexual desire and making love rather than with feeling love. (Dudley Moore's remake of *Unfaithfully Yours* fails precisely because he plays the role as a little guy. Preston Sturges's story furnishes a continuous eruption of surprises whose success depends on the comic collision of grandeur and pettiness. Such a dynamic contrast calls for an actor who can appear large, elegant, mature—there is none better than Rex Harrison in the original—and yet succumb to mean suspicions and jealousies which, because he has a big man's authority and bearing, he can promptly convert into grand scenes played to grand music.)

Carnal Knowledge is specifically about the problems men have in growing up, and the movie despairingly suggests that they don't, won't, and can't. At forty, the lover Nicholson plays is still measuring females' worth by the dimensions of their anatomical parts the way he did at eighteen. Although the story of *Heaven Can Wait* sends Warren Beatty into the body of a mature man and allows him to have a true relationship with the woman played by Julie Christie, he also seems to wind up eighteen years old, in a locker room, still a young athlete more worried about his physique than about his attachment to a woman. He has a sleepy gaze reminiscent of Boyer's, but he follows through not with a lover's motivation so much as an adolescent's, curious about love but easily distracted from it by projects, sports, other people. And Woody Allen, endlessly talking and making clever remarks, has endeared himself to millions of viewers—and many of them as fully middle-aged as he is—by his arrested development that shows up in his insecurities and obsessions about performing in bed, as well as in his discovery of such risqué subjects as orgasm and masturbation.

All three of these lovers are most interested in getting the girl into bed and rarely, if at all, in how she feels or in what she is really like. The freedom to show sex on the screen undoubtedly plays a role in the altered treatment of love on the screen, forcing its simplification. Where actors used to have to find ways to suggest sexual feelings and came up, as a result, with a repertoire of subtleties that extended their range as actors, the contemporary screen lover, in having intercourse on screen, may believe that the sexual act is an even exchange for—probably even a realistic improvement on—the old-fashioned, one-foot-on-the-floor days when actors had to communicate their feelings in other ways and, in consequence, communicated many more feelings. As it has transpired, however, grapic sex scenes limit the feelings a screen lover can convey (see chapter 10).

The stories themselves, especially from among these three, *Carnal Knowledge* and *Annie Hall,* suggest additional reasons for the altered treatment of love that are consistent with the changes discussed earlier with regard to loners and lawbreakers. The lovers have undergone a similar change over the decades, seeming less sure of themselves as men, less able, or less willing, to commit themselves to a person, a task, a faith. These adolescent men, ever dissatisfied themselves, bring little pleasure to the women they have affairs with. Jack Nicholson is relentlessly demanding of Ann-Margaret in *Carnal Knowledge,* as Gable is of Leigh in *Gone With the Wind,* but whereas Gable's demand carries with it an implied compliment to the women's attractiveness as well as an appreciation of her intelligence, Nicholson's demand springs solely from his imperative need. He picks Ann-Margaret up and drops her always in response to his needs. In looking at her, he sees only his own body's reactions; he doesn't seem to see her as a fully separate person. It is no coincidence that his final sexual choice is autoeroticism and his great fear impotence. Similarly in *Annie Hall,* Diane Keaton has to smoke marijuana to relax before making love because Allen is such a hasty, inconsiderate lover, too immature to take time with her. His needs are what matter. In all his '70s movies, he is brimming over with the urgency of his needs, while anxiously promoting his "great sexual technique," hardly a match for the *savoir faire* of Cary Grant.

During the three decades after World War II, the men in movies became boys. Women, a little more slowly and reluctantly perhaps, and by a different route—making a stopover as dumb sexpots or mannequins in the '50s—arrived at childhood too. The result has been some extremely well directed and acted, albeit dismaying, movies about characters less interested in other people than they are in themselves, as the post-war movies discussed here show. Such movies reflect a general distrust of relationships and a preference for detached, single pursuit of personal fulfillment through career, avocation, self-aggrandizement, and numerous nonbinding love affairs. For the men in these movies, women are sex objects rather than people. That is why the men ogle and leer rather than simply look; they aren't really interested in the potential depth and range of relationships and sex. Nor are they really interested in women, so they don't bother to look at them as if to read them. They seem to have trouble reading themselves; that is, for all the attention they devote to themselves, they do not achieve understanding of or comfort within themselves. However sincere these movies are and however fine the performances, the self-absorptions of male adolescents, especially middle-aged adolescents, are of decidedly limited interest. (Jack Nicholson's performance as a lover in *Chinatown* constitutes a clear exception to most of his roles, for he conveys the virility of a man sincerely in love, a true interest in the woman he loves, and the versatility of an actor who finds various ways to show what he feels.)

The men played by actors like Wayne, Cagney, Gable, and Grant are secure enough about themselves physically to forget about their bodies, to let their movements and gestures merge with and reflect an implicit confidence in their manhood. The later actors, by contrast, play men who all but writhe in self-consciousness. Jack Nicholson struts and preens, rooster-like, compensatory perhaps; William Holden, for all his physical beauty, carries it with a shrug and a slouch, as if he wished to hide; and Woody Allen, in a perpetual dither, all but breaks out in an acne of distress over his inadequacies. (Such a decline is already presaged in *The Best Years of Our Lives,* where Fredric March, as the banker, makes a speech in which he attempts to prove that "we lost the war." He's quite drunk, and his slurred, erroneous remarks are funny, but they do express his, and the other men's, malaise, their fear that they are losers. No matter how valiantly they won the war, the world seems no longer a place for winners. While March, Dana Andrews, and Harold Russell emerge in this movie as existential losers, heroically opposed to the insurmountable—a changed, Cold War world—the later men lose because they have too little courage, too little confidence, too little character.)

The men played by Jack Lemmon constitute an interesting variation on all the relatively contemporary male roles. With his success as the cowardly Ensign Pulver in *Mr. Roberts,* Lemmon established himself as a little guy, absolutely incapable of any sort of greatness. As we watch him develop through such movies as *Some Like It Hot, The Out-of-Towners,* and *The Prisoner of Second Avenue,* we see in him a person who is struggling awfully hard to be a grown man, disposed to behave responsibly and kindly toward others, but the crazy world keeps upsetting his life. Perhaps if gangsters, broken-down transportation, muggers, and burglars didn't hit quite so hard and so relentlessly, he would be able to acquire the poise, courage, and grace of one of the big men who preceded him on the screen. His endearingly mobile face is by no means limited to registering disbelief, befuddlement, and betrayal:

there's a strong, hard jaw beneath the gaping astonishment the poor devil is always cast into; those warm, frank eyes could direct a level, loving gaze at a woman (as they do at Lee Remick, during his sober interludes in *Days of Wine and Roses*). What we see in the essentially agreeable character of the man he plays is a man made for civilization, hanging on to it within himself but unable to salvage it in a world that seems to be sliding into the sewer right before his eyes. By means of the contrast between the decent young man and the foul world he inhabits and cannot conquer, Lemmon clarifies for us the demoralization that has taken root in and corrupted so many of the characters discussed here. They have lost completely his will to combat loneliness, alienation, and evil. Lemmon's businessman in *Save the Tiger* dramatizes and embodies the contrast within himself as he shuttles between the lonely, senseless life he leads and the rich, purposeful past he remembers. Partially estranged from his wife, cut off altogether from his daughter, caught in a tawdry business, he yearns for the time when he felt close to his wife; when his daughter was near; when the world was full of heroes, whose glorious names he loves to recite; when he himself acted heroically at Anzio. The camera leaves him leaning on a fence that divides him from the children whose sandlot game of baseball he watches with nostalgic longing. A captive of his youthful memories, a lonely outsider, he is somewhat reminiscent of Harry Caul of *The Conversation,* yet ever, like all Lemmon's men, affirmative of and in touch with something lovely and decent he can value though never attain.

In Paul Newman's impressive career, we see roles that mark rather clearly the changing stages in the portrayal of men. Unlike Jack Lemmon who, until he sank into "causey" movies like *The China Syndrone* and *Missing,* where he looks piously out of place, is always scrambling to achieve something like stature and self-control, Newman began bravely, in the '50s, as a '40s kind of man. In both *Somebody Up There Likes Me* and *The Long Hot Summer,* he sees himself as a man of stature and self-control: large, capable, energetic. Mature, established men acknowledge his potential, for he is made to succeed. One measure of this potential is his interest in a strong, intelligent, and energetic woman. By the end of the decade that sent a helpless Jack Lemmon out to sea with Joe E. Brown for a fiancé, Newman has drifted toward adolescence in *The*

Hustler. His fate in this movie brings to light the point so many movies of the '70s make: men may wish to achieve genuine success as adults with some control over their lives, but the process involves so much pain that they retreat to childhood for the comfort one usually expects when hurts come. The result is only an exacerbation of the pain they feel, since they have to suffer the indignity of being childish too. Newman's hustler cannot win the approval of the older men, and he can sustain neither his interest in the woman who loves him nor her respect for him. Like the men in *Sunset Boulevard, The Conversation, Carnal Knowledge,* and also *Five Easy Pieces,* for all his looks, talent, and intelligence, Newman is "bent and broken" by experience and not "into a better shape" at all. Initially brazen, energetic, and above all talkative, the hustler ends up in a heap, moaning and whining with nothing to say, waiting to rot by gradations into the confused opportunist of *The Sweet Bird of Youth,* the brutish, amoral ne'er-do-well of *Hud,* the seedy, drunken lawyer of *The Verdict,* whose every action is tediously slow, for whom the utterance of every word demands a colossal effort, and whose totality of lines seems to form a mere paragraph. He can no longer command a woman's love but falls prey instead to a worthless, little Charlotte Rampling, whose deceitful style has barely matured since *Georgy Girl.* The retreat to childhood yields a dream-like frolic in *Butch Cassidy and the Sundance Kid* and *The Sting* (as it does to some extent in *Paper Moon* and *Heaven Can Wait*), but behind even these somewhat sprightly Newman movies there is ever the disturbing sense of human suffering that robs men of dignity; of uncontrollable circumstances that force them to be impetuously resourceful like little boys, rather than maturely deliberate like men; and of the menace of ruin and death that makes life hardly worth growing up for.

The old-fashioned loner, epitomized by John Wayne, is out of date now. There are no more open spaces in which men can roam alone; technology has taken him, and women with him, to outer space, where dependency on team and machine precludes that emblematic long shot of the man on his horse, heroically still against a big sky. Self-doubt and introspection, moreover, have forced his kind out of the snappy "shoot-'em-up" Western and right into the "adult" Western, where, despite his victories, like the men of *The Best Years of Our Lives,* he feels like a loser but doesn't feel like putting on a brave face. Instead, epitomized by Gary Cooper in *High Noon*, he broods over the small difference a civilized man can make in a barbaric world.

It's one thing for the central character of a poem, J. Alfred Prufrock, to identify himself with Polonius—passing up the starring role in self-disparagement, but still selecting a crucial supporting role. It's something else, as Tom Stoppard proved, when Rosencrantz and Guildenstern hit center stage. They are men who feel powerless to initiate anything; they mock their own inability to say anything important; they feel they have no identitites. They are "lonely and anonymous" boys, helpless in this life. That sense of impotence and futility gripped the hearts of men in the movies for several decades. But it looks as if men, women, love, and character are coming back. Explicit displays of sex have had their day of fame and fortune and have bored most of us with a surfeit of gyrations and groans. Alienation, too, has just about wrapped up its road tour. Now, when moviemakers aren't promoting a love match between boy and robot, they are actually exploring once again the infinitely fascinating and sometimes even humorous subjects of strong character and close ties between men and women. Viva the life-affirming movies of the '80's: *Victor/Victoria, All of Me, A Room with a View!*

7.

Reflections of the Country: View from the City

One third of an ill-housed, ill-clad, and ill-nourished nation lived on the farm when Franklin Roosevelt took office in 1933. The population hadn't shifted much by the time he rang out those phrases of his 1937 inaugural address, but soon thereafter, in galloping strides once we'd entered the war, Americans moved to the city en masse. Most Hollywood dramas can be expected to have taken place in the city, for the city furnishes both an abundance of characters and story material. Many movies, though set in the city and concerned with the characters' lives there, also bring to our awareness the country setting that lies in those characters' past. Such movies show how a character's personal experience of the city both reflects and determines his attitude toward the country background, and explains the nature of his relationship to the city.

A backward glance at the way Shakespeare aligned the two settings in comedy and romance can help us to see the variations of traditional urban and pastoral meanings that show up in movies, for the interplay of city and country figures dramatically in his plays, as it does in some movies. In comedies like *As You Like It* and *A Midsummer Night's Dream,* and in romances like *The Winter's tale* and *The Tempest,* the city is the home of reality, the proper setting for mature, civilized people. Nevertheless, the city, with all its demands and pressures, is often a poor place in which to deal with relationships, for it furnishes no way or time free enough to resolve the problems associated with them. The country provides a simpler vacation setting, in which it becomes easier to resolve, or at least to understand, personal problems.

To some extent, the journey to the country resembles having a dream: simultaneously rejuvenating and maturing; confusing and clarifying; allowing one to release and indulge one's wildest wishes and to reconcile oneself to order. The journey to the country is, of course, a journey to nature and to one's own nature, and Shakespeare is careful, even in the pointedly dream-like atmosphere of *A Midsummer Night's Dream,* to give us natural details so we will know that the setting is a real place before it is a metaphor. The moon, for example, trembles with meanings, but to the artisans it's a natural source of light and a handy prop for their play. Such a journey is most important for its power to restore the balance between one's natural self and one's civilized self. In Shakespeare's vision, there must be a return to the city. The city may cramp one's natural self and thus do real damage to one's relationships, by drying one up emotionally, by frustrating one's desires, but the city, by means of the very exactions of loyalty and law which it imposes, also furthers the complexity and depth through which relationships prosper and last.

For Shakespeare's characters, the natural setting is lush, beautiful, and wild. It serves as an inspiration to poets and lovers, but art and love can flower only if the wilderness is tamed. The return of the three *Midsummer Night's Dream* couples, including the legalistic Theseus and Hippolyta, to the city signals their readiness to tame the wilderness and to accept the demands of reality while holding onto the happy memories of nature's lush beauty and freedom. Prospero's fifteen-year stay in the nature he loves and is forever taming constitutes in this sense his prolonged return to the city, his joyful penance for having been irresponsible in Milan—inappropriately on vacation in the city.

There is a noticeable difference in the way movies presented the country through the eyes of city-dwellers between the late '30s to the mid-40s, when the New Deal spirit was strong, and the mid to late '40s, when the Cold War mood took hold. In the "New Deal" movies, the use of the country and city settings resembles Shakespeare's in the sense that the two must be integrated in their minds before people can have strong and lasting relationships with each other. While the city retains a largely Shakespearean meaning, the movies adhere to a romantic view of the country. Nature offers not a wild, releasing, somewhat dangerous dreamland, like Shakespeare's forests, but a civilized ideal with which one can combat the corruptive forces of the city. The traffic in these movies, moreover, moves not from city to country but generally the other way. Characters adapt quickly to the city, which becomes the setting for professional success and an extended social life. People look strong, capable of mastering and enjoying a bustling environment. (Even the cute kids from backyard musicals graduate from *Babes in Arms* to win success in *Babes on Broadway*.) While they have no intention of returning to take up residence in the country, they carry it with them in their hearts. Characters are shown bringing with them a natural wholesomeness that refreshes the city. Having escaped the country's poverty yet held onto the simple faith in family, honesty, and candor they learned there, they are able to integrate city and country in their own minds, to nourish the city with their country idealism and simultaneously to acquire the charm of city sophistication. In the early "Cold War" movies, however, characters never feel comfortable in the city, which loses its Shakespearean meaning, having little to do with civilization and everything to do with corruption, which is itself a reflection of the irrational, violent animal that is man. Characters are more likely to confront their own true nature in the vicious, brutal city than in any natural setting. For these characters, it is too easy to succumb to crime, and the possibilities for personal satisfaction and fulfillment are narrow. Characters in these movies yearn for the country, which retains the romantic purity of the earlier movies but, because the characters themselves have fallen so hopelessly, takes on the quality of an unreachable dreamland, as if it were part of an imagined past to which they never really belonged.

In the New Deal movies, the city is exciting in the manner of a festive celebration. Human ingenuity, friendliness, and optimism prevail. The city is the true home of civilization, replete with services, conveniences, opportunities unknown to the backward country dwellers. In the Cold War movies, the city throbs suspensefully; buildings, pavements, machinery seem more at home in and more in possession of the setting than people do. In the New Deal movies, the country—the characters' place of origin—is a real place, with a name, and with specific, well known points and spots, to which characters still feel some connection. They even return for brief visits, although they plan to remain permanently in the city. In the Cold War movies, the country is a closed-off region to which the characters cannot return, at least not freely and easily, and sometimes not alive.

Mr. Smith Goes to Washington, The More the Merrier, and *The Clock* capture the New Deal spirit with its faith in human enterprise and good will perfectly. In all three, the women have preceded the men to the city, so we see the adjustment to the city as a *fait accompli* among the women and as a process among the men. The women are intelligent, efficient, self-sufficient—in a good position to be helpful to the men. This is exactly what happens initially. The women are established, comparatively worldly, and knowledgeable about getting along. Each has the city well under control and moves through majestic halls or dashes through dense crowds fearlessly. The man arrives on the scene, a quintessential hayseed, endearing to her for that very reason, as he spurs a reminder of something in her own life she holds dear. All three of these movies say that one needs help in learning the ropes and one needs help in maintaining an equilibrium in order to balance within oneself the city and the country.

James Stewart's Mr. Smith, wonder-struck by Washington at first, is soon drawn into its sewer of political corruption. It is Saunders the secretary (played by Jean Arthur) who helps him to clamber out, to fight corruption, by giving him all the practical guidance he needs. He helps her to an equal degree, however, by restoring to her an elemental kind of strength she has lost contact with, a belief in honesty rooted in his country origins. He makes her remember, simply by his presence, what she was like when she first arrived in Washington. "When I came here, my eyes were big blue question marks; now they're big green dollar marks," she confesses dispiritedly. Amused as she is by Smith's embarrassing gullibility, she is smart enough to see and admire the rock-hard conviction which could make a powerful man out of him despite the clownish eagerness of his deportment. It's not for nothing that he's named Jefferson and that he seeks out the Jefferson Memorial immediately upon arrival in Washington. That cultivated gentleman, after all, forcefully influenced American thought with his ideas about country values. Jefferson Smith renders them poetically for Saunders, conjuring up "the prairies" with "the wind leaning on tall grass and the cattle moving down the slopes against the setting sun" where "every tree, every rock, every stream, every star is filled with the wonders of nature." In Wordsworth's kind of simple phrases, Smith expresses the same romantic faith in nature's goodness.

A particularly apt touch in this movie is the casting of Harry Carey as president of the Senate. As the moderator during Mr. Smith's filibuster, this draftee from countless Westerns in which he played honest, folksy cowboys serves as a model himself of the happy union of city and country. The senior senator from Mr. Smith's home state may have gone astray in the city, and may no longer regard the country he left as a real place, but the vice-president is safely whole in the nation's capital because he is in touch with the country, smiling benevolently on young Mr. Smith from what Frank Capra, so justly pleased with his choice of Carey for the role, has called "a strong American face."[1]

The More the Merrier gives us Jean Arthur once again established in Washington, this time as Connie Milligan, not a bit jaded by the city as her Saunders was, but toughened by it in another way. She survives by adhering rigidly to schedules, routines, any kind of systematic arrangement. She is, in her compulsiveness, a sitting duck for the pranks of her two roomers—the urbane Mr. Dingle, played by Charles Coburn, and the unassuming newcomer to Washington, Joe Carter, played by Joel McCrea—because she has no elasticity left, no sense of humor. Though the men depend on her generosity for rooms in overcrowded, war-time Washington, she depends on them, especially on the young man, to learn something about true feelings. Consistent with her superbly organized life, she has managed to become engaged to a dull, unimaginative man, as rigid in his way as she is. Luckily, she is not impervious to Joe's homey directness about feelings. When he kisses her outside their apartment house, it is obvious from her bewildered look that he has surprised her into feeling much more than she thought possible. After all, Joel McCrea, like Harry Carey, is another reliable draftee from Westerns and has the same sort of "strong American face."

When Judy Garland meets Robert Walker in Pennsylvania Station, he is fresh from Indiana, about to go overseas, and she is fresh from a visit to the country, so their country origins figure significantly from the beginning of the movie. Like *Mr. Smith Goes to*

Washington and *The More the Merrier, The Clock* offers us a woman who is already at home in the city and a man who has just arrived and feels a little strange there. Garland's Alice loves the city and conveys her familiarity with it by the confident way she moves through its various settings: gracefully in quiet restaurant and church; aggressively in teeming subways. Walker's Joe is terrified, however. The skyscrapers on Seventh Avenue look so threatening when he first pokes his nose out of Penn Station that he scurries right back inside and doesn't emerge again until he has Alice to hang onto. "This city must seem very strange to you," she says as she watches him taking it all in with obvious uneasiness. In so saying, she sees the city through his eyes, probably remembering what she felt three years before when she came to live and work in the city. Before long, sitting in the Metropolitan Museum, they are trading stories of specific country settings each remembers and loves. Although she is now a confirmed convert to city life and devotes most of the movie to helping him feel as comfortable there as she does, his love of the land is as important to her as Mr. Smith's belief in honesty is to Saunders or Joe Carter's directness about feelings is to Connie Milligan.

The implication at the end of all three movies is that, however attached the characters may be to the country, their place is in the city; the city will sustain in them the attachment to their country past; the city needs them; they will prosper in the city. All three movies look forward to a bright future, even though in two of them the young men must leave their brides and go to war. There is no question that the brides will continue with their jobs and fare extremely well in the city, and that's where the men expect to find them when they return.

One way of marking the disconsolate mood that crept over movies in the mid-'40s is to look first at *On the Town,* a movie made in 1949 but set during the war and eager to impart a wartime optimism, and then at *It's Always Fair Weather,* a movie in which Gene Kelly tried, in 1955, to recapture the exuberance that characterized his earlier vehicle about three young servicemen cavorting about New York on shore leave. The 1955 movie, for all its excellent choreography and industrious comedians, can't seem to shake a certain lassitude that weighs it down from the first reunion scene in the bar, where everybody looks a little seedy and discontented, so different from those six radiant young adults dancing and singing their way through a beautiful day during World War II.

The serious dramas that convey a Cold War mood transcend the lassitude and wear a decidedly bleak face. The stark shots of buildings accentuate their unfriendly height, like giants in a fairy tale. The wide-angle shots of avenues contrasted with the sudden darts into dark alleys suggest variations of human vulnerability, either too exposed or trapped. Men may predominate over women in these movies, but they achieve no dominance over the city settings. Whether indoors or on the streets, the men look small and barely distinguishable from one another in comparison with Mr. Smith, country bumpkin, commanding the floor of the Senate, shot from below to accentuate his height; or the young couple of *The Clock* singled out for our attention by the camera three times in crowded Penn Station. In one way or another, moreover, the women are unequal to the needs of men, even when they are helpful, loving women. Movies like *Laura, The Lost Weekend, Out of the Past,* and *The Asphalt Jungle* present the city as a nightmare world. Its suspense and terror grow out of darkened phantasmago-ria unrelieved by comic or romantic overtones such as one finds in *The Maltese Falcon* or *The Big Sleep,* where danger is challenging rather than threatening because heroism and love still have a chance. While the city is a pure concentration of fairy-tale anxieties and fears, the country that lies in the background becomes a concentra-tion of fairy-tale wishes and delights. Both settings, strained by such fantastic exaggeration, seem unreal, the way places look in dreams—more frightening or more pleasant than real life.

Dana Andrews, the detective of *Laura,* epitomizes the moody, unattached, unhappy man of the dangerous city. James Stewart, goofy and gawky, triumphs in the United States Senate; Dana Andrews, tough, shrewd, and experienced, has, nevertheless, a hard time asserting himself among a handful of characters in New York. He is smart in a way and to a degree Stewart, McCrea, and Walker don't need to be, but barely smart enough to master his circumstances. Lacking their confidence in themselves, in what they know is right, he can be beaten by his own cynicism. He is further threatened by the superior enthusiasm and intelligence of the villain, played by Clifton Webb, not to mention the distractions engendered by his fantasy of the murdered girl, played by Gene Tierney, whose portrait he falls in love with. The girl comes to him fresh from the country, out of a dream, he thinks, as he wakes up from sleep to see before him the very vision of loveliness we know he longs to see. Once he is fully awake, though, he consigns her to the city setting where everyone is suspect, even she, the intended murder victim. Until the end, the detective is unsure about how to regard her; he imagines only two choices: she is either innocent or guilty; she is either an eager, talented young thing from the country who made good in the fashion world but got in with the wrong people, or she is part of the bewitching atmosphere of the city against which he must guard himself. Andrews struggles to the finish to get a proper reading of her, solves his case, wins the girl, and goes forward to a future likely to involve strange occurrences always tinged with evil, distrust, and uncertainty, the hallmarks of the setting where he must continue to wait watchfully for new troubles. The girl has brought nothing magical or restorative with her from the country to suggest any-thing else. Her country setting is cut off from the city, as implied by her defective radio, which failed to bring her news of her own "murder."

In both *The Lost Weekend* and *Out of the Past,* there are women, like Gene Tierney's fashion designer of *Laura,* who try hard to be helpmates to the men they love. In all three movies, moreover, these women have a connection to the country which serves to suggest something wholesomely, benevolently human about them. They alone in these movies sustain an integrated relationship with both city and country, similar to Shakespeare's characters and to the characters of the New Deal movies. The difference is that the integrity they achieve gives them no real power to be effective; they can't help the men they love and they can't exert any kind of moral or political influence. Their integrity is good largely for lonely survival. The men either cannot join the women in the country, or they cannot stay there, and are inexorably drawn to the city and its vile temptations. In the absence of his sensible and generous-hearted girlfriend, played by Jane Wyman, Ray Milland's alcoholic goes on his ghastly spree, all alone in a city whose flat, gray streets are empty, whose stores are inhospitably shut. And Robert Mit-chum, with his droopy-eyed, morose expression, looks awkward and out of place sitting on flat rocks in fields of tall grasses with his sweet girlfriend. Nature seems unnatural to him and, restless to get away, he leaves both girlfriend and nature behind in the country.

The country setting, to which the woman has access and the man does not, suggests a barrier in the very relationship between men and women. In the case of each couple, the men and women move in different directions; they don't work in tandem; they don't really understand each other; they love and admire each other, but they can't grow close to each other. They can't be in the country together, and even if they can like Mitchum and his girlfriend, the natural setting doesn't do what it does for Shakespeare's lovers, or for the lovers of earlier movies—bring them close to each other.

It's hard to imagine any of these later couples having cozy chats or trivial spats of the sort so familiar to people who live intimately. Instead, they have brooding conversations about his problems or silences during which the guilty distrust he can't shake off makes them occasional strangers. The men's range of emotional expression appears extremely narrow, posing special challenges of taut restraint to the actors, whose faces register hardly any affect (except for Ray Milland, who rants and raves during his delirium). James Stewart's Mr. Smith and Robert Walker's Joe Allen, with their versatile displays of enthusiasm, fear, wonder, anger, frustration, and happiness, seem, by contrast, more fully human than their truncated, Cold War counterparts, with their benumbed capacity for making jokes, waxing sentimental, gasping in fear, or laughing out loud. (William Wyler's 1946 masterpiece, *The Best Years of Our Lives,* anticipates the serious problems of disorientation and alienation experienced by post-war men. The men come home from the war, feeling backward and inept, almost as if they were country bumpkins, to face women who are self-sufficiently and energetically in step with the speeded up efficiency of the post-war world. The situation is sadly ironic. The inherent comforts and opportunities to which the women are already adjusted have been made possible by the men at war who, as Fredric March pensively remarks, "didn't see a thing" to prepare them for the very life they were forging when they stormed unknown beaches in Europe and flew over remote targets in Japan, feeling helpless and scared.)

While the men feel separated from the women who belong to or find easy access to the country, they are hardly at home with the women who belong intrinsically to the city either. Even in *Laura,* the movie among the *film noir* types which achieves an approximation to a happy ending for Laura and the detective, they bristle with distrust of each other during their first scene. That feeling runs parallel to their growing attraction and, for all we know, persists as part of their relationship forever. In *Laura, Out of the Past,* and *The Asphalt Jungle,* other sorts of women wait to excite men's passion and destroy them. Judith Anderson, in her best Lady Macbeth manner, looks darkly, shrewdly alluring. Mitchum's passion for the suavely sensual Jane Greer has him in thrall, resembling Milland's passion for liquor. Both men know and love wholesome, civilized women, but they are betrayed and inflamed by their passions, Mitchum's character coming literally to an incendiary end. Similarly, in *The Asphalt Jungle,* the mastermind played by Sam Jaffe is finally betrayed by his irrepressible urge to watch a voluptuous teenager dance to a jukebox melody in some roadside diner. The time he wastes ogling her body costs him his getaway. The mistress kept by Louis Calherne, played by Marilyn Monroe, is there only to satisfy physical desires. Sweet as he finds her, he does not confide in her any more than he confides in his adoring wife.

Every one of these movies ends on a note of yearning for some unarticulated wish yet to be fulfilled. The problems these characters face are not really any worse than the problems characters face in the three movies discussed earlier. But the problems seem worse to them, and if problems seem worse, measurement is a futile exercise. Corruption in the Senate and going overseas to war are big problems indeed. They seem less dire, however, not only because the characters are allowed to win something—if it comes to that, in the latter four movies the characters are also allowed to win something—but also because the characters face the problems as teams and, possibly more significant than anything else, the problems are outside of the characters.

The settings, too, are outside of the characters and exist as real places. The settings are not merely known; they can be mastered creatively, that is, shaped to match human ideals. For the later characters, the settings are more likely to seem but metaphors of their inner states, over which the people certainly have no control. Despite his success with the case, Dana Andrews's detective still looks rather glum at the end of the movie, not really confident that he can handle whatever lurks in the dark streets of New York. As Ray Milland looks out over Manhattan from his apartment window after his "lost weekend," he is "dried out" now, but his future is uncertain, and the harsh, forbidding expanse at which he gazes does not promise him mastery of it, despite his lofty vantage point, especially since the voice-over tells us that hundreds of lonely people struggle with their own demons somewhere within the vast conglomerate of concrete below. Both *Out of the Past* and *The Asphalt Jungle* end with characters (Robert Mitchum and Sterling Hayden respectively) in desperate flight to the country, the land of the imagined past, the lost land. Both men arrive only to die, both from gunshot wounds. Unable, for all their love of nature, to attach themselves to the moral ideals of the country as a kind of fortification—the way all of the characters from the New Deal movies were able to do—they have come staggering back, with the brutal law of the crime-ridden city laying claim to their dead bodies. Mitchum's car explodes before he can reach his country sweetheart. Hayden's death in the peaceful Kentucky pasture with the lovely horse mournfully bending over him and the loving Jean Hagen back at the road, too far away to help him, marks the closing shot of *The Asphalt Jungle,* a romantically perfect consummation of America's continuing love affair with paradise, long after it has been lost.

All of the movies discussed here suggest something about how a character's personal experience of the city is partially influenced by and reflects the movie's view of national morale—that nearly palpable quality of pride or fear, security or malaise people accept almost as a feature of their private lives. Similarly, attitudes toward the country background are ever connected to familiar attitudes toward America's innocence, vastness, and safe freedom. The change in attitude from affection to nostalgia for the country reflects city-dwelling characters' loss of faith in themselves. Individuals come to have only a tenuous hold on the course of their personal lives, subject constantly to crazy interruption from the outside, to irrational bursts from the inside. They bear on their tired faces the weariness of a nation that has been to war, has won, and knows, to its infinite dismay, that the war, though won, goes on and on. That is why Dana Andrews and Ray Milland look sad, almost defeated, even though each survives to survey the scene of the battle he has won.

In the three New Deal movies, both country and city are, in their own ways and despite their faults, congenial to people. They portray two faces of civilization, two compatible styles that make transfer from one to the other smooth and desirable. In the Cold War movies, neither city nor country seems equipped with any kind of apparatus or design to help people. They portray two contrasting projections of the characters' inner lives, neither of which serves as a firm foundation on which to carry on the business of everyday life. In the three New Deal movies, a bright future is implicit, paradoxically, in the very sights of Robert Walker and Joel McCrea going off to war and of James Stewart lying unconscious on the floor of the Senate. In the Cold War movies, however, people cannot build on hopes for the future because, just as they have a foothold in no setting, they are cut off from all time, adrift in timeless darkness.

Part III:

Acting

8

In a Dream of Passion: The Tragedy of Acting

Is it not monstrous that this player here,
But in a fiction, in a dream of passion,
Could force his soul so to his own conceit . . .

Hamlet, 2.2.577–579

Hollywood's wholesome self-love and fascination with theater loosed a flood of movies about show business. Backstage musicals like *Forty-Second Street* and *Footlight Parade*, and backyard musicals like *Babes in Arms* and *Strike Up the Band*, with their built-in song-and-dance numbers performed by those bravely perseverant, indefatigable young troupers, made sure-fire entertainment. Comedies about theater people on and offstage, like *It's Love I'm After* and *To Be or Not to Be*, exposed the vagaries and vanities of actors with a sophisticated, satiric edge as well as an affectionate understanding. And the musicals and dramas about making it in show business—the individual's hard road to center stage—celebrated the profession, parading it before us gaily, confidently in *Morning Glory*, *Stage Door*, *Easter Parade*, and *Singin' in the Rain*. (Judy Garland was forever struggling to keep up with her "betters" in movies, and parlayed her underdog status into performances of such vibrantly intelligent charm that her current revival-house audiences cheer and applaud her every "audition" and "debut" as if that inimitable talent were alive and "live," surprising them afresh.) All of the movies so far mentioned deal with anxiety, ambition, competition, frustration, and success. In all of them, life in show business is rough but also loads of fun. Talent is rewarded in a theatrical world that is fair and reasonable. Friends abound, moreover, and happy cooperation prevails.

Hollywood faced just as openly, though not so frequently of course, the dark, tragic side of theater, in which acting, while confirming the actor's genius to the public, becomes harmful, even fatal, to the private person. Movies like *A Double Life*, *All About Eve*, *Sunset Boulevard*, and *A Star Is Born* (1954) ultimately show us corrupted, thwarted, or ravaged selves, who have no notion any longer whether acting gave to or stole from them their identities. For these lost souls, acting is the great love of their lives, an ideal to which they aspire, the art for which they willingly exhaust themselves day after day, night after night. All could swear that they feel most alive—and most themselves—when acting, but a career of acting makes them unfit for real life. Such a career comprises a long, steady retreat from reality that takes in a highway of metaphors: the delightful secret garden; the baffling looking glass; the frightening twilight zone; the perilous seas of fairy lands forlorn; the dream of passion. The succession of metaphors suggests a journey farther and farther away from fellow human beings and the solace they might provide. These metaphors are useful not only to measure the actor's increasing distance from reality, but also to understand acting as a voluntary departure. People choose to be actors and in so doing choose that journey which turns out to be a tormenting, paradoxical quest that is flight, gain that is loss.

A Double Life pursues actor Tony John, played by Ronald Colman, on just such a journey. The very opening shot of him is already inauspicious. With his back to us—a faceless unknown—he stands in the foyer of a theater and studies paintings, busts, and photographs of himself. When he turns around toward us, he looks puzzled and abstracted. Two fans hail him, and he flees backstage where the fatal role of Othello is waiting for him. This beginning, so smoothly dispatched, gives us his story in embryo: in his search for himself, the actor looks to representations of himself. Although he finds no satisfaction there, his impulse is to continue his search through other representations, through roles, rather than to find himself through relationships with other people.

Acting involves passionate endeavor for Tony; he struggles to become Othello, as he says, ". . . trying to make someone else's words your own . . ." Behind that struggle lurks the fear that without the role he is nobody and has nobody. (When the waitress asks him his name, the roles he has played over the years come thronging into his mind; he cannot seem to remember his own name.) The role provides a way to become somebody. The actor achieves what Joseph Mankiewicz has called "a spotlight identity,"[1] what the young writer in *Sunset Boulevard* calls Norma Desmond's "celluloid self." The greater the actor's success in creating a self through the role, the greater, too, his ultimate sense of loss. For the role is but an abstraction, a playwright's idea of a person, into whom the actor pours his true, living person, without ever crediting himself with the substance he gives to the role, but thanking the role instead for giving an identity to him. So Tony John, in his final performance, speaks Othello's words, in alternate stumbling halts and smooth measures, as if he were making them up, as if he were saying them for the first time, as if, finally, he had words and thoughts. For that horribly long run of the play, he gave Othello his own life in order to become someone who is only a part in a play. It is no wonder that he looks for himself in paintings, stares into mirrors like Norma Desmond who, amidst a clutter of photographs spanning her career, watches her old movies over and over; like Norman Maine, too, who, while shaving every morning, chants, "Mirror, mirror, on the wall, / Who is the greatest star of them all?" As Tony dies at the end, Brita, his ex-wife, played by Signe Hasso, and Bill, her friend, played by Edmund O'Brien, remove the wig and make-up, trying to restore Tony to himself, but there is no self there. He wants to say something special, something moving by way of farewell to Brita, but nothing comes out. He has no lines of his own. (In an interview with Stephen Farber and Marc Green, Henry Fonda made this comment: "When I act, I put on a mask and when I do that I'm not self-conscious or shy at all, because I know that when I'm on the stage I'm going to be funny or bright or brilliant—I'm going to be another person who isn't me at all. You see, I'm no good on my own."[2]) For the actor, the role comes to appear much greater and more substantial than he. In yielding himself to a great role, the actor loses sight of his own power, which is simply life, with all its rich delights of free thought, learning, love and friendship, the very delights which

Karen, the playwright's wife in *All About Eve*, rates incomparably superior to "a part in a play" and urges on her actress friend, the great Margo Channing.

What intensifies the importance of the role, then, is precisely that it competes with relationships, becoming itself a friend, a companion, a lover. In a conversation with his ex-wife, Brita, whom he still loves but cannot get along with, Tony John says, "I don't know which is worse—with a part or without," much as a man might say, "Women—you can't live with 'em and you can't live without 'em." Indeed, to seal his meaning, he adds, "And with you, nothing but failure there," telling us implicitly that relationships with roles and with people are similar in his mind but, difficult as acting may be, at least it brings him some sense of personal success. It is tragic for him, finally, that he doesn't realize that the role is neither he himself nor a lover but only an abstraction that will ever lure him away from real people, real satisfactions, a real sense of self, to a death-in-life in which death, that last abstraction, becomes also the last lover.

This confusion of a role, and acting itself, with a lover plagues Norma Desmond also. This is what drives her great passion for the defeated screenwriter, Joe Gillis—gifted with words, as his richly metaphorical narration shows, but cynical and cold—who happens to land on her doorstep. Once she sees in him the hope of her comeback, she is obsessively in love with him and takes him as her lover, even though she hardly knows him and he is never kind to her. At the end, oblivious to the murder she has just committed—the victim none other than her young lover—she descends the stairs in an ecstasy: "The dream she had clung to so desperately had enfolded her." Joe Gillis's tenderly romantic words, marking his first note of compassion for her, here suggest to us that she glides into her fantasy of a renewed acting career as into a lover's embrace. In *Dangerous*, Bette Davis's down-and-out, alcoholic actress falls wildly in love with a man who enthusiastically helps her to revive her career, even though she hardly knows him and can, therefore, have no real interest in him as a person. And in *A Star Is Born*, Norman Maine falls in love with the woman who represents his new career. Because he has no energy left to go on acting, she will create a career for him that will give him a new self by being a great star herself. What initially attracts him to her is her having included him in her act when he was drunk and everyone else tried to keep him offstage. What continues to attract him to her is her phenomenal talent; he needs it and identifies with it so much so that, at the preview of her first big picture, he's glad that his own picture, also on the bill, is horrible. "We're in luck, Esther," he says, meaning that both of them will thrive on the superior quality of her picture. The career means much less to Esther. She is ready to give it up in a minute, to devote herself to her ailing husband, but what appears a sensible solution in her eyes he greets with anguished sobs. For him, the very marriage and his love for her are inseparable from his love for her career. That is why he seems, at the end, detached from his wife, more interested, like Norma Desmond, in the scene he is playing, as he deceives Esther in favor of the last lover and moves forward irrevocably to meet the embracing waves.

In *All About Eve*, a story less direful than the others discussed here, Margo Channing is on shaky ground where relationships are concerned too, even though her lover is a real man who truly loves her, not some abstraction. She can't believe Bill is really in love with her, for she isn't sure she is anyone at all behind what Joseph Mankiewicz calls "those magical Protean masks."[3] In her distrust of Bill, she recklessly propels her own suspicious fantasies to force a rupture in their relationship. It is no accident that their personal crisis is played out in a bedroom which is a stage set. She thinks she is finally getting at the truth—Bill doesn't love her; he loves Eve—but she is merely dissolving herself in another role. Clinging to her role, weeping alone on her stage bed, Margo Channing could, at this point, arrive at Norma Desmond's gateway of suicidal despair.

Death comes easily into the lives of miserable actors. In these movies, it serves as both a comment on the "inner emptiness they can never fill"[4] and a fulfillment. For those who yield up their love to abstractions, death is the only one that yields anything in return: the end of loneliness, the hopeless quest, the insatiable hunger for love. The death-like consequences of love for such abstractions as her past success, her youth, and her career mock the poor Norma Desmond in every macabre detail of *Sunset Boulevard*: her story is told by a corpse; her only baby is a dead monkey; she lives in a "grim sunset castle" with gaping garages and empty swimming pool; she plays cards with friends whom Joe Gillis calls "her waxworks." He finds her death-like setting merely disgusting, for in his brash, callous disapproval he fails to see that it represents the psychological depths to which she, a great actress, has fallen. In his smart, facile way, he cleverly compares her to Miss Havisham, another great actress with an equally keen appreciation for stage sets and melodrama. He means only to pass judgment on these crazy women who won't face facts, without noticing that the settings both women have created for themselves are perfect, pitiful, yet at the same time grandiloquent projections of the ghastly truths of their inner lives: demoralization; depression; detachment from life; desire for death. They really mean that they can't go on with life anymore.

Like tragedies, the movies discussed here portray greatness. In every one, the actor's greatness is explicitly dramatized. Tony John is "a great actor"; Norma Desmond and Norman Maine were "great stars"; Esther Blodgett is "a great singer"; Margo Channing is "a great actress." Greatness exacts from them a terrible price; even its rewards are costly. Seated on the pinnacle, loved and admired, the actor is alone, and he must meet the demands of the adoring public by enduring the long run or turning out a record number of movies and remaining great all the while. (It's that kind of pressure that prompted Marilyn Monroe to exclaim, "You're never finished.") Norma Desmond and Norman Maine restlessly mourn their lost careers; Tony John is afraid he won't be able to keep it up; Margo Channing, at a turning point in her life, worries that she is too old for the good parts, and that without the good parts no one will love her.

In every case, we are made aware of the actor's exhaustion and the ease with which his particularly exhausting career could lead to madness. Tony John does cross that dangerous border, and for the last third of the movie lives his life believing he is Othello, finishing himself off onstage at the end. His suicide, in his mind, seems to have little, if anything, to do with retribution for the murder he committed of the naive waitress. Like Norma Desmond at her end, Tony is hardly aware of other people as people; as he has retreated to his imaginary world of roles, he has taken other people with him cast in other roles. In dying, he is Othello, but he is also putting an end to an impossibly exhausting career that has driven him mad. In her witty way, Margo Channing speaks to this point when she says, "Performance number one thousand of this one, if I play it that long, will take place in a well-padded booby-hatch!" At the end of *Sunset Boulevard*, Norma Desmond believes she is on a Hollywood set being directed by Cecil B. DeMille. She recognizes none of the faces before her. (In *The Blue Angel*, Professor Rath goes mad right on stage, confusing the vaudeville rooster he is playing with the cuckold he is at that moment becoming.) The demoralization that comes from a sense of being nobody, of being hollowed out by acting, the loneliness that comes from the passionate pursuit of abstractions, all stir in actors a longing to be finished once and for all with a career that brings so much suffering.

The 1954 production of *A Star is Born* treats the actor's exhaustion and wish to be finished in a particularly poignant way by starring Judy Garland and James Mason opposite the roles that correspond so closely to their own lives respectively: Garland opposite the great, now broken-down actor; Mason opposite the strong, stable, reliable trouper. As Esther Blodgett, later Vicki Lester, she is the star Norman Maine creates, but she is also Judy Garland who knocked herself out from childhood, made money for MGM and her mother, who wanted, already at fifteen, to make enough money to buy her mother a house so she, Judy, could retire from show business and rest, but who went on and on until her agonies to get through yet another show and her somehow "miraculous" survival became part of every performance she gave. In playing opposite James Mason as Norman Maine, by furnishing so much warmth and sympathy for the actor who has given too much, who now needs to rest and drink as if to make up for all the years when he was overworked and parched, Garland intensifies our sense of his terrible plight and stirs our pity for him. The brilliant casting and acting of these two results in the subtlest movie version of this story despite the long, splashy musical numbers. Those numbers actually enhance the subtlety of the pair's interaction, for they enable Garland and Mason to dramatize the disparity between the happy life of "making it in show business" musicals— the kind of movies she makes in the movie—and the desperate need for that fantasy in the failed actor for whom his wife gamely provides home entertainment—the lavish songs providing evidence of her success as a star—after a day of work at the studio.

A Star Is Born is, after all, a story about acting and what such a career means to people. Though Norman's career is over, he can't let go of acting. He can't find anything else to do. (Great actors don't seem to move on to successful careers in real estate.) Not only does he direct his great passion toward Esther's career, but he acts most of the time in his private life. Except when he is drunk, he covers up and underplays constantly, acting the role of the successful, confident star. It is Esther's panoply of responses to him that brings forth what he really is and how he really feels. By her energetic song-and-dance routines, her worried, loving looks, her generous cheerfulness, we measure the drained, needy, unhappy actor she has married. Much has been said about Mason's job of reacting to Garland during her musical numbers, but reacting is built into her role, too, in a more complex and subtle way precisely because Norman Maine cannot stop acting. She must, therefore, support his act to spare his dignity and then, too, in those remarkable moments of naked feeling—with Oliver Niles, the producer, in her dressing room; with her old friend Danny after Norman's death—expose the devastation he works to conceal. Because Garland and Mason are doing double duty throughout the movie, acting one part and bringing out the opposite part, we come to feel those relentless pressures that drive actors mad. Much as these two really love each other, they can never just relax and be themselves.

All About Eve deals as seriously with the tragic aspects of acting as the other movies discussed here but saves the heroine from what Tony John calls "the nightmare stage," when the actor has wandered so far away and, as Brita says, has "release[d] feelings and imaginings that aren't his own at all," that what is but a "dream of passion" seems real life to him. What saves Margo Channing are her intelligent mind with its capacity for insight, her sense of humor, and, curiously enough, the advent of Eve. Margo's insight and wit reassure us, even when she is most confused and unhappy, of her attachment to reality. Of all the characters discussed here, Margo alone has friendships that last and conversations in which she is completely herself—open, honest, enthusiastic, making up her own lines, witty rejoinders, lightning repartees. In the opening flashback scene, her rendition of a funny interview and gales of laughter come to us from her dressing room before we even see her. And when we do see her, a few seconds later, she is seated at her dressing table, removing her make-up, and completely involved with the other people in the room, hardly glancing in her mirror. As the story progresses and she falls prey to the same fears and doubts that beset Tony John and Norma Desmond, she brings them out herself, instead of retreating with them into a lonely dream. The world Joseph Mankiewicz creates in this movie is not a tragic world, although potential for serious mistakes and failures exists. It is, rather, a comic world similar to that in Jane Austen's novels, where admirable people are defined by their capacity for articulation and their willingness to resolve problems through verbally fortified relationships: talking; arguing; screaming, if necessary; agreeing, speaking reason at last. (Addison DeWitt, Max Fabian, Miss Carswell, and Eve herself could move into and feel completely at home among Austen's stock company of divinely transparent hypocrites, idiots, and villains.)

Margo is indeed able to articulate her problems, as she does, for example, in talking to Lloyd Richards, the playwright: "So many people know me. I wish I did. I wish someone would tell me about me." She tries to regard herself objectively, understanding that she really has an identity in other people's eyes, even if she herself feels she is nobody: "What is [Margo Channing]," she asks, "besides something spelled out in lightbulbs?" and "I want [Bill] to want me, not Margo Channing, and if I can't tell them apart, how can he?" To balance such sober, direct approaches to her problems, Mankiewicz conveys her insight further by means of her sophisticated wit. In her first screaming bout with Bill, right before the memorable party begins, in response to his suggestion that she's being irrational, she lets fly: "Cut! Print it! What happens in the next reel? Do I get dragged off screaming to the snake-pit?" She's terribly upset during this scene, but she maintains a kind of control first by the absurd comparison between herself and the stereotype of a raving mad woman, second by the very act of differentiating between the two (she may be troubled, but she knows she's not crazy), and third by the delicious agility with which she, a stage star, wields the language of Hollywood studios and throws in a reference to a recent movie. (Joe Gillis refers to Norma Desmond as a fossil; Margo Channing is, by contrast, ever quick, adaptable, alive.) One look at Miss Carswell, played by Marilyn Monroe, and Margo, sensing the untalented trollop's need for respectability in a high-class milieu, introduces her as "an old friend of Mr. DeWitt's mother," effectively beating to the punch and silencing the acid-tongued DeWitt, who has brought this unsuitable guest. As she says to Birdie before the party begins, "The only thing I ordered by mistake are the guests," and as she correctly warns, in her now most famous line, "Fasten your seat belts; it's going to be a bumpy night."

Such examples of her humor represent her contact with reality and her creative way of assessing it. Her perspective presages a happy outcome, and that is what she wins, but not before suffering some blows at the hands of Eve. The rapacious Eve, who spends the whole movie trying to steal Margo's career (friends and lover, too, insofar as they can advance her career), becomes Margo's best reason for giving up her career. Eve endears herself to Margo by that first autobiographical pack of lies stagily delivered in the dressing room, when she recalls the birth of her interest in acting: "I used to make believe a lot when I was a kid . . . acting and make-believe began to fill up my life more and more. . . . The unreal seemed more real to me." Margo believes Eve because what she says must strike a familiar chord; after decades of great acting, Margo knows what Eve is talking about, sees herself in Eve, and immediately becomes protective of what she sees as her own young self lost in the dream of acting. Mankiewicz underlines the identification a little later when Margo refers to Eve as "a little lamb loose in our big, stone jungle," and Bill, minutes later, applies those words to Margo. As with all actors who come to grief through acting, identification comes too easily for Margo. She is not a bit like Eve. In contrast to Margo's spontaneous, frank way of talking, Eve's speech is a carefully calculated exploitation, rendered in a breathy imitation of deep excitement, of the compelling dreams that drive actors to the stage. These were undoubtedly Margo's dreams, and we see their effects in her anxiety about who she really is, but they are not Eve's dreams. Contrary to what she affirms in her first speech, Eve doesn't suffer from the actor's tragedy—the loss of self in a great performance of a role. She doesn't have enough artistic imagination; she has raw ambition instead. She who is unremittingly on her guard, ever conscious of her goal, ready to outsmart and outmaneuver everyone, suffers in the end from a worse emptiness than do any of the other actors discussed here. As Mankiewicz says, "She has been servicing a bottomless pit."[5] Seated alone on her couch at movie's end, having won the Sarah Siddons Award, she looks for all the world like a bitter, tired, thwarted being, without purpose or joy, on the verge of shriveling into Miss Havisham. In that last jaded, weary look, we see the helpless wish to be finished in a woman still at the beginning of her career. It may indeed be a flaw in the movie that Eve becomes a great actress when her imagination is limited to ordinary fabrications. Success in business or politics seems more compatible with her hard-nosed, cutthroat style. In any case, she does become an actress, and becomes, moreover, the victim of her big, offstage act; she must forever keep acting—ingratiating herself, manipulating, deceiving. Without the pretty cloak of her little wiles, she is completely exposed—a gaping appetite only. She hasn't lost herself to a great role; she's lost herself to petty pretenses.

Tony John, Norma Desmond, Norman Maine—these are passionate people who achieve theatrical greatness by throwing their hearts and souls into acting. Their careers resemble ardent love affairs. These actors reach the heights, not merely the depths, of tragedy precisely because they have the requisite greatness to be extraordinary. Each becomes a consummate artist and then finds the greatness itself too hard to master, finally too hard to bear. They don't have the strength to maintain a balance in their lives, but one can hardly blame them for that; an inordinately disproportionate talent might prove a crushing weight, fatal to anyone. Neither Eve's character nor her story is tragic, however. As the critic DeWitt says to her, she is a "killer." She lacks the passion for and complete faith in her art. She is incapable of falling in love, even with an abstraction. Her notion of love stops at recognition and success. Fame rather than art interests her. That is why she focuses on applause, which she likens to "waves of love coming across the footlights at you." Where the other actors are fulfilled by their tragic endings Eve, without passion, ideals, or scruples, is doomed to emptiness and fruitless frustration. When she looks into her mirror, she sees Phoebe, a limp, surrogate self, who, at movie's end, her hands in possession of Eve's award statue, clothed in Eve's evening robe, bows to herself in a three-way mirror. No amount of multiplication, however, can lend majesty to the reptilian little

Phoebe, as Eve sits friendless and alone on the couch with her drink in her hand.

It is this aspect of Eve's story—the absolute squalor of ambition unwarmed by love, ungraced by sensitivity—that ensures the resolution of Margo's story. At her engagement supper in the Cub Room, Margo herself, after playfully referring to "Eve Evil," acknowledges shrewdly that "Eve left good behind." Although Margo's story has been an unhappy one, verging briefly on tragedy, it is ultimately a comedy. Margo has the requisite greatness for tragedy, but by choosing to lay it aside when it threatens to overcome her, in favor of her love for Bill, she achieves a balance that saves her. The example of Eve has been so shocking that Margo is through with being "a great actress." Now she wants to be a woman. In her eyes, the fulfillment of her womanhood depends on her marriage to Bill, the man she loves. So, to the dismay of many contemporary feminists, she says, "Nothing's any good unless you can look up just before dinner or turn around in bed, and there he is. Without that, you're not a woman. You're something with a French Provincial office or a book full of clippings. But you're not a woman." In rejecting her career, she undoubtedly disparges it excessively, regarding it as near trivial in comparison with the sturdy private self she has found through her relationship with Bill. Feminists should not despair, nor should they take Margo's words as a political statement. (Militant feminists are apt to approach art as if it were politics and then to get mad at artists for having the nerve to express what they see and feel. Margo is one individual with her own individual circumstances and personality. She is reacting as her creator imagines this particular individual will. Both are simply going about the suitably dramatic business of expressing what Margo feels about her personal situation. Her words are meant to suit her, not to speak for all women.)

Margo has every reason to turn away from her career when she does: she's done it long enough; it's been too demanding; it's threatened her very sense of self and all of her important relationships except the one with Birdie; and in the end, it has cast before her a vicious rival who has no natural sympathies with or vestiges of her kind—whether her kind is humanity or womanhood—who would do anything "for a part in a play." Being a woman seems to

112

Margo, in this context, a "career" well worth pursuing. It promises a fulfillment that acting has ultimately denied: to be herself. This choice is one that Eve will never have.

Tony John, Norma Desmond, Norman Maine might have had the choice, but they didn't make it in time. They drifted off to their lonely destinies to fulfill their tragic lives. So in each of their movies, the actor is finally represented by a setting from which he has vanished: the spotlight shines on an empty stage from which Tony John can bow no more; Norma Desmond moves right into and is obliterated by the white glare of her close-up; the unvarying waves roll on, feigning innocence of the man they have taken to their depths. These actors end up as nothing on the screen—doesn't Hamlet warn us of just such an end in his tirade against acting: "And all for nothing!" But the message of these shots is mixed, for they leave us with our own sense of emptiness at having lost the actors. Like all tragic figures, they were magnificent, larger than life, each so original, one of a kind. Their absence, while terrible, is a reminder of the great presence that once was, before each flung himself down from his colossal height. Like all tragedies, their stories permit us to admire the rarity of greatness, to take note of its dangers, and possibly, to be grateful that we are closer to the ordinary. As such, we have a chance to savor those delights available to ordinary mortals, like going out to dinner with friends. That is how Margo ends up on screen—surrounded by people who know and love her. Margo Channing breaks loose of tragedy, and goes on to prosper in the sunlight of comedy and love.

9.

Eros and Thespis:
The Comedy of Acting

Acting offstage is one of the ways in which men and women may achieve the intimacy of a loving couple. There are several movies in which such acting occurs, and the acting falls generally into two categories: acting in concert, both individuals responding simultaneously to a specific, short-lived situation together by making up dialogue and playing roles; and acting for deception, one individual fooling the other, innocent party. Even though these two kinds of offstage acting result in very different stories and characters—people acting in concert command a shared knowledge that gives them authority over the plot; people acting for deception are likely to cause confusion and to become embroiled in it themselves—they have in common the process involving a fertilization and freeing of the imagination, a loosening of the inhibitions, all of which leads quickly to heightened sexual attraction, followed, in short order, by feelings of love. For a brief time, a couple can live free of their very selves. Without the burden of the real, rational, adult self, by pretending to be someone else, they can actually awaken and project something from the inner self that has lain dormant. By yielding to a sudden creative effusion which, like the lush verse of Titania and Oberon—the truly great poetry of the play—rides recklessly on the waves of impulse, people have a chance to be freely imaginative and childish again and thus to grow up once again, this time into people with a better understanding of their sexual natures and with a proper respect for the playful spirit true love craves. (See Stanley Cavell, *Pursuits of Happiness*, Harvard University Press, 1981.)

Before Clark Gable and Caludette Colbert of *It Happened One Night* have a chance to escape their latest motel cabin, her father's detectives have caught up with them and are swarming over the motel grounds. Within seconds, between the detectives' pounding on the door and their bursting into the cabin, Gable and Colbert have shed their real selves and have become a dull, clumsy, somewhat boorish married couple. He paces and talks energetically about absolute trivia while she sits frumpishly by, combing her hair and making a mess of the job. As the detectives and proprietor watch, the couple portray the lives of stupid, uncouth people so faithfully—they quarrel; he yells; she bawls—that the detectives leave to pursue their hunt for the heiress elsewhere. Left alone, the couple are exuberantly friendly to each other for the first time, excited about their success but also excited about each other. This scene marks the point in their relationship when they first feel attracted to each other. They have every reason to take a new measure of each other, for the little scene they just created has nudged them into a new relationship. It has revealed to them their perfect compatibility and has united them in a secret. From now on, their story is temporarily complicated but ultimately simplified by the fact that they have fallen in love.

A similarly masterly little scene in *Bringing Up Baby* yields Katharine Hepburn the results a whole movie's worth of botched plots denies: Cary Grant, the man she loves, takes a new look at her and likes what he sees. The midsummer madness of this movie ends in a jailhouse with Hepburn and Grant locked in separate cells, her vain promises of making everything clear and his desperate claims that she is only a principle of confusion confirming the distance between them. Suddenly, before our eyes, the zany, feckless, love-struck society girl becomes "Swingin' Door Susie," the moll of the Leopard Gang, complete with gangland patois, streetwise swagger, and sensational grace on that swinging cell door as the constable lets her out in exchange for the lowdown on the gang's exploits. The heretofore cranky Grant is amazed and delighted by her excellent show and makes no protest when she casts him as "Jerry the Nipper." His face clears and brightens; he sheds ten years and, for the first time since he's known this young woman, he doesn't criticize or attempt to interfere with her antics.

As Grant watches her act, he looks amused for the first time, which probably signals his first glimmer of understanding that he's been having fun all day with this woman, even if he did think he was miserable. All day long he's been crawling in bushes, falling down, wearing funny clothes, chasing a dog, saying rude things, behaving in a crudely undisciplined way—having, in short, as Stanley Cavell explains in *Pursuits of Happiness*, a childish adventure that will become the basis for his future happiness in love.[1] Unlike the day's playing, however, with all its oafish pratfalls, this acting has the special lure of any stylization. Born of a moment's whim and impelled by necessity, it emerges wholly shaped and pleasing, naturally calling attention to the actor's charms. Hepburn suddenly looks good to Grant, is dear to him. When she returns, dragging the dangerous leopard on a leash, Grant is so relieved to see her safe and so ready for love that he faints in her arms!

Although acting is a kind of playing and in these movies prompts a kind of childishness in the actors, making them feel daringly conspiratorial, it is a kind of playing that enhances adults' appeal to each other specifically as adults. They can admire each other's adaptability and wit; they can openly display their talents and captivate each other. Though not necessarily designed for the purpose, acting serves retroactively as flirtation. (At the moment, of course, acting is consciously designed for extrication.) Immediately after the scenes of acting in both *It Happened One Night* and *Bringing Up Baby*, the couples stop behaving like squabbling siblings and behave like young lovers instead. (In *The Palm Beach Story* by Preston Sturges, surely the Shakespearean comedian of our century par excellence, the married couple's very act is a brother-sister relationship, which they carry off so convincingly that they find each other irresistible: their love is revived; their marriage saved. Acting in concert, in their case playing roles that assume a shared childhood that further assumes the added excitements of incest, has given their love a badly needed boost, just as they were about to get divorced over lack of money. To the accompaniment of Rudy Vallee's serenade, intended to woo the woman for himself, she falls into a passionate embrace with her husband/brother.)

To Be or Not to Be shows us a similar transformation in a relationship. The Turas, played by Carole Lombard and Jack

116

Benny, a theatrical couple, compete with each other, betray each other, quarrel, lie, and cheat their way through married life. It isn't until they have to make up a scene offstage that they look and behave like adults. In the hotel scene, for the benefit of the Nazi guard, Benny has to play the notorious Nazi Professor Siletski, and Lombard has to play the gorgeous spy in cahoots with him. She in her shimmering satin gown, he is his Siletski beard, they gaze deeply, sensually into each other's eyes for a reading of the situation. As they bring off this scene, they are impressed with each other's courage, become purely attractive to each other, embrace passionately as soon as they are alone. Their scene has given her a chance to see her husband as an excellect actor, something she doesn't see onstage, where he butchers *Hamlet*. After the final bravura performance at the Opera House, moreover, when the whole troupe has safely escaped to England, Lombard, beaming with love, requests that her husband be allowed to play Hamlet. She can generously promote him for the role of roles now, without jealousy, for although his Hamlet is still awful, he has proven himself a great actor offstage. He has won her approval as an actor, just as she has won his, which comes to equal winning each other's approval as intelligent, attractive adults.

In *The Big Sleep*, Bogart as Philip Marlowe and Bacall as Vivian Rutledge have a delicious scene together when she visits his office. Demurely clad in checked wool suit, black gloves, and black beret, sitting on his desk looking very fetching, she is testy and contentious, while he is rude and tough. Despite their seductive glances, they can't get on a comfortable footing with each other but break into a nasty quarrel that peaks with her abruptly making a telephone call to the police. Before she can speak, Bogart grabs the phone from her and launches a scene that includes a third party at the other end of the line by making up marvelously absurd dialogue:

Marlowe: Why did you call? Here, talk to my mother. (Passes receiver to Vivian.)

Vivian: This isn't the police. My father should hear this. (Passes receiver back to Marlowe.)

Marlowe: Oh, you're the police! I wouldn't tell it to my daughter. (Hangs up.)

Their act takes a minute at most, but that's all the time they need to reach a comfortable footing, to feel out each other's capacity for compatibility and intimacy. By inventing a child's family, complete with mother, father, and daughter, they discover they can play house in a synchronized fashion. By being in tune with each other as actors, they emerge from the scene as lovers. The open, warm smiles they exchange once the receiver is back in its cradle tell us where this relationship is going.

Such pretending does anything but hide the self. It is one way for people to reveal themselves sexually in an artful way. Excessive loosening of inhibitions in the movies of the '70s seemed to preclude the need for anything so artful as acting in concert, but *Arthur*, with the spontaneously fabricated Dudley Moore/Liza Minnelli scene on the sidewalk in which they cover up her shoplifting, stirs hope for a revival of this particular form of artistry in movies. In *The Big Sleep*, acting is a form of flirtation and courtship, in which the actors show to full advantage how playful and sexy they are. In mere minutes of acting in concert, couples can reveal and share the complexity of what they have to offer as lovers: wit and imagination, and individuality of character. Pure Eros lacks finesse, and these couples shun his crude simplicity; Eros and Thespis together, however, make love itself a brilliant creation.

What we see in *The Sting* actually follows the pattern of what we see in the movies already discussed except that, in keeping with the spirit of the '70s, *The Sting* asserts the essential weakness of relationships between men and women, concentrates instead on the strengthening tie between the men, played by Paul Newman and Robert Redford, and sends them into the sunset at movie's end, leaving attractive Eileen Brennan behind. Before their departure, though, after they've given the villain the sting, when the male partners-in-confidence can safely return from pretend death—indeed from a perfectly acted scene—they open their eyes, smile, and then exchange a prolonged look of heightened understanding and love, exactly the way Gable and Colbert do when the detectives leave them alone once more in the motel cabin. (The end of *The Towering Inferno*, incidentally, features the same loving look of recognition and pleasure at shared success that would have belonged to a man and a woman who braved disaster together in a movie of the '30s or '40s. In this '70s movie, however, Newman and Steve

McQueen gaze long, admiringly, lovingly—across a crowded room, too—at each other while the highly original and dynamic Faye Dunaway has been relegated, just like Eileen Brennan in *The Sting*, to whore on call in her rumpled bed with the garish, orange sheets.)

The Sting's ending doesn't suggest homosexual love, although the couple's acting has aroused the same sense of sexual harmony we, and the couples, became perfectly aware of in the earlier movies. (As audience, willy nilly, we feel the end of *The Sting* as a happy consummation.) Rather, they are still children, a little old for that perhaps, but convincingly so nevertheless. In the American tradition of boys by Twain and men by Hemingway, the con artists don't return to childhood like the alienated men of '50s movies; they never left it. This bond between men that stops short of sexual involvement is one of the driving fantasies of several movies after the '40s, particularly strong in the late '60s and early '70s. The chaste tie to a member of the same sex puts off the evil day of complicated heterosexual entanglements with all their demands for permanence, constancy, reality, and maturity—that depressing litany of Latinate gravity!

Movies about people who put on an act initially only to deceive (rather than also to play and flirt) address, in highly inventive and psychologically probing ways, the subjects of fear and failure in relationships between men and women. In movies about people who act to deceive, moreover, the act itself must necessarily be prolonged (to bear the weight of the deeper problems and harder-won resolutions). The act demands an elaborate disguise, and one disguise of choice is a sex change. Movies in which a character disguises his or her sex force the character, and at some point also the person he or she is deceiving, to examine his sexual nature, to face fears of homosexuality, to learn by experience how the other half feels, to achieve a somewhat painful but rewarding adjustment to what he learns; all this, when he may have bargained originally for nothing more than a handy and brief release from his identity to escape danger.

In *Morocco*, Marlene Dietrich goes through her nightclub act dressed in a tuxedo and top hat. She passes among the patrons, singing and glancing in the standard, suggestive way, and ends by kissing a woman on the lips. This erotic act only heightens the attendant Gary Cooper's interest in the singer as, presumably, it was meant to do. Why was he not repelled by her masculine garb, her homosexual behavior? First of all, her act, though carried out with a woman, was nevertheless directed seductively at the man; his roused interest in and subsequent pursuit of her, followed by her ready response, make that clear. But it is also true that seeing a woman dressed as a man is sexually exciting to him. In her, possibly, he sees himself, his feminine self that he usually hides; in her, he sees someone he can feel close to because she seems to share his very sexual nature; in her, he sees a lover who can be his equal. With her, attraction becomes affinity. In this cold, lonely world, it is a comfort to find oneself in one's lover. (In one of the most poignant scenes of *Jude the Obscure*, Jude observes the sleeping Sue, who wears his shirt and trousers while her rain-soaked clothes dry. He is deeply touched—"his heart felt big with the sense of it"—to see her "masquerading as himself," visible evidence that he himself really exists and that she is a true companion. Similarly, once James Garner in *Victor/Victoria* knows for sure that Julie Andrews is indeed a woman, he is charmed by her male impersonation and smiles with pleasure to see her swagger jauntily in tuxedo through an impromptu number with Robert Preston.) Such comfort taken in the affirmation of self is equally true for women, who may be drawn to a man who can act like a woman. In *From Reverence to Rape*, Molly Haskell has pointed out that sensitive, gentle men, played by actors like Montgomery Clift, answered women's need for men who were "like women," disposed to understand and sympathize with them.[2] At the end of *Victor/Victoria*, Robert Preston is nothing but endearing, in drag for the "Shady Lady" routine, especially so to Julie Andrews, who looks touched as well as amused by his burlesqued version of her act.

When the sex change is a teasing suggestion rather than a true disguise, and is recognized as a cover by both sides, its use brings the same swift results as acting in concert does. The man and woman become aware of their sexual feelings for each other and move to establish a relationship as lovers. That is what happens in *Morocco*. When the attire is an effective disguise, however, so that the sex of the costumed person is misperceived, feelings of sexual attraction are erotically heightened on both sides: because secrets are exciting; because taboos are exciting; because unaccountable sensations are exciting. The disguise of a person's sex makes sex itself a deliciously sinful secret with an explosive surprise ever imminent. Prolonged secrecy coupled with dizzying confusion and the naked, heightened eroticism they foster—as well as the compounding urgency of maintaining the disguise—work to retard the establishment of a relationship, leaving the characters, and us, in the grip of purely erotic suspense. Even so, though a relationship seems retarded, if not also imperiled, the experience of sharing the sexually charged confusion still turns out to favor the growth of a relationship because so many feelings about the characters' sexual nature are also shared and confronted. That is why Rosalind and Orlando emerge from the forest of homosexual tangles more intensely drawn to each other and more deeply comfortable with each other than they were at court, where she wore skirts and he wore doublet and hose. The clothes may declare which is which, but her temporary change of clothes suggests that for true love it isn't always desirable to draw sexual lines so definitively; that true love may thrive on some crossing of those lines.

To escape the law, Katharine Hepburn must become Sylvester rather than Sylvia in *Sylvia Scarlett*. Once she is attracted to the innocent party, the painter played by Brian Aherne, her problems are plain and the resolutions are predictable enough, but the deceived painter has no easy way out of the confusion of feelings into which he is thrown by the appealing and forbidden young "man." On a moonlit night, Hepburn, as Sylvester, appears in Aherne's romantic artist's quarters on some pretext. Brought to considerable discomfort by the tense atmosphere, she is about to reveal her true sex when he interrupts her, "I know what it is about you." He pauses at length, giving her, and us, a chance to become excitedly tense about what he thinks he knows before he finishes his thought: "You should be painted!" His remark sounds funny and anticlimatic, but is dramatically sound, for it relieves the tension just a little before allowing it to gather again. His remark makes good sense, too, from a psychological point of view, for it is his unconscious confession of an attraction he has clearly been mulling over for some time and has now found a suitable way to express. You are so fascinating, he might just as easily have said, that I feel prompted, as all artists do, to make love to you through my art. In the scene that follows, the next morning Hepburn appears before him as a woman, and the revelation is a disappointment. The magical sexiness of the moonlit scene, in which the painter's purely erotic desire blooms, fades into the light of common day, and the movie sputters and coughs its way to a proper but dull resolution of the plot.

Later movies, notably *Some Like It Hot, Tootsie,* and *Victor/ Victoria,* will handle the resolution of such a plot with far greater skill and more credible fidelity to the psychological verities of the characters' feelings. In *Some Like It Hot,* one party, the woman played by Marilyn Monroe, is innocent. Intimacy between her and the men, played by Jack Lemmon and Tony Curtis, is arranged initially by the two men's acting as if they were the same sex as she. Here is a situation in which sexual feelings could be fatal to the act and must be severely restrained. But because secrets and taboos are so exciting, erotic feelings are so heightened that the deceiving actors come under increasing pressure to tighten up their act lest their sexual vitality explode. The more they tighten up, of course, the less controllable their feelings become. Sexual attraction charges the atmosphere of the whole movie, just as it does for identical reasons in *Twelfth Night,* for example, and it isn't only the disguised men who are responsible for that. The woman, though unaware of both her true feelings and the true situation, is roused by her new "girlfriends," responding with avidity to their interest in her. Released by their friendliness from her disillusioned, dejected state, she makes all kinds of overtures, calling Jack Lemmon "honey," climbing into his berth, rubbing his cold feet, cuddling up under the covers the way sisters (not to mention lovers) do. All of this leads to a wild party that comes so close to an orgy that Lemmon's desperate recourse is to pull the emergency brake on the train, just to give his overheated self a chance to cool down, lest he ruin his act.

What we see in the Monroe-Lemmon scene on the train is sexual attraction without an anchor, without a context. There is no relationship holding it down, so it can be easily misdirected, and, because Lemmon's life depends on sustaining the act, there is no direction in which his feelings can be allowed to go. It is attraction that captures, bewilders, and baffles the aware and unaware alike. Isolated from a relationship, it is intensely erotic and uncomfortable, the way sex often is in a dream, where too much happens too quickly and sometimes with perfect strangers. In this movie, even the heterosexual scenes of intimacy are uncomfortable, the air charged with sexual tension that finds no relief, and that is so because in these scenes, too, the deceptive act, while heightening desire, imposes a barrier, which is exactly the opposite of what happens with couples who act in concert. For them, acting demolishes the barrier, opening the way for desire and love. Tony Curtis, acting the part of Shell Oil, Jr., chooses, of all things, to present himself as impotent to the panting Monroe, so that their scene on the yacht resembles her scene with Lemmon in the berth: there is ever the exciting and disturbing sense of forbidden sex and the thrilling threat that the man's sexual vitality will explode and spoil the act.

Such an act cannot go on forever. Something has to spoil it, for life-saving though it has been for the two musicians, it has been life-denying, too. One danger in any act is that the actor will identify with the role. By disguising one's sex, one might really misdirect one's sexual feelings, which is exactly what happens to Lemmon as he loses himself in the role of the vulnerable girl who wants a rich man to be good to her, becomes engaged to Joe E. Brown, and has to be forcibly reminded that he is a boy, though he may already be too far gone to remember. Curtis, too, loses his grip for a moment when, clad as Josephine, he kisses Monroe on the lips in public. But that "homosexual" kiss spoils the act; Monroe recognizes the kiss, day dawns, and she becomes part of the act herself during its rapid dissolution. It is appropriate that Curtis should be the one to spoil the act when it has outlived its purpose, for he has benefited most from it. While Lemmon seems to be in the soup, even at the end, with a fiancé who's so agreeable he'll even marry a man, the experience of being a woman has changed Curtis in important ways, making him fit, as he never was before, to be a man who loves a woman. As Monroe's "girlfriend" he moves from heartless playboy to loving man. He is the "girl-friend" she confides in from the start: her career is going nowhere; she keeps falling in love with no-good saxophone players; she's taken to drink; she has no brains. He is the one she confides in from her happy conquest of Shell Oil, Jr. to his abandonment of her. As Lemmon drowns in the role of Daphne, Curtis as Josephine finds in himself a feeling and compassionate man who, having been a distressed "girl" himself, can't bear to see the grief he has caused Monroe. The tension and confusion of this movie resolve themselves in a way that makes future love for Monroe and Curtis credible, since it is finally based on their awareness of shared experience—struggling musicians who have made a mess of many relationships but have also, through the circuitous route of Curtis's acting, found the way to true intimacy within a strong relationship.

Dustin Hoffman and Jessica Lange find such intimacy by means of the same route. *Tootsie* often handles explicitly, through dialogue, what is implicit for Curtis and Monroe in *Some Like It Hot*. (Explicit treatment works here, partly because the script is excellent so the conversations sound natural and, more significant perhaps, because the characters are bright people inclined to conversation, used to thinking and talking about problems in a forthright way.) By pretending to be a woman, Hoffman discovers in himself an emotionally rich male lover. His imagination is enlarged by hearing from Lange the confidences one woman commonly makes to a mother, a sister, a close girlfriend, indeed, by experiencing intimacy as a woman experiences it. His bedroom scene with Lange is fraught with the same dangers as Lemmon's scene in the train's berth with Monroe: the physical self, which is what one most wishes to hide, becomes so terribly prominent and might, at any moment, burst its bounds. But in this movie, the man who winds up sharing a bed with a woman is also the "girlfriend" she confides in—the two roles were divided between Lemmon and Curtis in *Some Like It Hot*—so that in *Tootsie* the tension is alternately heightened and tempered in the most artful ways. In bed with the woman he loves but must not touch as a lover, Hoffman gently begins to stroke her hair, which has exactly the softening effect he needs to calm himself down so he can tolerate the situation and to discourage any suspicion in the woman's mind of his true identity. The measure of his success lies in Lange's words, "My mother used to do that." What a relief, and, within the intelligent bounds of this movie, what a compliment, to be compared to a loving mother!

Hoffman's awareness of what is happening to him and his ultimate expression of it lend him and the story a civilizing dignity. Where *Some Like It Hot* teetered wild and dream-like on the brink of nightmare, like the lovers' scenes in *A Midsummer Night's Dream,* even leaving us with the closing suggestion that Lemmon is lost to the nocturnal forest world where people do all kinds of strange, perverted things, *Tootsie* moves gracefully, consciously toward its resolution. Curtis spoiled his act on an impulse, a happy, life-saving impulse. Moved by Monroe's sad song, he rushes up and kisses her. Hoffman knows he has to spoil his act. After his highly charged scene with Lange on the couch, she thinks he's a lesbian; his whole relationship with her is in jeopardy. By deliberately weaving the revelation of his true identity into his television performance, onscreen before the world, he literally disrobes, presenting himself, through dialogue he is making up for the occasion, as a man who understands what it is to be a woman. For Lange, this revelation means the loss of a girlfriend, and she tells Hoffman sorrowfully, "I miss Dorothy." Opening his arms just slightly, he answers with simple delicacy, "She's right here." What he means is just that. The woman he puts on to disguise himself is a part of himself he found and projected, to his own surprised edification. "I'm a better man now that I've been a woman," he adds. His act has deepened him as a lover. He knows it, and she, we are left to surmise, will soon see in him the lover, mother, and above all, best friend she wants in a man. Their final relationship echoes the resolution of *Twelfth Night:* Orsino will be much better off with the sharp, resourceful Viola he has confided in while thinking her a close male friend and companion than with the obtuse Countess Olivia, who brings out only the lethargic, moping, one-sided lover in him.

Once Julie Andrews and James Garner have become lovers in *Victor/Victoria,* they reach an impasse because they can't find a way to spoil the act. "I think we're both pretenders, and that's not a very good basis for a relationship," she tells him, referring to her own act as a man pretending to be a woman and to his act as a legitimate businessman. In comparison with *Some Like It Hot* and *Tootsie, Victor/Victoria* probes most deeply the exact value of and defines most clearly the safe limits of acting.

Julie Andrews is driven into her act by the exigencies of starvation and the brainstorm of her sweet homosexual friend, played by Robert Preston. Her act offers various benefits: she is clothed, housed, fed; thought to be Preston's lover, she is secure from anyone's lascivious advances; she can enjoy the "emancipated" life of a man. In her eyes, her act is preferable to honesty until she sees and desires James Garner, at which point she needs to become a woman again. But she is reluctant to give up her act, increasingly so, strangely enough, as her relationship with Garner develops. Andrews's act may be remunerative, but its real value exceeds the monetary benefits for her. Acting as a man has brought out an elegantly aloof authority that she associates with being a man, with having confidence and control, whereas she used to be a helpless, flustered, feminine woman who fainted from hunger and agreed to sell her body for a meatball. When she throws Garner a flower at the end of a musical number (at which point she ritually unmasks to reveal her "true" identity as a man) or when she insists that he take her dancing at a gay club, she is pressing him to accept her as a man. (Portia of *The Merchant of Venice* also prolongs her act beyond the bounds of actual necessity, and for similar reasons: living as a man has proved both safer and more exciting than living as a woman, both dependent on the good will of men and prey to their selfish whims.) If Andrews's story is to have a decent resolution, though, she must reveal herself as a woman, which she will be able to do only when she understands what Hoffman understood about the Dorothy in him: she is as much Victor as she is Victoria.

Not surprisingly, in a way reminiscent of Cooper in *Morocco*, James Garner is drawn to the cool, sedate sexiness that emanates from Victor, as Julie Andrews ironically sings, "I Love My Jazz Hot." He enjoys her as he has never enjoyed another woman. (He happens to have a very hot, panting female at his side, presumably a typical example of his sexual choice—a parody of a '50s movie sort of woman, all breasts and shaking buttocks.) When he sees Andrews in performance, sexual awakening is written all over his face, and, though he does briefly have to deal with his possible homosexuality, his story takes quite another turn. He knows his instincts are straight, that his body wouldn't betray him, that Julie Andrews is really a woman. What he doesn't know is anything about a relationship with a woman. When he makes his entrance onscreen, before he sees Andrews, he is just an attractive hunk of a man with all kinds of undeveloped potential. His story is about the deepening of his sexual nature by his being attracted to a woman who presents herself as a man; a woman who can act. As his treatment of his vulgar girlfriend shows, he had been a crude, inept lover. Even though he knows soon enough that Julie Andrews is acting, it is precisely contact with a person who can act that enhances his sensitivity as a lover. The variety of feelings that play across his face—bewilderment; delight; self-doubt; wonder—as her acting introduces him to sexual subtlety, to forms of courtship foreign to him, indicate what changes are under way. (The choice of James Garner, an actor who, previous to this role, did virtually nothing with his face, was inspired. He foils our expectations as his are foiled; he surprises us as he is surprised.) His caveman approach to the girlfriend yields to a discreetly written billet-doux for "Victor." Furthermore, in artful pursuit of this keenly delicious excitement (in contrast to the "scrimmage of appetite" he formerly engaged in with women), he becomes an actor himself to gain access to Victoria's suite. Hiding in the bathroom closet, he peers out at the disrobing Andrews, and, when he sees what he came to see, he behaves with touching restraint: he smiles, sighs, and modestly closes the closet door. This is probably the first time in his life that he has felt deeply gratified in the presence of a woman, and the last thing he felt like doing was pouncing.

Once they consummate their love, it is time to spoil the act; instead, acting in this movie segues from acting for deception to acting in concert. But here, acting in concert doesn't serve a particular, practical purpose, as it does in all the movies discussed earlier in this chapter. Rather, it waits on Andrews's readiness to give up the role. It has none of the spontaneity or creativity we saw in the movies discussed previously, nor is it wanted to deliver the dart to yet unawakened lovers. For once acting has resulted in love, it's time to stop acting. Like Curtis and Hoffman before her, Andrews finally understands the dangers of a prolonged act, and that hastens her reconciliation to herself as a woman. She makes her last entrance looking supremely suave and womanly, ready to save both herself and her lover from a life of pretense, sure now that in her consummate womanliness she embodies those qualities she discovered while playing the part of Victor. Together she and Garner watch Preston turn her alluring musical number into a comedy routine, a deft mockery of acting, which is what acting deserves when it has overstayed its welcome.

The risks of prolonged acting show up in *Victor/Victoria*, as they do for Lemmon in *Some Like It Hot* and for Hoffman in *Tootsie*. "You and me, we're the kind of people other people want to be / Wandering free," sing Andrews and Preston at the gay club, keeping hold of their funny secret, playacting perfectly. Acting is indeed a way to achieve freedom, especially to understand one's feelings, a freedom so necessary to love. As Lemmon and Hoffman discover, however, a role can be a snare. Acting may help one find oneself, but it won't finally allow one to be oneself. Acting may help one to recover a lost sense of playfulness, but to keep on acting is to remain a child. Love needs freedom to bloom; to last out the years, it needs social sanction. The only resolution for any of these people who have perpetrated a sustained deception on the innocent public and on each other is to become themselves.

In returning to themselves, all these actors, and even those they have deceived in intimacy, bring with them a new perspective on relationships. In every one of the movies discussed in this chapter, someone has been anxiously preoccupied with getting a job, saving a job, meeting a deadline, or raising money. In the three movies discussed in the latter part, the sexual disguise is donned specifically to secure a job. By each movie's end, the job has served more than its purpose. Everybody has calmed down and turned to love instead. Acting lies in the past for all the couples, but it will be remembered and be dissolved into the relationship, just the way shared childhood, with its funny secrets, warm memories, and forbidden excitements, melts into, solidifies, and sweetens adulthood.

Part IV:

Problems of Aesthetics

10.

Why Sex Isn't Sexy in the Movies

> Frankly, I think there's far too much sex and violence
> gets by in the name of entertainment. I mean, I go to the
> theater to be taken out of myself. I don't want to see lust
> and rape and incest and sodomy. I can get all that at
> home!
>
> *Lord Cobbold, as played by Jonathan*
> *Miller, in* Beyond the Fringe, *1962*

Even granting that people do not uniformly agree on what seems
sexy, it is true, nevertheless, that portraying sexiness on the screen
presents special problems, and furthermore, that sex itself—a couple having intercourse—so often undermines the sexiness of the
scene. A movie, like any work of art, has to appeal to the viewers'
imaginations if it is to claim their attention and loyalty to the
subject. That is, a movie has to be entertaining, different from real
life. For such an appeal, a metaphorical structure is needed to show
life precisely not as it really looks but as it feels. In movies, that
structure is formed by the lighting, the music, the sets, the costumes, and by the actors themselves mainly through dialogue and
close-ups, all of which, while advancing a particular story, create a
particular atmosphere, too. Such metaphors represent arrangements of characters' feelings about an experience, and because we
recognize them, they draw us toward the people on the screen; we
understand what they are feeling.

Sexiness has far more to do with feelings—love, excitement,
and desire—and with the atmosphere those feelings engender than

with any actions. When it is presented on the screen, sex becomes more plainly physical than it ever really is. That is undoubtedly why, when Hollywood censorship came to an end, sex was routinely paired with violence for ratings purposes, as if the two were natural partners, like Astaire and Rogers. Sex and violence became natural partners, of course, when they became graphically visible, at which point they seemed doomed to be depictions of simple drives only—sometimes of the same drive, both of them looking like aggression—rather than representations of a richer, more complicated human experience, which is what one senses in the highly stylized and very sexy courtships, the dances, of Astaire and Rogers. True sexiness on screen has everything to gain from subtlety, surprise, suggestion, sidestepping. This is what Joseph Mankiewicz means when he says, "Lubitsch . . . could induce more enjoyable and provocative sexual excitement by his direction of a fully dressed young woman deciding whether or not to open a bedroom door than any one of . . . the most explicit hand-held full-screen close-ups of intertwined genitals presently before the public eye."[1] True sexiness is always akin to something artful. (A *New Yorker* cartoon of many years ago depicts a caveman sitting on a stump next to his cavewoman, saying, "You make me want to write something where all the lines end with the same sound.") For life isn't itself graphically realistic to our minds. We are always altering (coloring and discoloring) experience by means of memories, fantasies, and feelings. To show experience realistically demands our taking metaphorical work into account.

D. H. Lawrence's *Women in Love* provides a valuable example of what happens when the metaphorical structure is abandoned and sex is shown in a movie. In the novel, Lawrence writes as follows about a love scene between Ursula and Birkin:

> He seemed to be conscious all over, all his body awake with a simple, shimmering awareness, as if he had just come awake, like a thing that is born, like a bird when it comes out of an egg, into a new universe.
>
> He stood on the hearth-rug looking at her, at her face that was upturned exactly like a flower, a fresh, luminous flower, glinting faintly golden with the dew of the first light.

In the movie, these similes which intensify the scene's sexiness are removed. In their stead, we have gasps, shrieks, and pants, as the two struggle out of their clothes, with frantic close-ups of miscellaneous anatomical parts and a shot of Birkin's feverish fingers madly working to unbutton his fly (somebody must have been crowing over that zipperless touch of authenticity). Such a scene may be factually accurate, but it isn't sexy to watch. What happens, in effect, is that a scene that is sexy in the novel becomes pornographic by transposition to the screen. This doesn't mean that pornography was intended, but that is the effect for us because open displays of acts we associate with privacy astound us with their openness and not with what the people are feeling and because such acts make us voyeurs whether that's what we are or not. Visible sex, then, casts every viewer in the role of voyeur, threatening to make him a likely target of Birkin's tirade to Hermione, "What you want is pornography—looking at yourself in mirrors, watching your naked animal actions in mirrors."

Hermione probably does want pornography, and so do some viewers. It has its place and offers satisfactions to some people, but it is not the same as sexiness, nor does it have the same purpose. Pornography seeks to arouse by depictions of erotic behavior, while sexiness seeks to move, charm, and intrigue by evocations of an atmosphere that derives its shape from feelings of love. Sometimes pornography is exactly what is called for. The numerous instances when the hairdresser of *Shampoo* and a selected female fall, automatically and with passionless regularity, into coital position stress the shallowness of these encounters. He isn't truly sexy until he is clearly in love with one woman, and then he's standing on a hilltop and telling her of his love. They aren't even touching each other. *Blue Velvet,* in dramatizing an adolescent's sexual fantasies, shows beautifully a boy's struggle to combat his curiosity about pornography, which entices him, urging forward his compellingly elaborate plot, but which also makes him cry with disappointment at himself. He assigns his vilest imaginings to the movie's villain, whose pornographic excesses are of necessity shown on the screen as contrast to the tender chivalry, the more human sort of sexual feeling to which the boy aspires with both the exotic, troubled Isabella Rossellini and the conventional, healthy Laura Dern. The villain's sexual actions, while disgusting and full of menace, are also comically absurd, pointing out to us how distorted sex becomes by being made visible, something the young boy himself seems sensitive to; in his own lovemaking, his motions are discreetly veiled.

Pornography narrows while sexiness enlarges the range of sexual experience as conveyed by actors and as perceived by viewers on the screen. It is, therefore, very hard to keep a scene sexy, to keep it from seeming pornographic, when one attempts to show actual sex. One successful example comes to mind: the seduction scene in *Rachel, Rachel,* in which the cinematographer slowly blurs the picture, letting waves of mingling colors lap over the couple. What happens here is that the visible picture of sex has been artfully altered in such a way as to become instead a representation of the woman's feelings as she succumbs to the pleasure of her sexual awakening. Our attention, drawn to her feelings, is also drawn away from the mechanics of sexual action. There is, after all, a limit to the number of positions that can be used for copulation, and the positions themselves have nothing to do with making sex sexy on the screen. The absence of clothes, however, is something else and does not preclude stories in which character counts or in which characters can be witty, interesting, and inventive. Onscreen or stage, nudity can't help but be a kind of costume, so if designed and worn well, it can be a useful asset in all kinds of dramatic situations, as can be seen from the early Brigitte Bardot comedies to Ann-Margret's pitifully bare beauty in *Carnal Knowledge;* from the wrestling match in *Women in Love* to the gentlemen's swim in *A Room with a View;* from Anne Bancroft's sudden seduction in *The Graduate* to the leisurely striptease on ice in *Slap Shot.* But too many moviemakers, given freedom to show anything onscreen, just forget about character and courtship, about dialogue and acting, about the imaginative needs of the audience, and rush couple after couple from first meeting to bed in what seems like one take. That may be all right for real people in real life. Speedy sex with no art but plenty of adrenaline may be exciting in real life, but in movies it's boring, for dramatic fiction cannot satisfy an audience unless the characters have some substance, enough substance to have feelings recognizable to each other as well as to the audience, enough substance to take some time with each other's feelings.

A particularly vivid example of the way in which visible sex lessens the sexiness of the atmosphere and generally drains the characters of their sex appeal's subtlety is the 1981 remake of James Cain's *The Postman Always Rings Twice*. Jessica Lange enters as a sultry, tough, frumpy, openly wanton, and lewdly expectant broad. Jack Nicholson enters as a leering, calculating, sweaty, panting buck. One look at either of them—one look at the look they exchange with each other—and it's just a matter of time—minutes, probably—before they hit the hay. As soon as they're alone, Nicholson, in his best mad, gasping, lunging sex fiend persona, jumps her like somebody's wayward labrador. In some quarters, the sight of two virtual strangers clawing and chewing away at each other may be interesting, but in comparison with both Cain's novel and the original 1946 movie, the remake's sex scenes are somewhat vacuous and laughable, victims of a director for whom too much license has dulled all imagination so that a story of overwhelming passion turns into a tale of simple lust.

James Cain's novel is about the way passion takes people unaware. Like Alfred Hitchcock, Cain is fascinated by the plight of ordinary people suddenly caught up in circumstances that require superior character and intelligence. Where Hitchcock's misanthropy leads him to find amusement in his characters' weaknesses, Cain treats his own characters with compassion. In *The Postman Always Rings Twice,* Frank, Cora, Nick are all naive and a little slow, always behind in their grasp of events, repeatedly taken by surprise since they can't cleverly imagine or shrewdly anticipate, doomed never to be in control, least of all of their own schemes, which smart people, like the D.A. and Keats, the criminal lawyer, see through at a glance. What interests and moves Cain, particularly about Frank and Cora (played respectively by John Garfield and Lana Turner in the original movie), is their pathetic mixture of innocence and frailty. Without the great passion which destroys them, they might have got by in life on their simple good natures, their scant moral judgment, and their passable brains. (The same is true of Walter Neff in *Double Indemnity,* a nice, unassuming man who is unprepared for and unequal to the sudden moral complexity which passion brings to his life.)

Cain's protagonists are weak and sinful, but the author lends them a certain subtlety as they wrestle with their passion and their guilt. These are not ruthless psychopaths after all; they are people who would much rather not have become criminals, who want ultimately to be cleansed in some way. Both Frank and Walter, therefore, true to their religious upbringing, which impressed but failed to fortify them, tell their stories as confessions before going off to face execution.

The 1946 movie remains absolutely true to the spirit of Cain's characters and story. John Garfield deserves immortality for his look of naive surprise, with which he defines time and again the exact nature of the hapless Frank; and Lana Turner moves luringly about, staring dumbly out of her baby face, conveying immediately Cora's minimal grasp of her sexuality, and her provocative powers. The movie builds up each character with exquisite and fatal care by means of its own metaphorical structure. Frank comes to life and eventually to grief through his absolute lack of prescience; Cora comes to life through her provocative purity.

Frank is constantly caught off guard, and we see that in his first scene when the D.A. drops him off at the Twin Oaks, where he hopes to get a job, and he is uncomfortably surprised to learn that it is a powerful man of the law who gave him the lift, information a sharp-brained type might have culled during the ride. Cora appears before him in her shorts outfit, and he gapes in wonder; thus distracted, he is surprised by the burning hamburger he has neglected, an apt metaphor for his roused desire as well as for the pattern his life will follow. As the ever alert and skeptical D.A. says to Frank, "Accidents can happen in the weirdest sort of ways." He is saying more than even he suspects, for no matter how much Frank plans, he is invariably planning "accidents" which then turn out to be true accidents. During the first murder attempt, for instance, the cat climbs up on the escape ladder and accidentally kills himself on the fuse box, thereby botching the attempt. During the second attempt, as he and Cora try to simulate an automobile accident, the car hurtles down the hill before Frank can get out. Because Frank has no effective ways to control his life, it feels like a series of accidents to him. Each plan devolves into an accident of which he and Cora are the victims. He certainly can't anticipate one move of the lawyers, who swiftly drive wedges between him and Cora, who breezily turn up for lunch at the Twin Oaks, or even protect himself against the lowly clerk who barges in one evening to blackmail them. Finally, Frank is convicted for planning to kill Cora when her death really is an accident, a last surprise for a man who never could write the plot of his own life.

In her prim, neat way, as she stands before Frank in her white shorts, freshening her lipstick, while he and the hamburger burn, Cora half believes she is cooling down her sexuality and living up to the decent, proper standard she has set for herself. As we learn, she used to be hounded by wolves before she even knew what it was all about, so she married an unattractive old man to keep her pure and safe. Her white attire with its cascades of meanings—her naiveté; her girlishness about sex; her chaste ideal; her conscious-ness of sexuality and its dangers; the failure of her composed and blank façade to restrain the burning passion once it rages within her—is the perfect metaphor for her. Cora plummets into her passionate affair like a helpless little girl. During her elopement with Frank—before they consider murder—she soils her dress and shoes; disturbed by her dirty clothes, she wants to go back home and clean up. She knows she feels guilty, but given her sadly stunted conscience, guilt can't provide her its customarily restrain-ing advantages or give her an idea of where all this is going to lead. Metaphorically connected to her white clothes are the moonlight swims she likes so much. The untouched sands and gently rolling waves, photographed in a romantic, silvery light adumbrate Cora's wish for pure, young love, and her sense that Frank is her first love. Near the end of the movie, she asks particularly to go for a swim, hoping to recapture the happiness and innocence she must be convinced they once had. Like the white clothes, on which every smudge is intensified, the moonlight swims, with all their suggestions of cleansing and purity, are ominous, too. As her helpless, baby-voiced cry of "Oh, Frank, what are we going to do?" indicates, she is drowning in this affair; the visible scene in all its deserted beauty is eerily troubled as well, the water, here lightened by the moon, here darkened by shadows, dancing to the melancholy music. (The same metaphors—white clothes and wa-ter—are used in similar ways and with ever disturbing complexity in *Chinatown*.)

So much proves only that the original movie of *The Postman Always Rings Twice* succeeds, through a suitable metaphorical struc-ture, in bringing Cain's characters to the screen. It also succeeds, where the explicit remake fails, in bringing the novel's sexiness to the screen. The atmosphere generated by Frank and Cora, in both novel and original movie, derives from their relentlessly passionate desire. The more we see it fulfilled in the remake, the less we believe or take an interest in its continuing force. The original, therefore, capitalizes on the unrelieved tension that results from their trying to resist each other, from their trying to be just friends spending an evening together with Nick in the cramped quarters of the living room, from their trying to look casual dancing to Nick's singing. Once they plan the murder, the crime and the very guilt it induces only heighten their desire. They don't want to be criminals or even to have criminal thoughts, but conspiring together is itself sexually exciting. The scenes in which they plan the murder in breathless whispers feel like love scenes, charged as they are with their hot desire, so it seems a natural part of their relationship for Cora to make the murder of Nick a condition of Frank's love for her. It is precisely because the tension of secretly shared guilt enhances her passion that Cora is overcome with desire at the murder scene; the crime itself becomes suffused with their torrid love.

The Postman Always Rings Twice is a love story. Through the powerful attraction, guilt, murder, double cross at the trial, and the uncertain freedom after their acquittal, Frank and Cora are still together. They know that something big has happened to them, that they have real and deep feelings for each other which can survive suspicion and separation. They believe in and feel a tenderness for their love, which shows in their return to the moonlit beach, in Frank's delight with Cora's pregnancy, and in the sweet plans they make for a happy future right before the final accident in which Cora perishes.

The original movie makes plain the sincerity and depth of Frank and Cora's feelings; their desire for each other is serious and important. The remake fails as a love story, and the remake fails to capture the sexiness which the original sustains remarkably for its duration, because the rash of overheated sex scenes have a pornographic rather than a sexy appeal. Because we see consummation, the perfectly sustained tension, so heavily responsible for the sexy atmosphere of the story, never materializes. (Cain achieves this tension in the novel by heating up the steaminess—Cora's panting cries of "Bite me!" and "Rip me! Rip me!" certainly help—and then by carefully ending his chapters at the bedroom door, achieving the very effect of a fade-out that both stops the action we can see and sustains the mood, the way Lubitsch movies do.) In addition, the remake suffers from misdirection and miscasting. Nicholson and Lange play the characters like cunning animals rather than helpless people. It's that sort of interpretation that lands them fornicating on the kitchen counter like slabs of meat, instead of making love in the sexually inviting intimacy of a bed. Since Nicholson and Lange have built careers on intelligent, knowing looks, they are never convincingly helpless. On the one hand, they both look too shrewd to be unaware of what's going on, too crafty to be such bunglers, and on the other hand, their frantic physical behavior suggests impulses run amok rather than overpowering passion.

A contemporary movie that captures the spirit of the original version of *The Postman Always Rings Twice* is *Body Heat*. William Hurt and Kathleen Turner play to perfection Cain's kind of people, who just aren't smart or strong enough to stay out of trouble. Furthermore, the movie is very sexy; it shows little actual sex and concentrates instead on the atmosphere, which is achieved by two principal metaphors: the lurid lights that slap colors over the characters' faces like masks of exposed, hot blood or that erupt in blazing fires that are echoed in the flaming red skirt in which Turner executes her seduction; and the profusion of wind chimes, swaying to the hot, arid breezes, that stand in for siren songs, reminding us of Turner's seduction every time we hear them. As a muscial device, they penetrate the air with seemingly insouciant sounds that really ripple it with the tension of unknown, unpredictable, and dangerous darkness. Like the characters, passively attendant on the whim of passing winds, the chimes are played upon and roused. *Body Heat* owes this metaphor to William Wyler, who used wind chimes in exactly the same way, to create the same atmosphere, the sexual allure of crime, in *The Letter:* Bette Davis in her white mantilla faces the exotically black-garbed Oriental mistress; the wind chimes intone randomly in the shadows, playing up the suppressed but still throbbing sexual power of both women as they conspire in their criminal transaction. In both *Body Heat* and *The Letter,* moreover, the steamy heat of nature serves as a metaphor for the inner heat from which the characters can find no relief, which seems, fever-like, to infect nature itself. The winds in *Body Heat* are hot; the fans work to no effect in *The Letter,* where the moon glows and flares like a sinister, tropical sun. The fiery explosions of *Body Heat,* like the hot pistol shots of *The Letter,* like the crackling, flaming fuse box of *The Postman Always Rings Twice,* erupt in the sweltering night air, drawing our attention to the characters' burning passions rather than to the murders they are committing.

Sexiness in movies depends on an artful balance of substance and style. Pornography, a very distant cousin, a kind of parody of sex, can get by with a depiction that is completely graphic and, therefore, at the same time utterly raw and graceless. Sexiness in movies depends on the characters' emotional involvement and attachment, which can involve us imaginatively, and it depends equally on some finesse to reflect the stirrings of delight and desire within the characters: a stir in the air, like the cloud of dust that rises as Miriam Hopkins collapses invitingly on Fredric March's couch; a melodious passage of the cello as Clark Gable musingly follows Vivien Leigh up the stairs with his eyes; the metallic pitch of Deborah Kerr's "Sergeant" that only belies the soft, vulnerable woman behind her yearning eyes; James Stephenson's forgetting his legal distance for a second and leaning just perceptibly toward the semi-recumbent Bette Davis; Robert Walker and Judy Garland's enchanting pantomime after their wedding night as they gaze into each other's eyes across the breakfast table. All of these scenes are about sex, and they tell us more about what it really means to people—how it is shaped and colored by individual characters—than any display of physical action can. In such brief moments— five among thousands—true sexiness has been brought to the screen.

11.

A Painted Ship upon a Painted Ocean:
Movies about Art as Life

Even before the use of color photography reached true aesthetic heights in the early '60s, directors of movies used color to heighten emotional and moral experience through art and beauty. Anyone who sees *The Wizard of Oz* or *Gone With the Wind*, two outstanding movies of 1939 and two of the first technicolor movies ever made, must be affected by the way color contributes to a composition and by the role it comes to play in the actual telling of the stories themselves. If, as Kenneth Clark tells us, "color involves an unthinking response to sensuous delight," comprising the freely emotional aspect of painting, it is only reasonable for us to expect color to bring movies closer to the visual arts, to give us photography that moves us in the same way painting does, to give us photography that shares the narrative and thematic burdens once borne almost exclusively by the script.

In *The Wizard of Oz, Gone With the Wind,* and also in *Meet Me in St. Lous,* the way color is used to please the eye, the care given to camera set-ups, and the way we as viewers are made conscious of the design created by form and color betray an interest in painting. Each movie lives in our memory through its music, of course, and through its distinctive pictures: the first view of Oz— what charm, what pleasure, when Dorothy opens the brownish-grey door onto the land over the rainbow; almost any shot of the antebellum houses, Tara and Twelve Oaks, not to mention Tara revealed to the homecoming Scarlett as the moon sails out from behind a cloud, or the shot, frozen in silhouette, repeated throughout the movie, of Scarlett standing by the huge, gnarled tree, gazing over the land. There are countless portraits of people, especially Scarlett, framed in doorways, wearing costumes of pronounced color—the green dress made of drapes; the red dress, too sexy for Ashley's birthday party; the blue and white dress, too feminine for business at the lumber store. And we have the still, resembling a painting, that introduces each season of the year 1903 in St. Louis, before dissolving into motion; the portrait of the lovelorn Judy Garland framed by the window and sweetened by the scrim of white lace curtain; the two older sisters earnestly regarding their reflections in the mirror; all four sisters posed on the porch in white dresses, waiting to go to the fair on an exquisite spring day.

These three movies certainly make the best use of available materials and equipment, for cinematographers and directors with artists' eyes are in charge. What these moviemakers generally want to inspire by their use of color is our love for the appearance of what we see. Like impressionist paintings, these movies' pictures, fleetingly lovely, are meant to make us happy, lift our spirits, make us adore and remember the yellow brick road, the graceful staircase at Twelve Oaks, the shining white marble at the fairgrounds. Such "paintings" belong to a whole generation's happy childhood memories.

It was more than two decades before the actual color looked consistently good enough to rival the artistic black and white efforts of leading cinematographers. The greatest cinematographers and the greatest directors preferred, and generally stayed with, black and white pictures throughout the '40s and '50s, avoiding the color that was available. Artistically, from the point of view of visual imagery, no color photography of those decades could approach the black and white work of Gregg Toland in *Citizen Kane* and *The Little Foxes,* for instance, or even in the less experimental *The Grapes of Wrath. A Place in the Sun, From Here to Eternity,* and *Detective Story* would look intolerably cheap in the jukebox tones of the '50s. (Frank Capra, joined by many others involved in moviemaking, has objected with great indignation and good reason to the idea of tinting movies shot in black and white, like *It's a Wonderful Life,* for today's television audiences, as if the cinematographers had no artistic intentions that depended on the use of light and shadow, or as if contemporary audiences had no sensivitity to composition or could learn nothing about the integrity of art from seeing something a little unfamiliar. A movie shot in black and white is not necessarily missing something because color is absent. Now, unfortunately, we can see the colorized—what a word!—products Capra objected to: so pallid and ugly; all those beautiful stars looking as if they're wearing polyester, when we know it's fine-grained linen and shimmering satin because we remember how the play of light and shadow complimented texture. "Colorized" movies bear the same relationship to the originals as pornography does to erotic movies: in both cases, imagination and art are slaughtered.)

The garish spectrum of color was used, and overused, in the '50s largely to make a splash, to dazzle the eye, to give viewers what most television sets did not, and to make up, too, for a general verbal vacuity. (The imprisonment of the Hollywood Ten and the subsequent raids on American intellect, in and out of Hollywood, were hardly conducive to good scripts.) Occasionally someone like Vincente Minnelli, who, having started out as a painter, knew how to work with color, even bad color, came forth with a handsome musical, but all those drearily blue-skyed, brown-earthed, purple-mountained Westerns, not to mention all those yellow-haired, red-lipped, pink-skinned comedies, were so many eyesores. One notable exception is 1954's *A Star Is Born,* where music and color combine to carry substantial dramatic weight. Here the artistic effects anticipate the heavier, sometimes tragic, burden, inherited from expressionist painters, borne to excellent effect by moviemakers of later decades. Two shots stand out: Judy Garland and James Mason, heads together, stare into the mirror at the effect of his make-up craft, the reflection capturing for an instant the actual stars as they looked, in real life, ten years earlier, so fresh and young, which has everything to do with a story about retrieving one's lost or squandered past; and near the end James Mason, having looked lovingly at his pensive wife, seated motionless in her plain blue dress, lost in her own sad thoughts, separated from him again by a glass partition, glances up and then out over her head to welcome the gorgeous purple, blue, and black waves that surge forward to meet him, luring him like an exotic mistress. The view of the ocean played against Mason's face—his lips parting and his eyes widening in recognition—conveys everything without a word: he hears the wild waves' call; he feels compelled to follow his mysterious mistress and betray the wife he adores.

It is this dramatic use of color that appears consistently in five outstanding movies: *The Leopard* (1963); *Bonnie and Clyde* (1967); *The Garden of the Finzi Continis* (1970); *The Go-Between* (1970); and *The Shooting Party* (1985). By the time of *The Leopard,* color itself had been improved and so had the actual photographic work with color. Therefore, it was possible, as all these movies show, to make movies about art by visual rather than verbal means. People sitting around and discussing art, or being artistic before an easel, is enough to destroy any drama. One can do the one in a novel like *The Magic Mountain* or the other in a novel like *To The Lighthouse,* but neither will help anyone while away two satisfactory hours at the movies. The five movies mentioned above, by means of excellent color photography, use art as both subject and appearance in order to say something about human relationships to art and about conflicts inherent in those relationships: between high stylization and cultural collapse; between love of art and powerlessness to create; between beautiful surfaces and corrupt depths.

The Leopard depends on the skillful use of color to convey the difference between the subtle, antique shades of nobility and the vibrant gaudiness of the bourgeoisie. One of the most interesting shots occurs in a church where the Salinas attend mass. Seated in the family pew, the prince, played by Burt Lancaster, gazes blankly as the camera glides in, holds him, and then gently draws life from him, giving him in exchange the muted glow of an old, familiar painting, the flicker of gold fading into soft shades of brown. We have seen hundreds of such paintings—Titian's and Tintoretto's noble-featured faces hang all over Europe. In the movie, however, the moving camera has stilled the character, making us feel that Don Fabrizio, the prince, is like a painting, that is, a work of art, both beautiful and dead. And that is exactly the point: the prince is a cultured man whose limitations are such that, when Garibaldi has energetically assumed economic and social control, he himself cannot go forward. He knows that ugly jackals will follow the splendid leopards, but he would rather retreat to the beloved home scene of his childhood at Donnafugata than take the seat offered him in the newly formed senate; he would rather study mathematics and gaze at stars alone than become an active, public guardian of culture. It is not merely the old feudal order, which embraced a multitude of social and sexual injustices, that is dying; the prince himself is too learned and progressive a man to fight for that. But it is culture itself, about to be buried in an avalanche of crude vitality, a boisterousness that takes us straight from Garibaldi to Mussolini, that is dying because the prince is too refined and too weak to fight for it. He will sleep with the local wenches, visiting them in their dark, slatternly quarters, as a natural extension of his *droit du seigneur,* but in the light of day, he cannot imagine himself rubbing shoulders with the bourgeois riffraff. It is to his credit that he is honest both with and about himself; he is understanding, moreover, of his impecunious nephew's marriage to the rich bourgeoise and never tries to stop it, though he despises her family. He understands more than the animal desires that drive a young man after a blooming specimen like Angelica; he knows that his own brittle daughter, as richly endowed financially as Angelica, has no life to her, so his animated, aristocratic nephew must unite with the beautiful bourgeoise if only to keep life going, however vulgar its style may be. The prince himself cannot effect such a change, and so the camera yields him to us on the screen as he gracefully lapses into a painting.

This is exactly what happens to the Finzi-Continis, who, because they lead completely insular lives, protected from the rough streets of Ferrara, often shot in tones of gray, black, and white, just over the wall of their enchantingly green "secret garden," cannot act to save themselves as the middle-class Giorgio Bassani actually did. For them, the beauty of culture and the visual beauty of their patrician setting, with its serene lawns, white tennis courts, and overarching trees, become an assertion of a moral superiority which they firmly believe is theirs but which they all belie in various ways. The brother dies after a life of dissipation; Micol is a shamelessly cruel tease; the father, Professor Ermanno, devout and scholarly, sits enveloped by his dusky brown study, enshrouded by his ritual vestments, a man, like Don Fabrizio, although much less perceptive and warm-hearted, who feels he is beautified by his love of beauty. What we actually see, however, is a thin, wizened relic, still moving, but slowly, in mincing steps, still speaking, but slowly, in a high, broken, barely audible voice. If only the camera would dignify him, as it does the prince, and let him melt into a precious antique! Greater indignity still: the camera captures Micol as a lounging nude, brazenly bare by golden lamplight, in the company of her sleeping lover, the crude Malnate, as she stares blankly out of her heartless eyes. But the Finzi–Continis find dignity in their own way, a way not unrelated to the beautiful painting of Don Fabrizio at mass. For all their failure to be as beautiful in character as the garden in which they live, to teach their compatriots outside the garden walls how to live nobly, serving the ends of culture, they face death with exquisite beauty. After the Gestapo has driven into the now wintry garden and arrived at the house, the camera finds the Finzi-Continis ready to meet death. They are all standing still on the wide, elegant stair-case, composed, arranged so that each is fully visible, even the tiny grandmother looking taller than she is, beyond complaint and suffering, restored to a noble lifelessness in this group portrait.

In these two movies, interest in art is an expression of nostalgia. The wages of nostalgia are also death. For both Don Fabrizio and Professor Ermanno the yearning, love, and respect for a bygone time are manifestations of the men's aesthetic eminence and, si-multaneously, of their moral decline, if we regard morality as a measure of one's capacity to create goodness. They are sensitive to beauty; by their adherence to traditions, they may even create beauty or create a semblance of beauty simply by surrounding themselves with loveliness. But they are not truly creative because, unlike such literary forebears as Prospero or Darcy and Lizzy Bennett, they lack the moral responsibility to meet social change and save culture. They cannot and explicitly do not want to make, or even to face, something new. When the camera transforms them into original works of art, the men are punished and rewarded both.

Aesthetic awareness and moral decay strike up perhaps the most exciting and most complex counteraction of any movie in *Bonnie and Clyde*. The desperate protagonists are obsessed with art and with what they regard as its power to immortalize their innocence. The closest they ever come to creating anything is through exuber-ant photography sessions and through Bonnie's hackneyed verse. The movie opens, in fact, with a series of photographs which intensify the billing, evoking in us a sense of two people who once lived, who were probably dear to someone, who were cute little children, now shot dead forever to the sound of an amplified shutter, alive only in the black-and-white shades of unimpressive candids. It is no coincidence that these two people who love to shoot guns, whose pleasure in crime resembles and replaces the sexual and artistic joys they are emotionally too stunted to achieve, also love to shoot pictures. For them, both kinds of shooting seem like the childhood play of that particularly energetic and unimaginative brand of child who always needs plenty of equipment, never thinks of anything to do, and rushes about in aimless bursts of frenzy. When the brothers, played by Warren Beatty and Gene Hackman—the two women are played by Faye Dunaway and Estelle Parsons—are reunited, making the Barrow Gang complete, there is much boyish jumping around and affectionate shoving before Clyde hits on the idea to take pictures. Bonnie and Clyde strike magnificent poses, like little kids aping the sophistication of Hollywood stars, with much squealing and giggling between shots. They behave exactly the same way with the sheriff who becomes their prisoner at the lakeside, gaily taking pictures, supremely absorbed by their innocent play, absolutely oblivious to the outraged face of the stern, humorless law. After bank heists and shootouts, too, their getaway car seems positively propelled by their excited gasps and euphoric shrieks.

Their juvenile photography sessions say little about real art. Not even Bonnie's poem says much, though it is accomplished without benefit of a machine. The poem's primitive word choice and tuneless rhyme scheme, not to mention Bonnie's halting, first-grade rendition, undermine its artistic significance. Even the prophetic value of the last line—"It's death for Bonnie and Clyde"—is undercut by Clyde, who never achieves any insight and sees the poem only as a gift to him of eternal life, as if it really were a work of art and as if he were worthy of immortality.

Although Bonnie and Clyde are themselves artistically impotent, lacking even the capacity to recognize artistic style in anything more than clothes, which they wear with a certain dash, the movie itself takes pity on their aesthetic longings and creates beauty for them, making their idealized, innocent view of themselves come alive in the landscape. Bonnie and Clyde commit evil, criminal actions, but their story is told against backgrounds innocently green and sunlit; tender leaves, almost transparent, stir in the wind;

yellow spring grasses wave from the roadsides. Shot after shot shows us the restful, simple, dispassionate nature, untamed yet intrinsically civilized, that Andrew Wyeth painted for us, that Henry Thoreau wrote about. Wherever Bonnie and Clyde flee, they alight from their stolen cars after exhilarating criminal sprees always to find an eternal springtime, an asexual American Eden, Walden Pond—their gift from the camera. At the first motel shoot-out, with Blanche screaming and bullets flying, the camera filters through delicate leaves of overhanging trees. Even at the disastrous second motel shoot-out, resulting in horrible injuries to Blanche and Buck, we see through the dark a magically luminous green lawn. After a casual spree, when Bonnie and Clyde take a moment for a private quarrel, they argue against sweetly bucolic bales of hay resting in a pale green field. Having escaped the police yet again, after Buck's gruesome death, the two slide into a lovely, natural pool of pure water. At the lake where the Barrow Gang humiliates and then brutalizes the sheriff, the pure blue water, under a pure blue sky, embraced by long, leafy flora, soothes and softens us as it affirms Bonnie and Clyde's inner beauty. So powerful are these images of beauty that we do not even feel subversive in coming to share C. W.'s love for Bonnie and Clyde. The "laws" in their dark armored cars and dark uniforms seem cruel and faceless, while Bonnie and Clyde, sustained by the sympathetic camera, seem defensibly romantic. It is not surprising, therefore, to find them picnicking on a green hillside, near the movie's end, reading Bonnie's finished poem, making love for the first time, as if their story were a pastoral idyll. Nor is it surprising to follow them on their final shopping trip, Bonnie in a pretty white dress, and to watch them walk in that lilting way, still hearing the playful banjo of their childish hearts, the banjo that strikes up a celebratory tune to match the innocent laughter in the escape car after each crime.

For Bonnie and Clyde, art is as much an assertion of their imagined goodness as it is for Don Fabrizio and the Finzi-Continis. The camera shows us beauty that expresses the characters as they wish to be, and honestly believe they should be, regarded. In *Bonnie and Clyde*, we see the corrupt extremes to which fascinatingly deceptive uses of art can be taken. We may love art, this movie says, but we cannot trust it; we may feel wistful and sorry that art can serve anything less than high, noble purposes. If we are not careful, in fact, we may forget how dangerous and evil Bonnie and Clyde really are and so never learn that the desire for beauty may ride on the wildest impulses, just as carelessness on our part may make us forgive Oberon and Titania their every vile transgression because they write gorgeous poetry or relent toward the murderous Caliban merely because he loves to hear "a thousand twangling instruments." All three movies discussed so far are humbling because they unveil our weakness for art, our readiness to love it, as we are ready to love generally, without judgment. We emerge from scenes of so much beauty feeling disturbed, sad, exposed to ourselves, knowing that in our sympathy for Don Fabrizio, Professor Ermanno, and Bonnie and Clyde we are protecting an ideal vision of a gloriously innocent past in our own lives. Despite the weak reluctance of Don Fabrizio, the cold indifference of the Finzi-Continis, and the criminality of Bonnie and Clyde, these movies fill us with gentleness. They succeed in making us wary of art uninformed by morality, but they never disillusion us. Like true art, they make us wise lovers of beauty.

The Go-Between and *The Shooting Party*, however, do at times disillusion us. Those characters interested in art have not even the imaginations of the primitive Caliban; they cannot move us to anything but contempt because, with few exceptions—Sir Randolph Nettleby of *The Shooting Party* is one—they are perfect hypocrites. They do not love art at all, never mind being unable to create it. As it happens, they are destructive. Unlike Bonnie and Clyde, who fatally dream they can assert the beauty of a young, innocent spirit through their rebellious violence, the beautiful Edwardians have no dreams at all, though they are tirelessly skillful exploiters of art for their own often immoral and sometimes vulgar purposes. A chief cause of our distaste for the adults in *The Go-Between* and *The Shooting Party* lies in their utter selfishness and greed, which makes them fatal to the most vulnerable, children and lower-class adults.

The opening moments of *The Go-Between* alert us immediately to possible dangers. The camera follows an open, horse-drawn carriage rolling through summery-green English countryside; we are approaching Brandham Hall, a charming country estate. Leo, the twelve-year-old guest of young Maudsley, is arriving for a visit, and in the excitement of arrival, he stands up in the carriage to grasp a low-hanging branch. He doesn't fall out, but as he stands up, we see that this expectant, happy lad wears a heavy brown suit. At the same time, a voice, which turns out to be the grown Leo's, intones sadly, "The past is a foreign country; they do things differently there." In *The Leopard*, *The Garden of the Finzi-Continis*, and *Bonnie and Clyde*, art may not accord with reality in every sense, but it bears an unshakable validity in according with the characters' views of themselves, with their values and beliefs, with their yearnings for innocence and beauty. In *The Go-Between*, however, familiar symbols, like colors, are thrown into disorder with such ease as if to suggest that art itself may be merely a device. The innocent boy arrives in the color suitable to an old man; the voice of his future self steals away his initial reaction and warns us that what is about to happen will alienate the child from his childhood to such a degree that he will talk about it as a "foreign country" where "they" hold sway but where he himself doesn't exist. So we can already surmise that this is a story of spoiled innocence, and as soon as we meet the cast of adults responsible for the child's corruption, we see the deftness with which they spoil art, too.

One of the first things that happens to Leo, once he is on his own after his friend develops measles, is that young Maudsley's beautiful sister Marian offers to buy Leo a summer suit. She buys him a green one, and it is in the color of youthful freshness that Leo is corrupted; but we must be careful, for green has nothing to do with youthful freshness, any more than Marian's rocking in a hammock, clad in a frothy white dress, has anything to do with innocence and purity. Nor is brown necessarily the color of decay. During the cricket match, when Leo, in white uniform, falls while making his glorious catch, a cherub-faced, blond boy wearing a brown suit crosses the screen bearing a glass of water. We can measure Leo's fall by the appearance of this younger boy. Green is the color of the belladonna, which is filmed in an eerie, moonlit corner of the garden, where Leo finds and recognizes it. The picture, in shades of silvered green, dominated by the poisonous plant, is disquieting—too sensuous; too lurid; too evil for a child. It is the hidden underside of the Maudsleys, who will destroy Leo with poisons he won't recognize. (Ironically, they profess to know nothing of what grows in this garden, just as they profess to know nothing of Marian's infidelity to her fiancé.) Colors don't mean what we expect them to mean; nothing is quite what Leo expects. On the brink of adolescence, starved for affection and thus ready to succumb to the world of lovers on any terms (even as a lowly go-between), his imagination reeling with the heady scent of romance, Leo is never forewarned.

In one scene after another, Leo lays himself bare to beauty, only to suffer a shock that will initially confuse him and finally blast his youth. The trip with Marian to buy the suit, for example, during which she is all blushing smiles and flirtation, involves Leo in deceit, catching him so entirely unaware that, although he knows he is lying, he falls into the lie easily. To lie for the ravishing, generous Marian, to cover up her secret rendezvous in town, can't really be wrong. At an early evening picnic, Lord Trimingham, who has had trouble with the elusive Marian, his fiancée, is the first to employ Leo as go-between, hoping that the message he sends via the child will be harder to avoid than his own direct attempts to see her alone. As he sends Leo off on his errand, Lord Trimingham likens him to Hermes, an idle, cultured gratuity, meant to sugar over the insulting servility into which he has placed the child, and that it does. As Lord Trimingham's words—"carrying messages between the gods"—fall lightly on the air, the camera draws back to show us a pure, transparent sky above green banks decked, as with sweet flowers, by the pretty picnickers. Leo glides forward, as if he might indeed grow winged feet, a look of rapture on his face. He is charmed to be included, to play an important role in so lovely a world—he, a fatherless son of a poor, widowed mother—and has no way of suspecting even that the lovely world, with its graceful allusions and artful appearances, is all artifice. The happy pieties of antiquity are gone: Leo will never grow winged feet; on the contrary, his many errands will leave his body tired, his spirit spent. In another scene, he happens upon the farm where Ted Burgess, Marian's lower-class lover, lives. There Leo is delighted to find a picturesque barnyard. The rustic scene, tranquil and warm in the sunshine, is dominated by a high haystack. The enthusiastic Leo mounts its back, slides joyfully down its front only to cut his knee on an axe that was hidden beneath.

On another occasion, Leo is invited to join the gentlemen of

Brandham Hall in the smoking room after Sunday dinner. The camera hovers gently over an interior that epitomizes the privacy, prosperity, and dullness of gentlemen's clubs. The dark wood of desks, tables, and chairs gleams; the plush brown chairs suggest solidity rather than comfort; portraits gaze from paneled walls. Mr. Maudsley and Lord Trimingham have no conversation as such. They point out interesting objects in such a way as to make them uninteresting, thus joining the ranks of all those Victorian parents—Dickens created the best of them—who pretend that they themselves were never children. Leo, however, does have conversation. Having been invited to share this ritual occasion with the grown men in a setting that fairly breathes integrity, Leo feels safe enough to enlist their advice on a moral question. In a tactfully indirect way, he describes a situation, Marian's situation, in which a woman is engaged to one man and deceiving him with another. He lays his injured conscience at their feet, confident that the woman's father and fiancé are two people bound to share his distress, to take suitable steps, and to rescue him from an involvement that has lost all sense of sweet allure. As always, Leo's simplest expectations are foiled. Lord Trimingham's response to the child's implicit plea is a warning that Leo remember "nothing is ever the lady's fault." The two men stare sternly at the boy, who shrinks before them, stung and disheartened by this latest shock. Since Leo has dared to bring up the subject, he himself seems suddenly culpable. Later, Mrs. Maudsley, in the only effort she makes to stop her daughter's affair with Burgess, drags Leo through teeming rain, to the sound of a piano gone haywire with melodrama, insisting all the while that *he* is leading *her* to Marian's trysting place. The implication is that Leo is guilty for having guilty knowledge. So Leo is shocked out of all interest in life—on his birthday, too—and Ted Burgess is shocked into suicide—all to save the white-wedding-dress purity of Marian and the aristocratic aspirations of her parents. Sex is naturally interesting to Leo, but once his job as go-between has exposed him to desperately selfish passions and immoral actions, he feels overstuffed with knowledge; wearily, he tells Burgess he no longer wants to know "what horses do." The real evil of the story lies not, of course, in Marian's affair with Ted Burgess or even in her betrayal of Lord Trimingham. If they had settled it among themselves, it would be another story of an unfortunate triangle of the sort D. H. Lawrence wrote. The real evil lies in the brutal sacrifice of the child to save an outworn, absurd feudal notion that Don Fabrizio wouldn't have given a penny for.

In each of these scenes, the situation wears one sort of appearance—inviting, even seductive—only to prove ugly and dangerous underneath. At Brandham Hall, art is nothing but form, and every form is a kind of pageant designed to create the illusion of a beautiful and virtuous life that will confirm social superiority. The movie is full of processions—walking to church; going for a swim; going in to dinner; retiring to the gentlemen's room; going to the cricket match—by which the social-climbing Maudsleys can reach the aristocracy. Medieval pageantry grew out of a great religious faith; the Maudsleys' pageantry is spawned solely by their ambitions and their hypocritical concealment of their greed. That their pageantry means much less than it should is, like all their artistic uses, a subversion of art, but it is still empowered by passions strong enough to kill. In the face of such profoundly wicked hypocrisy, Leo has no chance to redeem himself, although he introduces the one truly religious note by singing a hymn about angels after his "fall" at the cricket match.

The Shooting Party is also about vile hypocrisy that cloaks itself in various forms of beauty and proves fatal to a man, Tom Harker, a local rustic similar to Ted Burgess in social place. In this movie, too, children are threatened—we worry throughout that harm will come to little Osbert and his duck or to little Dan Glass. Because the children are spared, however, the movie itself takes on a hopeful aspect at the end, saved from the bitter cynicism that closes *The Go-Between*. There is hope to be found, too, in Sir Randolph, a man greatly resembling Don Fabrizio in character and position.

The very name of the movie suggests the name of a painting. It evokes countless flat expanses in somber hues of green, speckled in the distance with brown beagles, proud horses, and red-jacketed hunters, under mild gray skies. The movie is framed, at beginning and end, with a shot of just such a painting that dissolves into faint stirrings at the opening and slowly freezes into stillness at the close. Immediately following the opening shot, we are shown one of those attractive studio photographs that one might mistake for a painting at first, picturing three women, each face looking confident, young, and alert. Unlike the amateurish candids of *Bonnie and Clyde*, this single shot is a true portrait in which every face is discernible. This photograph also dissolves into motion, so we are well attuned, within the first two minutes of the movie, to an interplay of life and art.

The movie positively inundates us with art, but all of it, except that connected with the two little boys, Dan Glass and Osbert Nettleby, is tarnished by the stains of imitation. From the easily recognizable opening "painting" to the familiar photographic composition, we are rapidly urged from one derivative form to another: the animal rights crusader with his red-lettered signs must be a twin of just such a man in *Tess of the D'Urbervilles*; John, the footman, sends Ellen, the maid, a love letter copied from a love letter filched from Lionel's waste basket—the letter, intended by Lionel for Olivia, relies heavily on misread lines from Keats's "Ode on a Grecian Urn"; Lionel and Olivia discover their love for each other by loosing a flood of clichés (at first, when one hears their "meaningful dialogue," one thinks something has gone horribly wrong with the script, but it's just Lionel and Olivia defining their true selves by staring spaniel-like into each other's eyes and trading empty phrases); Aline Hartlip deceives and humiliates her impotent husband Gilbert like the femme fatale of so many French novels, positively forcing him to assert his manhood by outshooting the others; for an evening's entertainment, everyone prepares a tableau vivant, the subjects chosen so predictable—Oscar Wilde is inevitably one—that even the actors are practically yawning; Tom Harker's death scene resembles exactly the death scene of poor Jo in *Bleak House*, complete with talk of oncoming darkness and responsive recitation of the Lord's Prayer; as all bystanders lean forward to catch poor Tom Harker's last words, he gives us not the expected condemnation of loutish aristocrats who get away with murder but the well-worn "God bless the British Empire!"; and finally, the shooting party itself is a tradition Sir Randolph feels bound to follow, though he derives no pleasure from it and rightly distrusts the viciousness it induces and shelters in Gilbert and Lionel. (Many shots of the hunters bearing rifles are derivative, too, in the sense that from a distance they resemble hundreds of such shots from war movies in which wary soldiers move cautiously among the trees. In *The Shooting Party*, these shots seem anticipatory since, from the vantage point of 1913, the great shooting party is just around the corner, but from our point of view, the shots are as familiar as the Great War itself.)

By steeping us in crude references to works of art we already know, by making us feel we've seen all this before, only done much better elsewhere, this movie is telling us that British culture is dying of poor imitation. The guests are much worse than their host, Sir Randolph, for they lack his goodness and intelligence, in addition to lacking all originality and creativity. They behave just like the Maudsleys, covering their stupidity and baseness with artful shows. Warm and perceptive, like Don Fabrizio, Sir Randolph is powerless to prevent the disastrous consequences of the coming events. Similarly paralyzed by his love of the beautiful setting, aching with his own nostalgia for a world that is dying before his eyes, Sir Randolph, too, is filled with a desire to retreat and talks of "taking to the hills when barbarian hordes overrun us," just as Don Fabrizio longs to escape the filthy jackals rising to power in Sicily. Sir Randolph cannot prevent the death of Tom Harker—some notion of fair play prohibits him even from acknowledging the "ungentlemanly" competition which leads to reckless shooting, a notion which taints him as the Maudsleys are tainted by denying Marian's guilt—but Sir Randolph can redeem himself; he can educate the gifted, lower-class child, Dan Glass.

Whereas the ruined child in *The Go-Between* thwarts our soundest expectations by representing the death of the future, the children of *The Shooting Party* restore our hope in the future. They are the only people in the movie with true originality. That is, they have the capacity to create life out of their own interests. Relying on no forms at all, they are completely sincere. Dan Glass pursues his interest in science, making precise drawings of animals during the hunt itself, while all the adults but Sir Randolph are rending the air with their shots; Sir Randolph notices the boy's talent at this time. Osbert, Sir Randolph's grandson, loves animals and has made a pet of a wild duck. At first, one mistakes Osbert and his duck for another derivation, as one is meant to. Throughout the movie, while the shoot, fueled by rivalry, adultery, jealousy, and cruelty, madly accelerates, we worry that Osbert's duck will be killed and that Osbert will be an easy target himself, out there in the middle of the river looking for his pet. Isn't that the sort of thing that happens in *The Wild Duck*? But Osbert surprises us; he is not an imitation at all. This tender little boy, so full of feeling, lives, and so does his duck. Sir Randolph's grandchild grows up to become an artist, while Dan Glass, Sir Randolph's adopted grandchild, so to speak, grows up to become a scientist. Together, these boys, with minds and hearts of their own, may save culture.

All five movies discussed here address the problem of art as an escape from life and the attendant risks such escape entails. *The Go-Between* is singular among these movies for its potential to alienate us from art. A movie in which beauty bears no relationship to goodness—where the belladonna ripens in the moonlight and the axe lurks under the haystack—can only discourage our love of beauty. What is ultimately so very discouraging is that the corrupt Maudsleys get away with so much. They do not suffer; they do not achieve insight; they do not even have to clean up the mess they make. Ted Burgess conveniently kills himself and Leo goes home to finish out his death-in-life. We may grow suspicious of the beauty in this movie, but we cannot deny it. Nor do we have to. It remains intact as it takes on a richer meaning through our eyes. For in living out the story through Leo, *we* suffer and achieve insight; therefore, in our sympathy for the helpless boy, we bring some goodness to what we see. In the absence of any good, strong adult, the movie depends, to a degree the other four do not, on our moral participation, for it is a fully charged moral tale in which a child is corrupted by beauty and evil. We are neither the Maudsleys nor Leo, however. It is our portion to restore the balance of art and morality by our outrage and pity.

In the other four movies discussed, the protagonists are fatal to themselves. They may recognize the truth about themselves or about their rapidly changing worlds—all but Clyde achieve such recognitions—but they are unable to meet the truth, to adapt to its new demands: the exigencies of Italy's unification; of Hitler's anti-Semitism; of the Great Depression; of the Great War. Instead, they retreat into their own worlds, naively seeking safety. Thus, they lose everything, just as Caliban does in refusing to accept the demands of civilization which Prospero holds out to him. Where there is love of art coupled with an awareness of its personal importance, there is hope of personal redemption. Don Fabrizio, Professor Ermanno, Bonnie, and Sir Randolph all know how they depend on beauty and know, too, that their relationship to art spells death. For it isn't enough to love beauty, to long deeply, spiritually, for its inherent immortality, or to defend oneself by means of the goodness art implies. One must act in some creative way to defend art, not oneself, and to let it nourish life. In times of critical change, it isn't enough to *be* good; one must be prepared to *do* good. The love of art can drain one's life away by weakening the will, by detaching one from the responsibility to deal with anything ugly or even with anything less than splendidly beautiful. (This is exactly what happens to Prospero in Milan and what almost happens again during the masque. If it can happen to Prospero, the best of us, it can certainly happen to the Maudsleys, the worst of us, for whom art becomes a bag of tricks for self-defense and exploitation.) That is why Don Fabrizio fades into a painting; that is why Sir Randolph is stopped forever in his tracks to become a solitary figure in a landscape painting at the end of *The Shooting Party*.

12.

The Heiress: A Successful
Transposition of Novel into Film

It is particularly fascinating that Henry James has attracted so many moviemakers to his work, and that the movies made from his novels *(The Heiress, The Innocents, The Europeans, The Bostonians, The Spoils of Poynton, The GoldenBowl)* have been at least partially, if not mainly, successful. As Leon Edel has pointed out, James's style is often cinematic,[1] but it is the inner life, replete with unvoiced thoughts, unauthorized feelings, and unknown states, that kindles James's imagination, that sets his stories ablaze. If this is true, if psychological conditions lie at the heart of his work, what does James offer the moviemaker? How does he enhance his chances for success on film when writers like Joseph Conrad and William Faulkner remain largely unfilmable? In addition to giving his novels a cinematic look, so that art director and costume designer can readily see what to do, James gives enough dialogue to prompt a screenplay about those aspects of the characters that can be dramatized. His greatest gift, however, is the hallmark of all his work, an interplay of subtlety and melodrama. In the hands of an imaginative writer and director, that interplay can be made to function just like drama between characters, forming an effective substitute for the invisible, unfilmable inner life.

If a movie is to be a successful adaptation of a novel, it must convey a fidelity to it by showing a "respect for the spirit of the novel" or by using the novel as "a source of inspiration. Fidelity is here the temperamental affinity between film-maker and novelist, a deeply sympathetic understanding. Instead of presenting itself as a substitute, the film is intended to take its place alongside the book—to make a pair with it, like twin stars."[2] *The Heiress,* written by Ruth and August Goetz and directed by William Wyler, does succeed as an adaptation of James's *Washington Square,* and it succeeds both by being true to the spirit of the novel and by becoming something else, a work that is true to itself as a movie and still no violation of the novel.

The Heiress is certainly true to *Washington Square's* time and place. The street and house reflect the "established repose" James describes; costumes and furnishings look natural; the actors look natural with them. Most of the significant dialogue, moreover, is taken directly from the novel, and whatever is added has an appropriate consistency of style and tone. The big change comes exactly where we should expect it, in the characters. Each character is altered in some way, and the alteration results in a simplification; the richer and more complicated the inner life of a character, the greater the degree of simplification. Such a change occurs because, as George Bluestone has explained, "dreams and memories, which exist nowhere but in the individual consciousness, cannot be adequately represented in spatial terms. Or rather, the film, having only arrangements of space to work with, cannot render thought, for the moment thought is externalized, it is no longer thought. The film, by arranging external signs for our visual perception, or by presenting us with dialogue, can lead us to *infer* thought. But it cannot show us thought directly. It can show us characters thinking, feeling, and speaking, but it cannot show us their thoughts and feelings."[3]

Morris Townsend and Aunt Penniman, neither of whose consciousness is of much importance in the novel, and neither of whom has a complicated inner life, are changed relatively little in the movie, while Dr. Sloper's vast, unspoken sense of decency, that makes such an interesting and all-important contrast to his mistreatment of his daughter in the novel, is pinched into nasty self-righteousness of conduct in the movie. Above all, Catherine's ever-enlarging scope of feeling and moral understanding are summarily replaced by her vengeful demonstrations of bitterness and guile. The main character, then, is intrinsically altered because her thoughts and very essence lie too deep for drama. But it is specifically one of James's purposes in the novel to show us that sometimes relationships fail because people are insufficiently subtle and penetrating to grasp what cannot make its way to the surface. Catherine fails as a daughter because she cannot bring to her father's attention what she really is. Furthermore, any overt act of bringing her real self to his attention would immediately alter what she really is in James's eyes. Her father, who judges shallower characters, like Morris and Aunt Penniman, with a swift, diagnostic accuracy of which he is very proud, fails completely to understand Catherine's character, regarding her as the "dull, plain girl" she seems to be rather than the tender, discerning, passionately moral girl she really is.

Another of James's purposes is to show us that what we really are is a valuable creation of our own efforts and becomes a private possession to cherish for life if we have made our characters beautiful. What we really are, then, need not, and sometimes cannot, be shared. For James, the artistic achievement of becoming a beautiful character is more important than making a happy marriage or being understood by one's father. Such purposes are antithetical to drama, and so one can see why the characters are changed for the movie. By changing the nature of the main character, the movie perforce must change the story too. The dramatic needs of the movie demand some kind of change, but the movie goes beyond simply forcing to the surface qualities that for James are inimical to dramatization; the movie makes of Catherine an altogether different sort from what James has given us. If the novel is about a father's failure to understand his daughter and her responding to the pain he causes her by deliberately, and all inwardly, forming a just and compassionate self in the face of injustice and cruelty, the movie is about a father's dislike of his daughter and her responding by learning to arm herself against pain by becoming shrewd and cruel like him.

Catherine's character, as a subject of her father's misjudgment and of her own creation, is the novel's leading example of subtlety. Dr. Sloper's guilt over the deaths of his wife and son, his wish and determination to be a decent father to Catherine, despite his disappointment in her, his myopic moral sense that leaves him blind to the questionable morality of his scientific curiosity about his daughter's miserable fate with Morris are other examples. Catherine's words to Morris at the end, words about such painful memories that are yet radiantly illuminated by her complete candor and self-control, have the effect of subtlety. The depth of what cannot be turned out into any kind of drama, however, is balanced in the novel by moments of shameless melodrama. Every character behaves melodramatically except Catherine. For James, melo-drama, and sometimes drama itself—whatever can be expressed or exhibited—is suspect, and he reserves it as a large, black cloak for his evil characters. In controlling her behavior, in disciplining herself to be fair to those who have made her suffer, Catherine avoids melodrama, maintains her integrity, and attains dignity.

Everyone else yields to excess at some point. In an effort to check up on Morris Townsend, Dr. Sloper visits the young man's sister, Mrs. Montgomery. The interview, and chapter, ends with Mrs. Montgomery, having already burst into tears, blurting out, "Don't let her marry him!" to the doctor's delighted ears. The sensational warning fills him with "moral satisfaction" as it con-firms his reading of the opportunistic young man and usually thrills readers. Later, when Catherine accompanies Dr. Sloper to Europe, where he hopes she will come to her senses and give up Morris, James reveals the two in an alpine valley, the setting described in a battery of patterned phrases designed for the sort of rapid impact we associate with melodrama: "very wild and rough"; "hard-featured rocks and glowing sky"; "cold and sharp"; "rugged and dusky"; "desolate and lonely." In such a landscape, the fright-ened Catherine senses her father's "still intensity" and knows that he is "dangerous" to her. Seconds later, he actually threatens her: "Should you like to be left in such a place as this, to starve?"

Morris Townsend and Aunt Penniman, in their subsidiary roles, have melodramatic moments too. Morris's smooth deception of Catherine makes his frank avowal of his scheming falseness crude and shocking: "He had listened and made himself agreeable . . . in order to get a footing in Washington Square; and at present he needed all his self-command to be decently civil." Such admissions gain melodramatic weight next to his light, tactful touch with the deceived Catherine. Aunt Penniman's very fantasies take the form of melodrama, which James satirizes with a rash of outworn phrases. "She liked to think of poor Catherine and her suitor as the *guilty couple*—being shuffled away in a *fast-whirling vehicle* to some *obscure lodging* in the suburbs, where she would pay them (in a *thick veil*) *clandestine visits*." (my italics)

What James achieves by his interplay of subtlety and melodrama is a way to orient us morally. The melodrama establishes the world as a wicked terrain that tempts characters to become wicked too. Those who are heroic in his eyes, however, traverse the terrain, resisting its temptations by learning caution, discernment, and delicacy of feeling. Goodness, because it demands a kind of artistry, always has greater depth, complexity, and subtlety for James than evil, for which cheap melodrama will do.

The Goetzes and William Wyler achieve the feeling of the novel by their own interplay of subtlety and melodrama, despite the fact that they change the story and its characters, notably Catherine and her father. The arrangements of the interplay are completely original in *The Heiress*. The movie's moments of melodrama occur largely at the end and give the story of Catherine's striking change of character a great weight. The novel's scene in the alpine valley becomes, probably for economy's sake, the movie's scene in a Parisian café, where Dr. Sloper, displeased at Catherine's obdurate fidelity to Morris, makes two abrupt, violent gestures that are meant to equal his threat to abandon her to starvation in the novel. (The cozy Parisian setting accords ill with melodrama, and only the excellence of Ralph Richardson and Olivia De Havilland's acting—those tense, unhappy faces; his effort to suppress his terrible anger; her frightened eyes—saves the scene from seeming silly.) Back at home, Catherine finds herself the target of such scathing abuse that Dr. Sloper, in unleashing his diatribe becomes, for the duration of the scene, a simply villainous, rather than a self-righteously erring, man. The villainous impression is undercut shortly thereafter when Dr. Sloper softens toward Catherine, not wishing to cut off his "only child" from his will, while she hardens. Her sweet round face becomes angular, her soft, large eyes stare scornfully, and her voice, once naively high, now sounds deep, cold, and stern.

The course of the movie's end, beginning with Dr. Sloper's sudden, angry gestures in Paris followed by the cruel outburst at home, is lurching indeed. The effect is certainly melodramatic, but the violence of the drama is at first confusing about the characters and ultimately in violation of them, especially of Catherine. She isn't thinking about what is right, as she does in the novel; she is just reacting in anger. Her grim refusal to attend her father on his deathbed and the trick she plays on Morris at the very end show us that this Catherine has traversed the wicked terrain and been corrupted by the cruelty of Morris and Dr. Sloper, which is exactly what does not happen in the novel. In the movie, she makes this melodramatic assertion: "I can be very cruel; I have been taught by masters," when, for James, her heroism springs from her capacity to resist evil teaching, to learn goodness from it.

The movie's end is troublesome in terms of the novel, but it does have a validity of its own. Many people do learn cruelty from cruel treatment. James's heroines, however, do not; they learn to cultivate goodness, a process that may be hard to dramatize and even harder to believe. Yet there was no reason to shy away from subtlety at the movie's end, which is a melodramatic geyser as the tight-lipped Catherine mounts the stairs while Morris pounds on the bolted door, desperately shouting "Catherine!" to a riot of Aaron Copland's brass. Wyler could have used the novel's final scene between Catherine and Morris, but not once the script had steered Catherine's development in the direction of bitterness. (One must admit that the movie's melodramatic ending provides audiences with a certain amount of pleasure and satisfaction. Some people love to see mercenary Morris getting a large dose of his own medicine.) Even so, it is with subtlety that Wyler achieves his greatest success in the movie, if not with the essence of individual characters, then certainly with what he is able to suggest about them in their relationships with each other.

There are some supremely effective small touches. In an early shot of Washington Square, a ringer for Dr. Sloper walks a white bull dog. The purebred animal, harboring the power and aggression we associate with the breed, but demonstrating none of it as he walks in leashed obedience, is just the dog that belongs to Catherine's friendless setting, just the dog that Dr. Sloper and Morris could become were their respectable social appurtenances removed. (The subtlety of this touch could have been effectively balanced with melodrama by other shots of animals roused to violence.) The ironic use of the song "Plaisir D'Amour" is masterly for its frank articulation of the sweetness Catherine craves and thinks she is winning from Morris and, simultaneously, the sad loss she has no idea will be her true inheritance. (Aaron Copland's score, incidentally, with his enthusiasm for brass, has too modern and too triumphant a sound for the story, where defeat dogs every character. To balance the gentle piano rendering of Jean Martini's song, a melodramatic organ or even a heavily insistent score for piano, such as the one Michel Legrand composed for *The Go-Between,* would have commented richly and truly on the story.)

The movie is subtle sometimes on the very occasions where the novel is melodramatic. In the movie, for example, Dr. Sloper meets with Mrs. Montgomery at his house. He asks for information about her brother, and when the crucial question of Morris's motives arises, Mrs. Montgomery says nothing. She lowers her eyes, a tense silence follows, and Dr. Sloper has his answer. While there is, from the outset, no question that Dr. Sloper is right to regard Morris as a fortune-hunter in the novel, Morris is presented more subtly in the movie. Wyler expressed his own intentions this way: "His character was a subject of controversy—should he be charming and believable to her or should he be a fortune-hunter. I was told after the film came out that people were disappointed at Townsend's turning out to be a fortune-hunter, that they had expected a happy ending because he had been charming through most of the picture. Well, of course they didn't expect it. Neither did Catherine Sloper. If she had, she wouldn't have fallen in love with him. The way I played Townsend was rather straight so you would believe, as she believed, that he was honest and straightforward."[4] We see Morris from both Catherine's and Dr. Sloper's points of view in the movie, so we are invited, by means of their dramatic conflict, to participate in a moral conflict of the story, by feeling it as if it were our conflict.

The movie's greatest examples of subtlety are to be found in the photographic set-ups and in the sets. Throughout the movie, there are medium-close shots of threesomes. As in the proverb, so in the movie, the presence of three people suggests impediments to the intimacy of any two and makes the atmosphere tense. For one, Catherine, Morris, and Dr. Sloper sit for a brief chat in the small front parlor. Seated between the men, trying to please both— to win her father's approval, and to reconcile the men to each other—she succeeds in reconciling them to each other only at the expense of her own inclusion, for they, tacitly joined in their recognition of her clumsiness, isolate her. In a later scene, Catherine, Dr. Sloper, and Mrs. Montgomery meet briefly in Dr.

Sloper's study, another small room, and here again Dr. Sloper and Mrs. Montgomery tacitly join each other in judgement of the flustered Catherine, who is on view, as before, trying to please and failing. Near the end of the movie, Catherine, Dr. Sloper, and Maria, the maid, are gathered in the front parlor. Dr. Sloper announces his grave illness and approaching death. Maria begins to weep, but Catherine is silent, wishing only to leave the room where she feels trapped, as she makes evident by jumping up the minute her father finishes speaking. In each of these shots, Catherine feels like the stranger of the group, although she is in her own house and in the company of her father, while someone else is really the stranger. Each shot tells us about Catherine's isolation, a particularly treacherous isolation, in which she is never alone in privacy but always shut out and lonely.

The sets are used with great artistry in this movie. No room in the house ever feels comfortable; there is either too much or too little space to accommodate the furniture and number of people. Dr. Sloper's study and the dining room are small and cramped and give the sense of trapping people, especially Catherine, in the web of Dr. Sloper's hostility. The living room, where Catherine is left alone by her Aunt Penniman to be courted by Morris, is too vast for a love scene and only makes her feel awkwardly exposed. The parlors' sliding doors heighten the sense of entrapment when one is inside and the sense of exclusion and distance when one stands outside and watches them close. The steep, dark, narrow staircase, with its suggestions of an arduous climb to a summit that will yield no exhilarating vista, conveys all it should about Catherine's hard condition in the house, her abortive prospects, and the force of character she acquires in our eyes each time she passes over the depressing treads without succumbing to depression. When Morris makes his first amorous pursuit of Catherine, he backs her playfully against a door, trapping her between it and himself, which confirms a link between him and her father, but suddenly the door moves, leaving her suddenly unsupported, as she always is left in this house where no one loves her.

Such imaginative uses of detail and composition constitute the very means by which the movie becomes "twin stars" with the novel. One comes away from both knowing one has been privy to rending moral strife and heartbreak within a family. In both, one has witnessed a father ruining his daughter's life without precisely intending to, and one has watched her character take a turn neither we nor he anticipates. In both, one is alternately touched by subtlety and jarred by melodrama. Despite the substantial changes in the characters of Catherine and Dr. Sloper, the movie is artistically complete in itself and stands proudly as proof, moreover, of the "temperamental affinity" between Henry James and William Wyler.

13.

The Elusive James:
Another Turn of the Screw

Almost all of the works by Henry James that have been filmed carry his story and spirit to the screen by dramatizing the author's interplay of subtlety and melodrama. Though, as in the case of *Washington Square* and the movie *The Heiress,* the movie made from a James novel may necessitate or inspire changes, it pays loyal tribute nevertheless to its true parent, the author of the novel. The short novel *The Turn of the Screw* has never met with precisely that kind of success, and the reasons for the failure lie in the novel's intrinsically defiant elusiveness. An examination of two movies that are based on the novel—one excellent, *The Innocents,* made in 1961; the other atrocious, *The Nightcomers,* made in 1971—should help to explain not only why this particular novel may forever elude the moviemaker, but also how a movie's requirements may, in general, rule out certain kinds of fiction.

In James's novel, the characters are not merely ambiguous; they are unreachable. One way James achieves that effect is to put the narration at a third remove, giving us an unnamed narrator who is, with others, in the company of a Mr. Douglas who once knew a governess who has written down the story which Douglas reads and the unnamed narrator records for us. From the beginning, then, the story is set up to be tantalizingly out of reach, just like ghosts. (As it happens, this group of people have been entertaining one another with ghost stories; when we come on the scene, it is Douglas's turn to tell one. For his contribution, he chooses to read what he says the governess says is a true story.)

As the governess's story unfolds, we discover that we never

know anything for sure. No matter what the characters, with the possible exceptions of Mrs. Grose and the uncle, say or do, they successfully elude our best judgment. Elusiveness becomes the ultimate terror, casting us into a moral nightmare where none of our usual tests work. We don't know who is good and who is evil. We know that the governess is terribly concerned with such moral questions, but we also know, from Douglas, that her story took place during a "really great loneliness," which sounds ominous, for loneliness intensifies people's needs and distorts their perceptions sometimes. Therefore, the story may be more truly a psychological nightmare about an agitated young woman who imagines all kinds of things, and not a moral nightmare at all. Before we get carried away with suspicions about the governess's reliability, however, we have to keep in mind Douglas's admiration, indeed his love, for her, and to remember, too, that he met her after the tragic events at Bly which constitute her story, and found her a rational person. Her position at Bly was her first. She went on from there to a successful career as governess to Douglas's little sister. So says Douglas anyway, but now let's go ahead and get carried away with suspicions: we hardly know Douglas, so why should his good opinion of the governess influence us? Just because he supports her belief that the children were possessed by ghosts shouldn't make the rest of us lose our heads. Douglas introduces the governess's story and then vanishes into thin air as he reads, joining the ranks of the unreachable. He doesn't even have a chance to take a bow at the end of his reading. (Lockwood, probably the weakest character in *Wuthering Heights,* is at least allowed to return and finish what he has begun by rounding off the novel he opened.) It is possible, therefore, that James, in callously dispensing with Douglas, is telling us something about Douglas's reliability. Actually James is telling us nothing. He is merely offering suggestions, the result of which is that everyone in the novel, as well as the very story itself, is unfathomable.

We know from the vivid variations in the governess's style that the story tests her reliability as a narrator and, by association, Douglas's reliability as a judge, but we also know that the story gives us no firm clues whatever. Every phrase is a clue to something, but we can never be sure to what. The prose is charged with feeling and meaning, so we know we are caught in an atmosphere of alarm, but exactly what is alarming eludes us. The more we read, the less we know for sure but the more we feel the pressure of James's prose. The turn of the screw is meant for us.

In "The Tell-Tale Heart," we read a story of a narrator who implicates himself from the beginning and ends up foaming at the mouth, confessing his crime to the police. Poe's style for his narrator is cleverly suspect: the more the man denies his madness, the more certain of it we become. The more logically he reasons, the more we are struck by his crazy ideas. James's governess implicates herself in a similar manner, also from the beginning, raising doubts about her soundness of mind. Her initial perceptions of the children, for instance, are exaggerated. She sees in Flora "a creature so charming as to make it a great fortune to have to do with her. She was the most beautiful child I had ever seen . . . I slept little that night—I was too much excited." She goes on effusively about the girl's "angelic beauty," her "placid heavenly eyes" like "one of Raphael's holy infants." She extols Miles's "fragrance of purity" and "sweetness of innocence," calling him "something divine." Because common experience teaches us that children are not as she describes Flora and Miles, we must distrust her. In idealizing them, she puts them out of our reach; under the impress of such flamboyant language, they come under suspicion too. We know they can't be as she describes them. But no one provides alternatives to help us see what they might really be like.

What she tells us about herself directly raises further doubts about the value of her insight. She listened, she tells us, "for the possible recurrence of a sound or two, less natural and not without, but within, that [she] had fancied [she] heard." Is she unusually honest and intuitively acute, or is she deranged, hearing things? When she speaks of "the teachings of my small, smothered life," she may be regarding her rural upbringing in a parsonage from a new, more worldly vantage point now that she is away from the place, or she may be hinting to us why she must always take a grossly limited moral view of what she sees, including the children, of course. Like Poe's narrator, she never hides the intensity of her feelings. He assumes they enhance his mental powers—especially his judgment, of all things!—and says so, thereby only certifying his madness. She may assume the same thing about her intense feelings, but we can't be sure because she doesn't say so and besides, unlike Poe's narrator, she doesn't sound so emotional all the time. Sometimes, in fact, she sounds quite rational, as when she draws her habitually decisive conclusions, but we still never know what they really mean to her. We know only what they sound like; we don't know how they reflect on her or how they reflect the truth, if they do at all.

For most of the novel, while we are writhing in tormented confusion, she balances bursts of rapture (as cited above) with stout observations. "There was no ambiguity in anything." "If he (Miles) had been wicked he would have 'caught' it, and I should have caught it by the rebound—I should have found the trace. I found nothing at all." "I had left a light burning, but it was now out, and I felt an instant certainty that Flora had extinguished it." "On the spot there came to me the added shock of a certitude that it was not for me he (Quint) had come there. He had come for someone else." "The four (Quint, Miss Jessel, Miles, Flora), depend upon it, perpetually meet." In every one of these instances, she sounds rational and clear. The trouble is that the clarity is excessive: the readers are forever groping in poor light while she suffers not even from "ambiguity," and can advise Mrs. Grose to "depend upon" her feelings of "certainty" and "certitude." She doesn't sound completely crazy, like Poe's narrator, but when she sounds most rational, it's just possible that that is when she is making least sense. She herself undermines her staunchness near the very end of the story: "I suppose I now read into our situation a clearness it couldn't have had at the time." The airiness with which she dispatches this remark once again leaves us nowhere. She has accused two children of evil entanglements. If she has self-doubts now, where, if she's so scrupulously moral, is her self-reproach for what she did to the children? She does not stop to explain. Rather, she continues, as ever, to indulge in her expressions of feelings: "I seemed to float not into clearness, but into a darker obscure, and within a minute there had come to me out of my very pity the appalling alarm of his (Miles's) being perhaps innocent. It was for the instant confounding and bottomless, for if he *were* innocent, what then on earth was *I?*" She raises a most important question here, but she doesn't pursue it, leaving us to plumb the depth of her insight and coming up entangled in seaweed, wondering afresh just what her motives are, just how good or evil she is. Does she want to save the children? Does she want, once she has gone public with her suspicions, to prove she is right? Does she want to understand the children or herself? Is she a morally upright woman? Is she a woman so afraid of sin and guilt that she projects them onto little children rather than face them in herself? Is she right about the children? The point of the novel is that, no matter how we answer these questions, we may be right and we may be wrong.

Conversations in the novel are constructed to achieve the same obscurity as the governess's narration, which is only to be expected, for they are subject to her narrative control. We rely on her to tell us what everybody has to say. As we read the conversations, it is never certain that any two people are on the same subject. They may be, but they may also, by the hovering presence of what they omit, be bypassing each other continuously. In that case, they are not properly having conversations at all. If indeed we take an extreme view, the novel may be a story that is purely psychological. Nothing really happens at all; there is no real drama; it's all in the governess's mind. Without corroboration, proof, evidence, any view is possible, and it is just that terrible anxiety over moral abandonment, for us as much as for the governess or for the children, that James conveys. It is, of necessity, the only thing he conveys clearly in the whole novel. This fact alone may preclude the possibility of turning the novel as written into a movie. It's only fair to ask that somebody know, and let us know, what's going on in a movie, whereas we can survive without knowing that in a novel, where we have other ways than visible drama of getting at the characters.

Conversations in which people miscommunicate can make interesting dramatic variations in movies as they contrast to true conversations in which people understand each other. Consider, for instance, the efficacy of such miscommunication between Guy and Bruno in defining the characters and shaping the plot on the first train ride in *Strangers on a Train*. A whole movie of such conversations, however, is likely to become intolerable and, what's more, to fail dramatically, which a movie may not do. People have made movies that disgorge us from theaters abuzz with fabulous elucidations of the ponderously umbrageous pretensions on parade. *Last Year at Marienbad* ranks as the finest example. That movie resembles a pageant: its characters are not really people; its language is not really talk. We have no definite idea what, if anything, is going on or did go on "last year," or even who's alive and who's dead. All those "meaningful" shots, like the one of the formal garden in which trimmed hedges cast shadows but people don't, are deliciously titillating, but the effect evaporates quickly, taking the whole movie with it "into thin air." Onstage, where artifice and illusion are, paradoxically, natural, the pageantry of a highly stylized play, opera, or ballet is beautiful and convincing. In the movies, it is all too apt to look ridiculous.

The Turn of the Screw has been made into a stage play, an opera, and two movies. (Two more movies were made for television.) Both stage play and opera resemble the novel closely, while the two movies are essentially new, somewhat independent works. The success with which this particular novel can be staged should not be surprising, for the stage's very removal—its being a platform at a distance from the audience—meshes perfectly with the novel's exquisitely achieved inaccessibility. The stage, moreover, provides comfortable, natural-seeming hiding places. When characters are in the wings, behind screens, in corners, we sense them as vague presences, exactly what a ghost story calls for.

In his play *The Innocents,* William Archibald assumes that the ghosts are real and that they do possess the two children. The title he has given the story carries, therefore, an ironic weight, as it also emphasizes the playwright's focus on the children rather than on the governess. Even so, throughout the play, the children are elusive, not merely because of what they withhold in conversation, but physically, for they are always on their way offstage, playing hide-and-seek upstairs, outside somewhere, or prowling about in strange, unused rooms. Both audience and governess are perpetually trying to find them. When they are on stage, the drama takes on the stately formality of pageantry. Miles sings a song, presumably for Quint, one of those mournful, pretty ballads that flatter so the singularly pure English soprano voice: "What shall I sing/To my Lord from my window?"

As he sings, unpleasant vibrations disturb the air. The play treats us to a pageantry of terror, complete with musical effects; the vibrations accompany each ghostly visitation and confirm the governess's sense that "the innocents" are not playing a conventional game of hide-and-seek "upstairs." This pageantry satisfies our sense that the unknown has been made palpable. Benjamin Britten's opera, named after the novel, succeeds in the same way and for the same reason as the play does: it is a magnificent piece of pageantry. The arias and duets, the entrances and exits, the stilted placement of figures on stage, the lighting effects—large moon-like spots that announce themselves as well as the ghostly visitors—the music—now trembling, now trumpeting; scaring us no matter how it sounds—all conspire to do credit to the elusiveness of James's little novel.

Because movies thrive on the intimacy and certainty of close-ups, they can actually outshine the theater in carrying illusion over the brink to reality. Characters in movies aren't in costume; they're dressed. We can forget the dark theater in which we sit and the screen at which we stare when we become absorbed in a movie as we cannot forget the stage that calls attention to itself as the performers' world, separate from ours. In a movie, there are no sets, lights, props, stage; all before us is the real world these people with real faces inhabit. Pageantry can work in movies if there is a dramatic story in which something valid is conveyed about relationships. This accounts for the success of D. W. Griffith's sweeping historical pageants and Cecil B. DeMille's biblical pageants. Their movies work not because of the pageantry but in spite of it. History and the Bible happen to provide the prototypes for most great characters and plots, without which a movie falters. For moviemakers engaged in transposing to the screen a story that may not even exist but, if it does, that finds its freest expression through the very strictures imposed by the stage, a collision is inevitable unless someone swerves off the road. Both movies made of *The Turn of the Screw* represent "swervings," and in both instances James's novel, unchecked, unharmed, and ultimately unfathomed, proceeds safely down the highway. *The Nightcomers* crashes into a concrete barrier, which is exactly what it deserves for driving a vehicle that could not pass inspection. *The Innocents,* however, skillfully steers itself onto a new road tangential to the highway; all passengers survive.

The Nightcomers is a vile piece of vulgarity in which only the names are unchanged. Otherwise, there is no resemblance to the novel. Quint and Miss Jessel are not ghosts but, regrettably, living servants. They engage in a grotesquely miserable affair, and the two children, no less disgusting in their perennially besmirched clothes, smile lewdly at the excesses of sadomasochistic sex they are permitted to see. The point of such a movie is anybody's guess. Many movies of the '70s are full of tasteless displays so dear to the hearts of the newly liberated—an unavoidable and perhaps also beneficial binge which provided empirical instruction leading eventually to more artful uses of freedom. In *The Nightcomers,* however, there seems to be something pointed in picking on Henry James, who lends himself less than most writers to overt sexual manifestations, for any original screenplay about kinky sex and child pornography should have served the purpose if all a moviemaker wanted to do was jump on the uncensored bandwagon. The only way to account for this travesty called *The Nightcomers* is to see it as just that. It isn't the first: James has brought lampoons on his head by the dozens because, for all his greatness as a psychological novelist and master of structure, he is also a terrible stylistic tease and nowhere so much so as in *The Turn of the Screw.* Someone probably became so furious at him that this cinematic stream of invective, this repulsive spewing forth seemed but a just revenge for James's coyly aesthetic daintiness. The impulse is understandable but off the mark. James may never take us into the bedroom in any of his fiction, but he lets us know what goes on behind the closed door in the manner of all the best Victorians when he wants to. *The Turn of the Screw* is possibly about sexual perversion; just as likely, if not more so, it is about the governess's suspicions of it. The novel is fundamentally about not knowing what is going on. That can be a perfectly legitimate subject for a movie as long as there is some anchor of certainty somewhere. Both *The Go-Between* and *The Fallen Idol* deal pointedly with children who do not know what is going on, and any mystery movie makes a game of ignorance, but in every one of these cases, knowledge, though hard won, can be won.

The movie of *The Innocents,* though not a "twin star" of James's novel, is an excellent movie. It stays as close to the novel as it can while still maintaining its integrity as a movie and then glides away to its own waters. Even though the wide screen is too vast to house comfortably a setting that suffocates with Victorian sentiment and sensation, the photography and the acting are perfect representations of the novel's prose. Shot in black and white, the movie conveys the novel's melodrama through the sharp contrasts of dark and light; the novel's vagueness through gray tones. Throughout the novel, the governess gives practical assistance to the cinematographer of *The Innocents*. When life is relatively tranquil, she speaks of the "grey prose of my office," telling us over and again, "The day was grey enough," "the afternoon was damp and grey," "in the grey, gathering day." When horror strikes, she stresses white and black: "you're white as a sheet" is a favorite exclamation. She shudders "in the darkness of the night . . . so bowed with evil things," sees Miss Jessel "dark as midnight in her black dress," and Quint with "his white face of damnation." She gives away her love of melodramatic composition in this description: "The place with its grey sky and withered garlands, its bared spaces and scattered dead leaves, was like a theater after the performance—all strewn with crumpled playbills." When we read such prose, we are bound to see a black-and-white movie reeling through our minds. It is precisely such prose, composing frame after frame for us, that makes James look so good, so right, on the screen. *The Innocents* is completely faithful to the novel's appearance. It is faithful, too, in its pace. To accommodate all the instances when James's characters "hang fire" or tacitly "take meaning" from each other, the movie allows the innuendo, pregnant pauses, and speechless stares, all of which Deborah Kerr, as the governess, handles with exquisite aplomb, to force the action to the slowest possible speed, without actually crawling into artily affected slow motion, so that the atmosphere is charged and ever recharged with tension.

The treatment of the characters, however, constitutes a departure from the novel. The movie bravely offers a definite interpretation and for that very reason succeeds as a movie. The distant figures of the play become accessible people in the movie. While *The Nightcomers* makes them accessible by robbing them of their complexity, *The Innocents* advances the importance and enhances the effect of their complexity by organizing it for us, that is, by interpreting it. The movie's interpretation is consistent and valid, implying that the neurotic governess, swept off her feet by the children's uncle, whom she must never contact once she becomes their governess, is frustrated in love and overpowered by guilt at feeling so strongly attracted to a man she hardly knows. Out of her guilt and naiveté, she projects her own "evil" thoughts onto the children and ends by destroying little Miles. She alone sees the ghosts; it is made clear to us that the children never see them. The children seem a little weird, but their lives have been weird in the tradition of so many orphaned Victorian siblings. As for "talking horrors," however, only the governess experiences the ghostly horrors for a certainty: she sees a picture of Quint and thereupon she sees Quint; Mrs. Grose tells her Miss Jessel often wept, whereupon the governess sees Miss Jessel weeping. The governess is photographed, moreover, sliding in and out of camera range as if she were herself a ghost, while plump Mrs. Grose waddles endearingly and the pretty children scamper about. For the movie, the definite interpretation works beautifully and does so within the confines of the eeriness James created in the novel. What such an interpretation does is to insist on clarity, to place within our grasp what eludes us in the novel. The title of the movie is no longer ironic; nor is it ambiguous. The children are innocent little children, neither the angels the governess first adores nor the devils she finally abhors. *The Innocents* may well be the best movie that could be made of *The Turn of the Screw,* but it had to be made at the expense of James's leading character: elusiveness.

The Nightcomers is a nasty violation of the novel. The physicality of its characters, the ugliness of the language, and the crudity of the acting—Marlon Brando may be capable of a great deal on the screen, but not one Jamesian character comes to mind that he could play—sever it completely from the novel. *The Innocents,* with its English cast so well trained in stage technique, does justice to the novel as far as it possibly can. The acting is flawless, with Deborah Kerr reaching new degrees of subtlety in her presentation of a woman whose sexuality is composed of wild imagination, tremulous desire, guilty restraint, and lady-like reserve—a volatile mixture. As in *Black Narcissus* and *From Here to Eternity,* she builds her role carefully, on a gradual incline of impending explosion. She fills us with dread as, with her misplaced passion, she embraces and holds the children, her voice quivering with emotion held in check only by the thread of her perfectly enunciated King's English.

This movie's interpretation of the story is formulated perfectly. Its logic is well-wrought and irrefutable. If it were a matter of physics, one could probably launch rockets by its accuracy. The real message of James's thriller, however, is that the human psyche is sometimes impenetrable, opening between people what James so often calls "an abyss." How can we know the ghosts from the haunted when we can't even tell who are the ghosts and who are the haunted? Where shall we look for answers, in the mysterious universe or in the mysterious mind? Are universe and mind merely metaphors whereby we fashion reality out of the void? Novels may ask such questions, but when movies try that, as *Last Year at Marienbad* does, they come out looking absurd, for they strike one as being, finally, about nothing. Movies have their own integrity to safeguard. They can't nudge us into rumination with words, words, words that we must absorb privately at our leisure; they can't charm us into credulity with theatrical presences. In opera or ballet, the integrity is inherent in the splendor of design, movement, music; it doesn't matter if the story is inscrutable, farfetched, or even idiotic. In movies, the integrity is inherent in the candor with which the characters are presented; the story, therefore, is paramount and had better mean something intelligible to us where those characters are concerned. *Last Year at Marienbad,* all evanescent, and *The Nightcomers,* all fleshly, represent two cinematic failures. The makers of *The Innocents* "give up the ghosts" and concentrate feelingly and thoughtfully on the problems of the living. In so doing, they salvage their chance to bring a fascinating, intelligent drama to the screen.

14.

Endings

It is a popular piece of fiction that old Hollywood movies always tie everything up neatly, religiously eschew realism, and offer audiences a happy ending. It's a myth that was trumped up as a gimmick to advertise the great strides of the late '60s, which ushered in a rigidly fashion-conscious decade, when REALISM and TRUTH were served up in a generous soufflé of slogans that understudied, and sometimes took over, for convictions. To say that all old movies have happy endings; or that old movies foster a double standard; or that old movies never deal with anything serious; or that old movies take a narrow moral view is as good as saying you can't trust anyone over thirty.

The unhappy ending became popular in the late '60s. As it did so, it often led, inadvertently perhaps, to flawed attempts at ambiguity, in which the endings are merely left unresolved, suspended, perhaps because someone—writer or director—hoped the unfinished ending would prove profoundly meaningful, though what meaning was intended is often a mystery. Sometimes, it appears, the moviemakers weren't sure what ending suited the characters, so a curve was thrown in as an interesting surprise to substitute for a workable, believable ending, as in *Georgy Girl;* or the moviemakers, having so much fun with open sex, infidelity, abortion, and promiscuity, forgot they were telling a very unhappy story and let it fall into a confused heap of crocodile tears and mirthless laughter at the end, as in *Alfie* and *A Touch of Class;* or the story should have had a happy ending, but no one worth his trendy salt would have stooped that low, as in *An Unmarried Woman.*

Ambiguity can be used to good effect in ending a movie. Ambiguity is not the same as irony or confusion. When ambiguity is handled well, it makes perfect sense, allows us to see two meanings that belong together, that flow inevitably out of the story and out of the characters' natures. Ambiguity works when it grows out of a story that has recognized all along a duality of moral claims. It isn't a device, a special effect, that a writer or director can throw in to wrap things up with a little dazzle; it has to be part and parcel of the drama. The meaning should be clear, for ambiguity is a way of asserting the validity of two meanings that belong together and cannot be sundered. Such an assertion is bound to establish a mood of uncertainty and dissatisfaction, thereby vexing the viewer, but however unsettling the emotional effect may be, the ambiguous ending is in itself a definite way to settle the story. Only when ambiguity is handled badly does it seem ironic or, worse, confusing. The ambiguous ending is a way of addressing the fact that life is far from perfect; that most important episodes in life leave us happy and sad; that such episodes simultaneously fulfill and disappoint us. Many movies were made in the '30s and '40s and in the '60s and '70s with artistically valid, ambiguous endings. It is well worth examining some of these successes, as well as the failures, to see just how ambiguity works in bringing a movie to its close.

Frank Capra, often known as "Mr. Capra-Corn," created movies with some of Hollywood's most intriguingly ambiguous endings. With the Dickensian populations of his movies, as vibrant a collection of eccentrics, opportunists, villains, and sweethearts as any the great novelist imagined, like his spiritual ancestor, Capra is "corny" only in style and then only when occasion permits. When it comes to what really counts, he rises to high artistry with an easy grace that rivals the last scene in Miss Havisham's misty, moonlit garden, or Dombey's reunion with his daughter in the dusky ruins of his house, or Lady Dedlock's return to both lover and child at the gates to the pauper's burial ground. After generations of arrogant critics got over applauding the entertainment, patting the good jester on the head for being so very amusing, they settled down to notice that Dickens had something to say, and that what he had to say lodged in those funny people's conversations, in rustic streams and bypaths, in London's grandeur and squalor, in the greatness of ordinary people, in the joint sense of fulfillment and loss imparted by his endings.

Three of Frank Capra's movies are remarkable for the Dickensian way subtlety—a subtlety so noiseless and natural that it can be easily missed—propels each movie to its ambiguous conclusion beneath a seemingly obvious, simple surface: *The Bitter Tea of General Yen; Meet John Doe;* and *It's a Wonderful Life.* In each, the main character is an innocently good person forced into a moral awakening with such strong religious overtones that it disturbs as much as it exalts him, like the dubious joy of modern conversion that T. S. Eliot describes.

The missionary portrayed by Barbara Stanwyck in *The Bitter Tea of General Yen* comes on screen with a clear sense of her future. There's no mystery about it whatsoever: she's going to marry her missionary fiancé and together they will do God's work in China. There's no mystery about her either: she looks initially like one more healthy, smiling, dull American woman. Once she is taken prisoner by General Yen, however, her life is imbued with mystery, and her character is altered and deepened by it as she sits evening after evening at dinner, confronting the fabulous but sinister East in her captor and the folksy but corrupt West in the parastic American businessman, played by Walter Connolly, who hangs around as Yen's advisor. Though she resists Yen's culture, much as a young woman would protect her virginity (which is partly what she is protecting), she is stirred by it, takes it with her into her dreams, where her wish is not to be restored to her American fiancé but to be ravished by Yen. What happens to her is not merely that she unpropitiously falls in love with a Chinese; in yielding to such feelings, she yields to the complexity of culture and of human nature. In recognizing his immense dignity, his integrity as a man, a leader, a warrior, and a lover, she recognizes also the simplicity of her missionary goals, the simplicity of the American sense of history and culture she has brought with her.

Built into every aspect of the story is a sense of ambiguity that necessitates the ambiguity of the ending. The purity of her and her fiancé's missionary zeal is coupled with ignorance; Yen's exotic milieu is infused with decadence; her erotic response to Yen frees her as a woman and threatens to confine her as a sleazy mistress; Yen's suicide is a brave, decent liberation of the young American woman and a cowardly escape from his imminent military defeat. So, too, as she emerges from captivity, escorted by Connolly, she greets the prospect of this liberation with tears in her eyes. There can be little doubt, when all is said and done, that it is probably good that she returned to her American friends and fiancé; she belongs with them after all. Her experience with Yen has enlarged her capacities as a woman and a missionary, so she will go on to lead a good, purposeful life. Yet her tears at the end tell us that, held in thrall by Yen, she cannot now cheer for the freedom she once prized so highly, or even believe wholeheartedly in the mission that will shape her personal and professional life.

Capra himself wrote humorously of the troubles he encountered in bringing *Meet John Doe* to an end: "We had a startling opening and a powerful development that rose inexorably to a spectacular climactic wow. But—we had no acceptable SOLUTION to our story. The first two acts were solid; the third act was a wet sock"[1] The ending we have now, evidently Capra's fifth attempt, is anything but a "wet sock." It is exactly the sort of disturbing and uplifting conclusion the story calls for. The movie is a comedy that grows, right before our eyes, into a tragedy. What begins with "Take Me Out to the Ballgame" ends with Beethoven's Ninth. What begins as a story of ordinary, brave people struggling through the Depression ends with people surpassing themselves in a struggle for spiritual salvation. What begins with Barbara Stanwyck and Gary Cooper looking cute, worrying about money and cashing in on "a circulation stunt" ends with Calvary on Christmas Eve. The movie warns us, all along the way, that the moral landscape of our lives is never fixed. What is simple or trivial under one set of circumstances can stun us with its solemnity under another. Therefore, Stanwyck's gimmick to save her job is initially a good, clever idea, completely justifiable; Cooper's pretense of being John Doe so he can get some food into his stomach is likewise completely justifiable. They both begin as harmless opportunists, and who can blame them? Lying and cheating to support your widowed mother and little sisters or to fill your stomach are signs of a healthy will to live. That's why Stanwyck and Cooper look so cute at the beginning. Once their stomachs are full, however, they acquire heavier moral responsibilities (exactly Bernard Shaw's point in *Major Barbara*). There is a lag, however, before they fully understand the changed situation. Through the drama of two people caught up in a morality play, the movie's script races anxiously through a sequence of pep talks, speeches, and harangues, ingeniously turning each declaration into a question. Every pronouncement just makes us wonder.

The movie forces us as much as the main characters to grapple with the fact that good does sometimes come from evil. We may not like it at all; it makes Stanwyck and Cooper squirm and finally impels them to drastic actions. But the fact is that the corrupt D. B. Norton, played by Edward Arnold of course, puts up the money to bring John Doe's message—in reality the message from Stanwyck's late father, the good, generous doctor, the thoughtful idealistic model standing in the movie's heavenly background—to a nation of spiritually starved people. The D. B. Nortons of the world are fascists, however, and they want only power for themselves. ("What the American people need is an iron hand," says Third Party candidate Norton. When we first see him, he is reviewing troops of motorcycles at drill practice. Only the iron cross and "heil" salute are missing.) Eventually, when Norton no longer needs "the John Doe vote," he will break the American spirit instead of sponsoring John Doe to revive it. Because Stanwyck, Cooper, and the newspaper editor, played by James Gleason, stay with the moral fight and keep trying to figure out how good and evil are related, they learn something valuable about the sad complexities of life, lessons that will help them fight evil in the future. The cynical hobo, played by Walter Brennan, who distrusts everyone, who sees in every person's imperfection an affront to his own inviolable innocence, learns nothing. (He summarily adjudges everybody a heel and dreams ever of roaming, beyond the moral fray, in rural fairy lands, accomplishing nothing besides protecting himself.) The movie asserts that it is impossible, and certainly undesirable, for anyone to remain innocent. It is impossible, moreover, for any large human matter to concern only good, though good people may aim at good ends. If a matter does not taint them with evil, they are not fully human and not apt to do humanity any good. That is why John Doe should not commit suicide on Christmas Eve. As Stanwyck says to him, in her tearful plea, someone already died for our sins; John Doe, not God but a plain mortal, can't accomplish a thing by such a gesture. He doesn't jump; he marries Stanwyck instead, which hardly constitutes an unequivocally happy ending. Life and love are better than suicide, but Christmas Eve, in this movie, bears the sadness of Good Friday. The little people may still love John Doe, but D. B. Norton still has the money and can still use it to subvert the forces of good. The newspaper editor, in the movie's last words, may crow triumphantly that you can't lick the people, but we see how easily, with a two-minute tirade and a cut-off microphone, Norton does lick the people at the rainy convention. Cooper may get Stanwyck at the end, but she has rushed from a sickbed to save him from suicide, and the bride he now carries down from the tower is heartsick and unconscious. He walks away somber-faced. No one is smiling but the temporarily misguided newspaper editor.

Involvement in this grim story that begins so liltingly has deepened the main characters' humanity. They know more about life now, and they know, above all, that they are fit for life, not for death. Their early joyful scramble to stay alive has brought them, through permutations of the moral scenery, to a sober sense of the duty life exacts. The simple joys of "O Susanna!" belong to a never-never land of moonlit rural scenery, the only setting in which the hobo feels at home, a setting to which John Doe must never return. Like Jefferson Smith, an earlier Capra hero, he is for the city now, where the conquest of America must be his life's work, not because he wants it—he wants to play baseball—but because it is also the life's work of D. B. Norton. Beethoven's music of joy, a deep joy born of terrible suffering, is now John Doe's portion.

It's a Wonderful Life plays in a similar way with the confluence of Christmas and Good Friday. It is worth asking why this story of George Bailey's frustration and eventual resignation to, if not acceptance of, so much less than he wanted out of life has become a traditional Christmas movie right beside, if not overtaking in its appeal, the happily ending *Miracle on Thirty-Fourth Street* and *Christmas in Connecticut*. Like John Doe, George Bailey chooses life over death. Like John Doe, he learns that ordinary people can be very important. Like John Doe, he learns that the forces of evil are powerful indeed, that they can be opposed but never truly defeated. At the end, Old Man Potter, the nasty, stingy banker, still has his piles of money—*and* the $8,000 he stole from Uncle Billy. Potter's absence from the festivities at the end marks his isolation, accentuating the love that has brought everyone else together at the Bailey house, but in his lonely absence, he also stands out, carries weight, continues to be powerful. Like D. B. Norton, he drives people to despair and suicide while remaining untouched himself.

It's a Wonderful Life is about a good person's painful reconciliation to life. The last shot looks for all the world like an absolutely happy ending, with George awash in loving friends, wife, children, Christmas tree, monetary donations, and "Hark, the Herald Angels Sing." What has brought him to this happy scene, however, are shocks and surprises that make him feel how little he can master his life, how little reward there is for being good, how steadfastly his dreams go unfulfilled. He wears a smiling, singing face, but if we look closely at the tired, haggard features, it will be clear that his smiles connote not so much simple happiness as relief at being rescued from the nightmare of having no power to do or have anything at all. (In this sense, his attitude toward life, and toward his life, is not unlike Hamlet's—both men ultimately have to acknowledge and appreciate life, however much they may hate it, because it's all the world has to give.) Behind the smiling face is a man who has been chastened into appreciating the limitations of what he has; who has been edified by the sad truth that life is often hardest for the good and selfless. George Bailey's happiness at the end is neither fulfillment nor reward. The ending is ambiguous— reminding us of sadness in our joy—because his happiness is an act of heroism wrung out of an aching heart. That probably accounts for the compelling appeal of this Christmas movie. *Miracle on Thirty-Fourth Street* gratifies the child in us by giving us Santa Claus. *It's a Wonderful Life* gives us greatness of spirit and stirs us with sympathy for a fellow mortal born to win by loss, to know joy by suffering. These are the very paradoxes that give soul to the Christmas story.

All three of Capra's main characters are heroic for the way they behave when they are brought up short and plunged unexpectedly into profound suffering. Each endures it and recovers, ready to go on with life. Barbara Stanwyck's missionary returns bravely to a life that is no longer her heart's desire; Gary Cooper's John Doe, still grief-stricken, descends to the musical strains of a joy he does not feel; James Stewart's George Bailey accepts his "wonderful life" because expulsion from existence is so much more horrible. Each one chooses to involve himself with life, and each expects of himself to lead a good life knowing now full well just how hard that is. It is their suffering—akin to tragedy, but lacking tragedy's motives or reprieves—that modifies the ending of each movie and informs it with poignant ambiguity.

Ambiguity is serious business, and it usually suits best a serious story—like Capra's three movies—that can bear the weight of a moral struggle. There is room for ambiguity in comedy, too, however, and there it is anything but poignant. Preston Sturges's masterly *The Lady Eve* has us in stitches right up to the brazenly ambiguous ending, where moral subtleties are clearly affirmed, just as they are in Capra's dramas. What makes the difference is the degree and depth of suffering. While ambiguity always furnishes a combined sense of gain and loss, it does not require agony. A good jolt of moderate disturbance will do.

From the beginning of *The Lady Eve,* Charles Pike, played by Henry Fonda, is resistent to knowledge. He cleaves to innocence and chastity. His pompous speech to his fellow ophiologists in the South American jungle fools no one; he may believe he is engaged in "the pursuit of knowledge," but he doesn't recognize the forbidden fruit when he's hit on the head with it by Jean (later disguised as Eve), played by Barbara Stanwyck. She tries subtler ways, too, to ease him into some knowledge of human nature, but he stubbornly refuses to heed her hints. "Don't you know it's dangerous to trust people you don't know?" she asks, and, "The best [women] aren't as good as you think they are, and the bad ones aren't as bad." Therefore, because such advice means nothing to him, when he is confronted with evidence of her tainted past, he becomes cold, self-righteous, unforgiving, clings to his innocent and chaste ideal without once considering that he may be tainted himself in some way, that he may not merit an ideal.[2] By becoming the Lady Eve, Jean confronts him with his ideal—a ravishing, poised, aristocratic creature who, he surely supposes, belongs with him right back in the perfect garden—and in that guise again clunks him on the head with the forbidden fruit. On their wedding night, as Eve, she fabricates for confession a heavy record of girlhood promiscuity, which draws from Charles the same smug, unforgiving reaction as before. He is so indignant, so impatient, moreover, to put distance between himself and his sullied bride that he stops the train in the middle of nowhere, gets off, and falls into the rain-soaked mud. (Here is another broad hint of his own sullied condition, which he naturally doesn't get.) At the end, he runs into Jean again, whom he greets with a passion of which he never before seemed capable. By comparison with Eve, the wicked vamp, Jean now strikes him as the sweet, smart, loving girl she is and has been all along. Though she is ready to clarify for him the relationship between herself and Eve, he stops her: "I don't want to know." He never knew before that he didn't want to know or that there was something important that he didn't know.

As Charles and Jean run down the stairs of the ocean liner at the movie's end, the scene races with them in a torrent of ambiguity: Charles seems to have acquired some knowledge, but he still seems ignorant of the facts; he has been humbled by what must be some sense of his own imperfection, but he still seems to lack common sense (at one point, he is conned into making out a check for "thirty-two thousand dollars and no cents/sense"); he is clear about his feelings for Jean and cleaves to her, but he looks awfully puzzled; he does and he doesn't grasp the connection between Jean and Eve, so the end is funny. But the end is also disquieting; the lovers are happily restored to each other, but there is some doubt that they can be happy. After all, it is his hatred of Eve that confirms Charles in his love for Jean, but they are "positively the same dame," as Charles's bodyguard keeps telling him.

Charles has had to reconcile himself to imperfection, to give up his stony pride and settle for the best woman he is likely to find. In choosing Jean at the end, he abandons his essentially worthless ideals of innocence and chastity in favor of love, humor, forgiveness, companionship, and knowledge. He signals some readiness to accept ambiguity as a feature of moral life instead of thinking, in his obstinately literal and narrow-minded way, that an apple is an apple is an apple; a snake is a snake is a snake. As the stateroom door closes on this "married" couple, we, left outside, laugh at this resolution that bears suspicious signs of continuing irresolution. He's getting the girl, and he's getting clunked on the head again. There is no other way, both Bible and John Milton have told us for centuries: the greatest happiness is inseparable from, even dependent upon, knowing the worst. (If Rappaccini's daughter had had Jean's sense of humor, she might have been able to teach her prissy lover a thing or two; then both might have lived to enjoy a comic rather than a tragic ending at the hands of their creator, that absolute master of ambiguity.)

The ending of *The Lady Eve* works because the movie has known all along where it is going and what it wants to say about the folly of childish ideals and the virtue inherent in the Fall. Every step, every detail—Charles's ritual falls; the snakes; the apple; the references to knowledge—prepares us for that splendidly ambiguous reunion of Charles and Jean. Attempts at ambiguity fail, though, when they do not grow naturally from the beginning but are tacked on as a piece of ingenuity. This is exactly what happens in movies like *Georgy Girl, A Touch of Class,* and *An Unmarried Woman,* where everyone involved—writer; director; actors—seems undecided about the characters and what should happen to them.

Thanks to the sensitive performances of Lynn Redgrave and James Mason, *Georgy Girl* almost succeeds as a wistfully sweet story of a worthy young woman who loses the young man she loves and marries a worthy older man in the end. It's the song, bearing the burden of a final speech or dialogue, that renders confusion, closing the movie with this inane observation: "You're rich, Georgy Girl, you're rich, Georgy Girl!" as if money constituted a motive with her or as if all she were getting in Mason were his money, when in reality the money pales next to his husbandly assets like loyalty, kindness, and reliability.

In *Alfie,* too, a song is used as a closing comment and serves only to confuse us about the character. After Michael Caine's Alfie has indiscriminately broken hearts and ruined lives in his two-bit imitation of Don Juan, and Shelley Winters, to our relief, has given him the brush, the sympathetic strains of "Alfie" waft unaccountably over his head as he wanders alone in the deserted streets, suggesting to our ears that Alfie is a sweet fellow who means no harm rather than a proven cad strangely without capacity for love or compassion. Alfie goes out of our lives accompanied by a cute little mutt and these heart-tugging lyrics: "What's it all about, Alfie? / When you sort it out, Alfie . . . / When you walk, let your heart lead the way, / And you'll find love any day, Alfie." It is as if he were just a well-meaning, good-hearted, but confused guy when he hasn't been looking for or been interested in love during the entire movie. Both *Alfie* and *Georgy Girl* suffer from lack of concentration on the characters and from perplexity about the meaning of the sexual freedom they have displayed: is it healthy sport or is it decadence? To this question, the movies squirm, fidget, and end by saying yes, which leaves us, at best, skeptical about their sincerity.

A movie that plays fast and loose with our sensibilities, however, is *A Touch of Class,* which seems to think, on the one hand, that a sexual frolic among full-fledged, adulterous adults is as cute as puppy love, and on the other, that such an adulterous affair will benefit from allusions to *Brief Encounter.* Nothing doing, though. *Brief Encounter* is made of whole cloth: serious people find themselves seriously in love. *A Touch of Class* is not about people who take love seriously, so their tearfully watching *Brief Encounter* on television is a most transparent piece of cheating on the part of the moviemakers. (Though probably not intended as such, *Brief Encounter* is the only "touch of class" in the movie.) Glenda Jackson starts out resembling the snappy, independent woman Rosalind Russell, Barbara Stanwyck, Bette Davis, and Carole Lombard often played, but thanks to a story which refuses to develop any of its characters, which refuses to be about love and then insists that its main characters are very much in love, which insists further that it is a frivolous sex comedy and then keeps making blunders like asserting that these characters do feel something, she comes off looking as silly as Lauren Bacall in *Designing Woman.* (Jackson's character happens also to be a designer.) The movie cheats all the way through, wanting to have everything its own way and never bothering to make sense or remain faithful to the characters. And so, after the couple have given each other up—the man's best friend has piously and rather illogically recommended giving a woman up as the ultimate proof of love—the movie closes with Glenda Jackson again in a taxi. That is where she was at the beginning, when George Segal stepped in to share a ride. When a new gentleman appears at the end, asking to share a ride, she assesses his good looks, ascertains he is married, and quippingly refuses, as if the bad experience she has just been through were equivalent to a credit card muddle rather than an unhappy love affair. In the manner of Lucille Ball, she gives that adorable, knowing look that says: I know better than to step into that hornet's nest again! Where *Georgy Girl* and *Alfie* are easily reparable because they have some integrity, since they have honestly developed some real characters, and need only revisions that will yield endings true to the characters, *A Touch of Class* is rotten to the core, constantly in violation of its characters, loyal to no affirmation that is made about them, just having a good time splashing in the pool of sexual freedom and then having the gall to pretend that it's as heartbreaking as *Brief Encounter* or as heartwarming as "I Love Lucy." Take your pick.

An Unmarried Woman has troubles with its ending because ideology seems to take over. In *Reds,* that sort of thing happens, too, but only for a brief time, when Louise Bryant precipitately calls time out for a gratuitous eruption over her lover's male chauvinism, which someone forgot to write into John Reed's part, for he's been a most consistently respectful partner to his wife throughout the movie. Similarly, Jill Clayburgh's unmarried woman, involved with a paragon of liberated, sensitive masculinity, as played by Alan Bates, makes her big decision not to go on vacation with him, and the movie ends with the message—and it feels very much like a *message*—that she can go her own way and doesn't need him and doesn't have to do what he wants (even if it's what she wants, too), as if he'd been bullying her rather than loving her, as if his wanting to be with her were some insidious way he had of gaining political power over her. There's no shortage of movies in which domineering men put pressure on women to do what the men want just because they need the satisfaction that comes from having their way, from exercising control, in a relationship. See *Citizen Kane, Dragonwyck, Gaslight,* or *June Bride.* But the lover of *An Unmarried Woman* just isn't that kind of arm-twister.

The movie starts out being about a woman who discovers, after the sad blow of being left by her adulterous husband, that a new man she falls in love with offers her a far more mature and more satisfying relationship. The rejection that seems so terrible at first turns out to to be a boon after all. The natural ending for these two lovers is a commitment to each other. But suddenly, as the movie is winding up, it veers off the road and bumps around in the shrubbery before picking up a new direction. Now it is a movie about a woman who discovers that it is worth more to her to be "an unmarried woman" than to be fully committed to a relationship. *Looking for Mr. Goodbar* can say that at the end, because such is the absolute truth for desperate young Theresa Dunn, but when

An Unmarried Woman veers off like that, it's just putting on the "fashionably unhappy ending" agony and the "women don't need men" style. For this particular woman likes relationships with men, and she's good at them. (It was her husband who wasn't up to the relationship in their marriage.) Her choice of lonely self-sufficiency and the sudden upgrading to career of her job at an art gallery at the end look suspiciously like a quick bit of pandering to the crew that will yell and scream if a woman finds fulfillment in a relationship with a man. (It makes sense for Bette Davis's novelist in *Old Acquaintance* to end up alone with her career; she's not good at relationships with men, and her all-absorbing work is a believable alternative.) With no special talents of her own, she'd rather cart paintings around Manhattan than win fame as the subject of a talented artist's portrait or win fulfillment in a marriage with him. Such are the misguided ambitions of unimportant people. Unmarried and untalented, the unmarried woman walks away from the camera, deluded, to boot, by the phantom of fulfillment through solitude and convinced, as are many in the audience, that she is making an important "statement." As George Cukor has said, "For certain material, 'honest' unhappy endings are really dishonest."[3]

Several movies on this side of the '60s manage to steer clear of ideology and to arrive at ambiguous endings perfectly suited to the characters. Two excellent examples are *The Graduate* and *New York, New York.* There is no better ending imaginable for the overindulged and underenlightened young graduate than his impulsively forcing a resolution to his problems. As he sits at the back of the bus with his stolen bride, the vacillating shades of right and wrong, happiness and misery, safety and danger, drowning and rescue—shades which have beclouded this morally weak young man throughout the movie—play across his face in an alternation of happy smiles and sober stares. He has won the girl he thinks he loves, but to elope with the daughter of the woman who, by means of initiating him sexually, gained power over him, when he still has no idea what he believes in or what he wants to do in life, may be a Pyrrhic victory if it is any victory at all. By marrying into her family, he has attached himself to his bride's mother fully as much as he has escaped her clutches. He has derived a sense of freedom from acting, from snatching the bride away from the altar as she was marrying another man, but that face in the bus lets us know that he is, in those final moments of the movie, becoming enlightened about the way action limits one's choices, even when it has been carefully deliberated. His rash action, therefore, will likely demand years of his trying to master an inner turmoil he is just beginning to understand.

New York, New York, for all its shapelessness as a story, is consistently firm and true regarding its characters, thanks, undoubtedly, to the unflagging enthusiasm of the two stars. Liza Minnelli and Robert DeNiro carry this long, unwieldy movie largely alone and never forget who their characters are. The rocky relationship between two people who are so right and so wrong for each other must come to an ambiguous close. The final shot of Liza Minnelli in the elevator is a perfect comment on the character's acceptance of the closing in and shrinking of life's options. Dustin Hoffman's graduate leaves us at the beginning of his awareness, having just made his first important choice. Therefore, the moral toll shows in pronounced, rapid switches of facial expression. Liza Minnelli's successful movie star in *New York, New York* is a mature woman at movie's end, who has thought about and understood her failed marriage. She is unspoiled by suffering as well as by success, and that shows in the subtle economy of her facial expressions. As the elevator door closes, we imagine her rising slowly out of our view and out of her ex-husband's life as the boom lifts us with her above New York's streets, leaving him below on the sidewalk. Standing there, resolute and tall, she knows she is making the right decision. To resume relations with her impossible ex-husand would only end in pain. Yet, in giving up the abusive, selfish man she married, she is also giving up the love of her life. Their respective talents promised a perfect songwriting partnership, but they were never able to work together. Their one song, like their sweet son, is a joint but never shared creation. (This movie, incidentally, embodies all the problems of the much more tidily constructed and decidedly shallow *The Way We Were* but probes the causes, the undercurrents, of a relationship's failure—the psychological forces that collide to destroy what certainly was true love—perhaps because it never once stoops to the crude sources of incompatibility served up by the Christian, blond, conservative Redford mismatched with the Jewish, brunette, communist Streisand.) So

Minnelli remains perfectly still in the elevator, staring ahead of her, the face, dominated by the large, sad eyes, portraying the serene gravity that is both her penalty and her reward. Her face recalls us with a sigh to the aged dignity of Gary Cooper, far removed from his harmonica-playing days, as he carries Barbara Stanwyck away in his strong arms at the end of *Meet John Doe*.

Freedom from the production code in the '60s broke out in all kinds of rashes: sexually joined, writhing bodies; decapitations; toilet seats; four-letter words; and, at long last, miserable endings. The outbreaks undoubtedly served a purpose, if only to permit moviemakers to experiment with freedom and to learn just how intricately woven is the fabric of reality and imagination in art. For a while it seemed as if "realism" as defined by the above-mentioned rashes, was cinematic sine qua non to judge by the frenzy of shocking scenes and frightful endings as seen in *Easy Rider, Midnight Cowboy, Straw Dogs,* and *Chinatown.* (Although the ending of the book *Chinatown* offers a relatively optimistic resolution, it was scorned by Roman Polanski in 1974 in favor of this ending: Faye Dunaway, shot through the eye—an injury of choice in the '70s—sprawled dead and ghastly in her bloodied car. It is an obvious surrender to the violent trend, so jarringly unsuited to the carefully paced, subtly mysterious ambiguity of a story supported all along by disturbingly beautiful images of interfused purity and impurity.) The real lesson of such movies is that the absolutely happy ending and the absolutely unhappy ending have limited uses, the former doing very well for musicals and very light comedies; the latter doing very well for nightmare visions, like those above, that seek to affirm a totally negative prospect. Ambiguity is forged by the fact of human complexity. Most drama, therefore, if it is to satisfy our longing to understand moral and psychological strife and to feel for our fellow man's struggle to achieve a modicum of goodness and joy, must indicate that life offers us something but not everything; that, while one problem is resolved, another is left unresolved. The ambiguous ending reaches the heart of human life as it is experienced by most people. Such an ending is a true test of a movie's merit, moreover, for the conclusion that implies some lack of resolution must grow naturally out of the characters' range and intentions and must also be completely clear in its meaning. The skill and restraint demanded by such endings pose rigorous challenges indeed for writer, director, and actor.

Reprise: Thinking about Movies

In the '30s and '40s, Hollywood studio heads may have been insensitive to the feelings of artistic people, but they employed great writers, photographers, actors, directors, painters, dancers in droves, and gave them a tremendous amount of work to do. The opportunity was there for every kind of artist to do distinguished work. Those who had character as well as talent to recommend them—Joseph Mankiewicz, Gregg Toland, Bette Davis, William Wyler, Vincente Minnelli, Gene Kelly come immediately to mind—stopped complaining about the artist's plight in the highly remunerative "struggle against injustice" of Hollywood, found ways to assert themselves, and concentrated on developing their art. Hollywood movies of subsequent decades, while less pleasing to me personally—less delightful to wind through memory—are just as interesting to think about for several reasons. They show us what happens to art, for instance, when moviemakers are motivated by fear of costs rather than by love of movies; when moviemakers are inhibited by political strictures rather than by the Hays Office; when artists become self-conscious about creating "true art" in the style of European moviemakers; when the struggles to make movies are no longer about achieving freedom of expression but about knowing what to do with freedom; when being totally "realistic" is all the rage; when chances to practice one's art are greatly reduced. Like most uncongenial conditions, these threatened, tested, and ultimately refreshed moviemaking as an art.

Movies thrashed around and floundered in the '50s and '60s, and practically drowned in the '70s. Indeed, for all their attempts

193

to make statements, to be meaningful, to surpass the blithe banality of Hollywood's Golden Age with the profundity of their terrible truth, movies of the '70s so often merely tease us into a guilty sense that we should recognize something very significant to think about. But these movies actually convey a decline of ideas, which manifests itself in sparse dialogue, seemingly aimless camera work, fitful eruptions of impulsive action, and a relentless insistence on humorlessness that makes us thirst for any jokes, even the bitter barbs of *Lovers and Other Strangers*, that very funny and very distressing farewell to the power of relationships. As these movies try to transcend mere drama about relationships and to make important statements about important issues instead, they prove that, however important an issue may be—be it tyranny, racism, feminism, nuclear arms—any issue, as a dramatic subject, remains subordinate to the big subjects of character and relationships in which every issue finds its reason for being an issue at all.

William Faulkner spoke to this point when he accepted his Nobel Prize, saying, "The problems of the human heart in conflict with itself . . . alone make good writing," and movies have always been, no matter how silent or "purely" visual, linked to writing, dependent on the imaginative writer's capacity to get close to "the human heart." Whether a movie is written by a professional writer, slapped together on the spot by a director, silently shaped by a few subtitles, improvised by actors, or written by actors—the way Bette Davis and Mary Astor huddled in a dressing room on the set and wrote scenes for *The Great Lie*—a movie is a piece of writing and depends on our understanding of what fiction can do with words. It is other things besides, but its successfully credible evocation of a total world in motion corresponds exactly to what happens in novels. That is why André Bazin justly claims that both movies and novels are "enrich[ed] from within by the originality of their characters, their psychological flavor, an engaging individuality."[1] The big subjects, therefore, inevitably remain as big as ever during the '70s, and some movies' apparent denial of their importance is precisely what becomes significant in defining their lapse of faith in plain humanity and their concomitant rush to deck characters out in prestige-leading issues.

There is no cause for despair, for we must hastily acknowledge that these decades also show us how movies as an art form survived the '50s, '60s, and even the '70s. Some great movies were made in each of those unhappy cinematic decades, and the totality of movies made then—undoubtedly in part because of their affected imitations and experimental blunders—brought forth resolutions to some of the problems suggested by the uncongenial conditions enumerated earlier.

The '80s have brought us heaps of "kiddie fare" to accommodate the majority of this decade's moviegoers, who are, in fact, children. Movies bulging with muscles and the exertions they justify, like *Rocky* and *Rambo*, and movies evoking a young adventurer's dreamland, like *Raiders of the Lost Ark* and *E.T.* abound with a revived insistence on the innocence of what happens in movies. Much like the old Westerns and the '40s war movies on the one hand and the immortal *Wizard of Oz* and decidedly mortal *Blue Bird* on the other, such movies are popular with adults as well as children because they generously confirm our wish and need to master our surroundings, to conquer evil forces with our natural goodness. The childishness of such movies is undeniable, lavishly displayed in the fairy-tale assumptions that invest our physical selves with natural goodness and protect us, in our smallness and weakness, from those who are naturally wicked by rewarding us with magical powers. But the childishness of these movies is also sincere, and that gives them a validity shared by their prototypical fairy tales: the validity is both psychological and aesthetic, for childish fantasies give us ideas, sometimes even useful, practical ideas, about surviving, and they do so in the form of terrifically entertaining fiction, serving up deliciously pronounced characters, plots, and settings. One can do worse, then, than be simply childish, as movies of the '70s proved: one can wallow in affectation and adolescence, bemoaning the decay of one's pure romantic hopes into a piece of cynically rotten cheese. Adolescent fantasies make great poetry now and then out of all those fleeting inner promptings on which they principally rely, but they don't make great fiction because they have so little sense of character. Even the childish movies of the '80s have a respect for character.

Many movies of the '80s are truly adult, sturdily confronting the problems of adults in relationships rather than focusing on wishes and fantasies. These movies' attitude toward relationships, moreover, constitutes a revival of faith in character and people's capacity for attachment to each other. One happy result is movies in which the script really matters again because people have something to say to each other. Blake Edwards's *S.O.B.* and *Victor/Victoria*, Steve Gordon's *Arthur*, and Sydney Pollack's *Tootsie* all have a satirical front, possibly rigged as a defense against sentimentality (of the very sort that turns up in a maudlin way in *On Golden Pond* and in a refreshing way in *Moonstruck*), but in each one the spirit of playfulness and verbal wit creates true comedies, in the classically life-affirming, character-promoting sense, in which people are drawn to each other because they are independent and imaginative, full of conversational promise.

Restored faith in character is central to the scripts, and therefore to the conversations, in *All of Me*, *A Room with a View*, and *Blue Velvet*. The diversity of this trio is itself telling in terms of the literary richness they represent, with a broad comedy, a sweet romance, and a dark drama all concentrating on the intertwined rewards of maturity and fulfilling relationships. The scenes with the mysteriously sordid types propel the powerful undercurrent in *Blue Velvet*, but the movie would have no story, and the boy would have no character, without the conversations and the relationship they build with his blond girlfriend. Although this movie, in a manner of speaking, gives Andy Hardy a chance to face his unspeakable adolescent fantasies, it is not promoting them or telling us, reductively, that he is no more than the sum of them the way movies of the '70s, like *Carnal Knowledge*, *Shampoo*, and *Looking for Mr. Goodbar*, do. Rather, the movie promotes his rejection of those fantasies in favor of civilized manliness, especially vis-à-vis women: his mother, his aunt, his girlfriend, and even the woman of shadows, toward whom he is finally a true gentleman, cloaking her nudity in a raincoat and gallantly escorting her to the hospital.

It is fitting indeed that as our current decade draws to a close Steve Martin finds inspiration in the love story of the beautiful Roxanne and the epistolary Cyranno. This story, in which words rather than looks have the real power to foster love, is exactly suited to adults of the '80s.

In tempering the excesses and eschewing the vulgarities attendant upon the rages for realism, the movies of the '80s demonstrate a renewed appreciation for the sophistication, wit, and life-loving spirit of Hollywood's Golden Age, a renewed respect for subtlety as a way of answering the often conflicting demands of freedom and beauty, as well as a renewed and even enhanced confidence in moviemaking as art, which will choke on graphic depictions and verbatim accounts but will surely find sweet nourishment in imagination, honesty, and intelligence.

Notes

2. Women's Work in the Movies of the '30s and '40s

1. Gary Carey, *More About All About Eve* (New York: Random House, 1972), p. 40.

3. When Ideology Goes to the Movies

1. Marjorie Rosen, *Popcorn Venus* (New York: Coward, McCann & Geoghegan, 1973), p. 144.

2. Molly Haskell, *From Reverence to Rape* (New York: Holt, Rinehart and Winston, 1973).

3. Rosen, *Popcorn Venus*, p. 174.

4. Marilyn French, *The Women's Room* (New York: Summit Books, 1977), p. 277.

5. Blank and Pitiless as the Sun: Movies of the '50s

1. Haskell, *From Reverence to Rape*, p. 222.

7. Reflections of the Country: View from the City

1. Frank Capra, *The Name Above the Title* (New York: Macmillan Co., 1971), p. 263.

8. In a Dream of Passion:
The Tragedy of Acting

1. Carey, *More About All About Eve*, p. 24.
2. Stephen Farber and Marc Green, *Hollywood Dynasties* (New York: Putnam, 1984), p. 143.
3. Carey, *More About All About Eve*, p. 22.
4. Ibid., p. 29.
5. Ibid.

9. Eros and Thespis: The
Comedy of Acting

1. Stanley Cavell, *Pursuits of Happiness* (Cambridge, MA: Harvard University Press, 1981), p. 127.
2. Haskell, *From Reverence to Rape*, p. 358.

10. Why Sex isn't Sexy in the Movies

1. Carey, *More About All About Eve*, p. 69.

11. A Painted Ship upon a Painted Ocean:
Movies about Art as Life

1. Kenneth Clark, *The Romantic Rebellion* (New York: Harper and Row, 1973), p. 255.

12. The Heiress: A Successful
Transposition of Novel into Film

1. Leon Edel, "Why the Dramatic Arts Embrace Henry James," *New York Times*, March 4, 1984, pp. 1, 23.
2. André Bazin, *What is Cinema?* (Berkeley: University of California Press, 1967), p. I:141.
3. George Bluestone, *Novels Into Film* (Baltimore: Johns Hopkins University Press, 1957), pp. 47–48.
4. Axel Madsen, *William Wyler* (New York: Thomas Y. Crowell & Co., 1979), pp. 293–94.

14. Endings

1. Capra, *Name Above the Title*, p. 303.

2. Cavell, *Pursuits of Happiness*, p. 65.

3. Gary Carey, *Cukor and Co.* (New York: Museum of Modern Art, 1971), p. 38.

Reprise: Thinking about the Movies

1. Bazin, *What is Cinema?*, p. II:155.

Bibliography

Affron, Charles. *Star Acting.* New York: E. F. Dutton, 1977.

Basinger, Jeanine. *The It's a Wonderful Life Book.* New York: Alfred A. Knopf, 1986.

Bazin, André. *What is Cinema?* 2 vols. Berkeley: University of California Press, 1967.

Bergman, Andrew. *We're in the Money.* New York: Harper and Row, 1975.

Bluestone, George. *Novels into Film.* Baltimore: Johns Hopkins University Press, 1957.

Braudy, Leo. *The World in a Frame.* Garden City, NY: Anchor Press/Doubleday, 1976.

Capra, Frank. *The Name Above the Title.* New York: Macmillan Co., 1971.

Carey, Gary. *Cukor and Co.* New York: Museum of Modern Art, 1971.

———. *More About All About Eve.* New York: Random House, 1972.

Cavell, Stanley. *Pursuits of Happiness.* Cambridge, MA: Harvard University Press, 1981.

———. *The World Viewed.* Cambridge, MA: Harvard University Press, 1971.

Ceplair, Larry and Steven Englund. *The Inquisition in Hollywood.* Garden City, NY: Anchor/Doubleday, 1980.

Curtis, James. *Between Flops.* New York: Limelight Editions, 1984.

Davis, Bette. *The Lonely Life.* New York: G. P. Putnam's Sons, 1962.

Friedrich, Otto. *City of Nets*. New York: Harper and Row, 1986.

Funk, Lewis and John E. Booth, eds. *Actors Talk About Acting*. New York: Random House, 1961.

Geist, Kenneth. *Pictures Will Talk*. New York: Da Capo Press, 1978.

Harmetz, Aljean. *The Making of the Wizard of Oz*. New York: Limelight Editions, 1984.

Haskell, Molly. *From Reverence to Rape*. New York: Holt, Rinehart and Winston, 1973.

Higham, Charles and Joel Greenberg. *The Celluloid Muse*. Chicago: Henry Regnery Co., 1969.

Jowett, Garth. *Film: The Democratic Art*. Boston: Little, Brown, 1976.

Kanfer, Stefan. *A Journal of the Plague Years*. New York: Atheneum, 1973.

Kantor, B., I. Blacker, and A. Kramer. *Directors at Work*. New York: Funk & Wagnalls, 1970.

Kobal, John. *People Will Talk*. New York: Alfred A. Knopf, 1986.

Madsen, Axel. *William Wyler*. New York: Thomas Y. Crowell & Co., 1979.

Mast, Gerald. *The Movies in Our Midst*. Chicago: University of Chicago Press, 1982.

Minelli, Vincente. *I Remember It Well*. Garden City, NY: Doubleday, 1974.

Navasky, Victor. *Naming Names*. New York: Viking, 1980.

O'Connor John E. and Martin A. Jackson, eds. *American History/American Film*. New York: Ungar, 1979.

Pells, Richard. *Radical Visions and American Dreams*. Middletown, CT: Wesleyan University Press, 1973.

Roffman, Peter and Jim Purdy. *The Hollywood Social Problem Film*. Bloomington: Indiana University Press, 1981.

Rosten, Leo. *Hollywood: The Movie Colony, The Movie Makers*. Salem, NH: Ayer Co. Publishers, 1941 (reprint).

Schickel, Richard. *The Men Who Made the Movies*. New York: Atheneum, 1975.

———. *The Stars*. New York: Bonanza Books, 1962.

Thomson, David. *America in the Dark*. New York: Morrow, 1977.

Walker, Alexander. *Bette Davis*. Boston: Little, Brown, 1986.

Index